BOB WILSON
Behind the Network

MY AUTOBIOGRAPHY

BOB WILSON
Behind the Network

MY AUTOBIOGRAPHY

Bob Wilson

Hodder & Stoughton

First published in Great Britain in 2003 by Hodder and Stoughton
A division of Hodder Headline

A CIP catalogue record for this title is available
from the British Library

ISBN 0340 830 32 8

Typeset by Palimpsest Book Production Limited,
Polmont, Stirlingshire

Printed and bound in Great Britain by
Mackays of Chatham plc, Chatham, Kent

Hodder and Stoughton
A division of Hodder Headline
338 Euston Road
London NW1 3BH

For Louis and Max
May your lives be as blessed
as your grandpa's has been.

Contents

Acknowledgements

This book began its life in my longhand writing. At times, it has been illegible and found wanting grammatically. It appears as it does now courtesy of an extraordinary labour of love conducted by my wife Megs. It is the second book of mine that she has converted from scrawl to type, from jumbled thought to legitimate prose. It has helped that she knows and understands me better than anyone else, but none the less I owe her a huge debt for making some sense of my work.

My thanks also go to my two sons – John, for his journalistic eye and advice, and Robert for his brilliant photography, exemplified by the front cover of the book.

Likewise, I would like to express my appreciation of the great team that represents Hodder and Stoughton, led by the remarkable Roddy Bloomfield. From the moment I laid out my synopsis to the famous editor, he has added his own special enthusiasm. 'Just keep writing,' was his advice after he had read the first two draft chapters. I needed that encouragement, Roddy.

This story of my life has surprised me. It has reminded me of just how lucky I have been. Thank you to all those who have been part of it.

PHOTOGRAPHIC ACKNOWLEDGEMENTS

The author and publisher would like to thank the following for permission to reproduce photographs:

Alantic Syndication/Daily Mail, BBC, Colorsport, Empics/Sport & General, Express Newspapers, Guardian, KR Hailey Photographic, Jean Havilland, Mirrorpix, News International, Popperfoto.com, Kenneth Prater, Press Association, John Wells Photographic Service.

All other photographs are from private collections.
Whilst every effort has been made to trace the copyright holders of these photographs, the publisher would welcome any information regarding ownership.

Foreword

By Michael Parkinson

This is no sloppy, ghost written, scandal sprinkled story of a professional footballer. Instead it is a meticulous account of how a well educated, middle class boy from Chesterfield became a professional footballer. Put another way it is the story of how a sensible son of loving parents decided to make his living in the most hazardous occupation in football – that of goalkeeper.

It is well known that you don't have to be barmy to be a goalkeeper, but it sure helps. Bob Wilson developed into one of the best goalkeepers of his generation. He was brave and athletic but most of all intelligent. He was (and is) charming, articulate and socially adept, which in his chosen profession tended to set him apart from the mob.

His life story substantiates this feeling of a man involved and in love with his job and yet able to take a backward step and place sport in a sensible context. He had two brothers who he never knew because he was a baby when they were killed fighting the Germans in World War II. His research into their life and death is both inspiring and moving.

Then when he and his beloved Megs had thought they had safely shepherded their children into adult life their daughter Anna developed a rare form of cancer. Bob Wilson's story of how Anna and the family dealt with the inevitability of loss and the consequence of suffering could only have been written by an exceptional man.

That said I don't want you to think this is a gloomy book. I have known Bob and Megs for more than 30 years and it has been a friendship characterised by laughter. There is humour in the book and a huge sense of an athlete celebrating the fact of being paid to play football for a living and later talk about it on television. The job the hobby, the hobby the job. One lucky man. Forget all the other books by and about football you might have read. This one is not only different, it is outstanding.

Preface

'If a man's gonna make it, he's gotta be tough
And I knew I wouldn't be there to help ya along.
So I give ya that name and I said goodbye
I knew you'd have to get tough or die.
And it's the name that helped to make you strong.
I tell ya life ain't easy for a boy named Sue.'

'A Boy Named Sue' by Johnny Cash

The lyric of this famous song may appear to be a slightly bizarre introduction to my journey through life, that is until you start to comprehend how difficult it can be to accept a feminine Christian name when you are born a boy.

That's exactly what my dear mum and dad bestowed on me, their sixth and last child. It hardly softened the blow that three of my four brothers and my lovely sister Jean had previously been given my mother's maiden name as well. Yes, Primrose was and is that name. This is a story about a boy named Primrose.

The sentiments expressed in Johnny Cash's song 'A Boy Named Sue' had no intentional bearing on my mum and dad's choice, although ironically as my life has unfolded there have been times when the 'get tough or die' option has materialised in a slightly less dramatic form. You simply cannot survive forty years in the world of football, let alone thirty years in the television spotlight, without facing the sort of criticism that challenges even the most hardened and optimistic spirit. But what's in an unusual name anyway? What really counts is how you live your life. How you face it, enjoy it, improve it and how you cope with its unpredictable and at times cruel side.

'The primrose path' is defined in most dictionaries as 'a pleasurable way of life'. For this particular Primrose, pleasure and success have indeed played a leading role, but the way has also been strewn with drama, sadness, even heartbreak. At times, intense despair has touched my life, but never enough to extinguish the joy that can be gained, as long as there remains enough desire and belief. Happily, those attributes had been established from day one.

My mother was an extraordinary lady, the daughter of a Scottish Presbyterian minister, the Reverend Robert Primrose, after whom I was named. Understandably religious, she was also blessed with a caring and humanitarian nature that surmounted all barriers, however challenging. 'It will all work out for the best' was Mum's favourite saying. At times, she drove us all mad with it as she tried to make sense of the latest family trauma that seemed to have no meaning or solution. Miraculously, she was more often than not proved right, although her faith was tested to the full. How could it not have been when two of her children were to die before their twenty-first birthdays? Somehow she was still able to persuade my dad and those around her that 'everything is sent for a reason' and that 'every cloud has a silver lining'.

Had she not taught me with such conviction, I doubt this primrose path of mine would have been sustainable, let alone so pleasurable.

1

Scot or Sassenach?

'O flower of Scotland when will we see your like again
That fought and died for your wee bit hill and glen'

Roy Williamson

I glanced nervously, but hopefully not too obviously, at the craggy face alongside me. It was a famous face, one known throughout the world as a consequence of the owner's brilliant skills with a football and predatory goal-scoring instinct. He had made his name during the 1966 World Cup finals in England, when his burning desire for glory was extinguished by the host country in a dramatic semi-final at Wembley. I had been on the terraces at that game; now, in the tunnel that led from dressing room to pitch, I was about to come face to face with this legend, in more ways than one.

Eusebio Ferreira da Silva possessed the sort of face that you were unlikely to forget. He had an infectious smile and exuded a confidence bordering on arrogance. Five years on from the World Cup he was now captain of his country. Portugal remained attractive and dangerous opponents for anyone. For a Scottish goalkeeper about to represent his country for the first time, it was a moment when the self-doubts far exceeded the norm.

What made matters worse was that I was riddled with other insecurities, notably a strong suspicion that a huge proportion of Scots, led *en bloc* by the Glasgow press corps, seriously doubted their new goalkeeper's nationality. Questions were being asked about me and have continued to be asked ever since. Bob Wilson, Scot or Sassenach? The date was 13 October 1971, the venue Hampden Park, Glasgow. More than 50,000 fanatical fans had turned up to see a European Championship qualifier between Scotland and Portugal.

My selection had been deemed controversial in the extreme despite a recent international law change. A few weeks earlier, the FIFA regulation stated a player could play for the country of his birth only, in my case England. Overnight the ruling had changed to allow a player to choose between the country of his birth or that of one of his parents. Mum and Dad were both Scots, their respective families without a trace of English blood among them. Why the big deal? Surely a country not renowned for producing the greatest of custodians would welcome with open arms a keeper at the pinnacle of his career and generally acknowledged to be one of the best around at that time?

Ten to eight on a damp Glasgow evening was not the moment to worry overmuch about the debate. More pressing matters were at hand. Seize the moment. Argue the point later. Just go out and win them over with a display of talent. After all, was this not the most rewarding moment of my career, the moment when a schoolboy dream would come true – to play for Scotland?

Just over twenty-two years earlier, Christmas day 1949 was significant for the unwrapping of a gift that fired my ambition. The label on the present was written 'To Robin, with love from Uncle David and Auntie Anne'. Doctor David Lees, a Scot, and his wife were close friends of my parents. As I eagerly opened the soft package, I anticipated an article of clothing, possibly a scarf or gloves. Imagine my delight when I discovered a blue goalkeeping jersey, blue to represent Scotland, a keeper's jersey sent to sustain a little boy who couldn't get enough of football and who had already enjoyed some success 'between the sticks'.

The rest of that Christmas day was spent with the jersey worn proudly and a lot of moaning to my dad and brother Hugh, demanding they kick a ball at me. Any sort of ball, proper football, tennis ball or, to avoid broken windows and the like, socks rolled into the shape of a ball. Even at the tender age of eight I put myself in the shoes of a heroic keeper of the time, Scotland's Jimmy Cowan.

The house in which we played was where I had been born on 30 October 1941. It was called 'Threepwood', after the farm in Galston, Ayrshire, where my dad was born. The Second World War was raging when my mum recognised the familiar signs. It was no surprise to her; she had been there five times before. I was about to arrive, the sixth child of William Smith Wilson and Catherine Wingate Primrose, known as Kitty. What was perhaps surprising was that my mum, quietly and without drama, slipped upstairs away from a gathering of RAF crew, in order to give birth.

So far the Scottish thread holds firm but the first weakness appears on inspection of the birth certificate. Naturally, it indicates the town where the baby arrived, in my case Chesterfield, Derbyshire, England. Pretty conclusive and damning evidence if you accept that country of birth is more important than the blood that courses through the veins. I have always had to argue the point and one way is to exact a response to the question, 'If I had been born in Tokyo, would that make me Japanese?'

Had my dad had a choice, I guess he would have preferred to have been the Borough Engineer and Surveyor of Edinburgh, Dundee or Glasgow rather than a market town south of the border, but as that wasn't to be, his instinct was to go where the best job presented itself, and that was England.

It's almost certain that he would not have pursued such employment had his parents lived long enough for him and his brothers and sister to sustain the farm but both died at a relatively young age, his mother just thirty-seven, and their children were brought up by relatives. My dad was educated at

Bablake School near Coventry, and a school prize presented at Christmas 1909 reflected his tartan taste. Given as the Resident Boy's Prize for 'excellent conduct' to William Smith Wilson, *The Poetical Works of Robert Burns* was a book he would read and enjoy for the rest of his life.

As the First World War unfolded he saw service in France and Belgium in the Highland Light Infantry. For a spell he was Intelligence Officer with the 145th Infantry Brigade. Many were the times he would recall the desperate conditions encountered during that dreadful war, between 1914 and 1918, stories of the trenches, where 'tartan trews' replaced the kilt, where reckless orders from officers were sometimes disobeyed and where life was lost daily with a disregard that bordered on not just desperation but insanity.

Dad would only go so far when pressed about his involvement in the heat of battle. I remember, as a very young boy, opening an army trunk of his that had been well buried in a usually secure shed in our garden. There were military documents including maps, and a holster with a pistol. He was surprised that I had chanced upon them and totally non-committal when I asked him whether he had used the gun in earnest. The conversation was abruptly cut short and none of these remnants of his First World War experiences were ever seen again.

Dad simply refused to talk about specifics, only generalities. For instance, he often recounted the battle of the Somme where British casualties amounted to 420,000, French losses 204,000 and German losses totalled a huge 670,000, and all for a thirty-mile strip of land only seven miles at its widest and lacking any worthwhile strategic position. Insanity seems the appropriate word. To my dad, the benefits of such experiences were the camaraderie they provided, fighting for a cause, fighting for his country. Although a proud Scot, to the day he died he believed passionately in Britain as a whole.

To me, he was an older dad. By the time I was born he was

forty-nine, ten years older than my mum, to whom he had proposed when she was just sixteen. The letters he wrote to her as a soldier in France and Belgium are truly fascinating. His love for her was obvious. Separated by land and water, he expressed himself eloquently while the 'ochs', 'ayes' and 'wee dearies' replicated his everyday way of speaking.

The age gap between them was never a huge problem except perhaps to my mum's parents. My dad wrote to her father to ask for her hand in marriage, and the response from my grandfather was remarkably philosophical, especially considering his position as a Presbyterian minister. Replying from Valparaiso in Chile, where he was preaching at the time, the Reverend Robert Primrose wrote:

> My dear boy, your news did not take me by surprise. I have known for a long time where your heart was centred and also where my darling daughter's heart was centred. There is no man to whose keeping I would more confidently trust our darling wee Kitty. She is like her Mother, one of God's best and truest.

My grandmother, also named Catherine Wingate Primrose, was similarly direct:

> I have great confidence in you Bill and feel as though you are my son already. You have a canny way of entwining yourself around our affections.

I wish I had known my Scottish grandparents. I consider it a huge void in my life that all four were dead long before I was born. My curiosity particularly surrounds my mum's father, the man after whom I was named. *The Reverend Robert Primrose VD RNVR. Preacher, Lecturer, Padre and Sailor* is the title of a book written about him by J.H. Leckie. The account of his life is lavish in its praise, especially his preaching. 'Spellbinding' is the description given to a minister whose special talent was taking on churches that had become run down. Time and again, by the sheer force of his personality and his preaching, he would build these churches into a thriving Christian community and then move on and repeat the exercise elsewhere. He was also described as expansive, warm-hearted and a fine athlete.

From all accounts he was quite a character from youth. On one occasion, his father had prohibited him from playing in a football match because it was considered unbecoming for a divinity student. The young Robert Primrose thought differently. What he hadn't anticipated was that his dad would be a spectator at the game. Even then initiative took over and Robert Primrose took to the field disguised. Afterwards, at the family table, he listened with a smile to a glowing paternal tribute to the prowess of 'the wee fellow with the beard'!

That game took place in a Glasgow park just a stone's throw from Hampden Park, where some ninety years later the goalkeeping grandson of the Reverend Robert Primrose walked out into that famous arena, without disguise, to face the full glare of a demanding football-mad nation on his international debut. The noise was deafening, the adrenaline rush huge. As the Scotland and Portugal teams lined up for the anthems, I glanced down momentarily at my jersey and the proud lion rampant on the badge.

In the stand high above me there was a humorous moment as a proud Scottish lady wearing a tammy on her head turned to her daughter-in-law, similarly clad, and said, 'Och Megs dearie, I never realised Bob was such a giant of a man.'

Quietly, but with a smile, my wife replied, 'Mum dear, he's not really that big. Just look carefully at those on either side of him.'

I was also aware of my nearest team-mates. Captain Billy Bremner, 5ft 5ins, Jimmy Johnstone, roughly the same size, and Archie Gemmill, barely 5ft 6ins. I towered above them at 6ft 1in, a veritable giant. Even if I'd heard my mum's words it's doubtful whether it would have warranted a smile at the time. I was now locked into serious concentration, so desperate to perform well. The lift I required came as I headed away from the centre circle to my goal. Unbelievably, considering the adverse publicity, I could hear the fans chanting the name 'Wilson!' and applauding generously. At least they were happy I was there.

The mixture of skill and luck upon which every footballer depends, didn't desert me on that memorable night. Scotland won 2–1. Eusebio failed to score, was substituted at half-time and I played OK, nothing brilliant, but competently enough maybe to get picked again. Victory would certainly have won over a few more votes, but I was under no illusion – persuading the masses might always remain a problem. Scottish blood I had in plenty but the place of birth and the accent were so indelibly English.

Half an hour after the final whistle I could be found wandering around the pitch by myself surveying the empty terraces, taking in the cold Glasgow air and marvelling at the strange turn of fate that had brought me this far. I was thrilled to be there, knowing exactly what it meant to my mum and dad and to all my family.

If I could have been granted a wish at that moment, I would have asked for the terraces to be full of Scottish fans so that I could, for a brief moment, take on the mantle of my grandfather and namesake, the Reverend Robert Primrose. I wouldn't have preached or even said a lot, but I would maybe have adopted his impish humour and made a final plea in presenting the case for my Scottish heritage.

The members of the press who had so cruelly questioned my selection hadn't done their homework well enough when researching my family tree. Had they done so they would have discovered that this same Hampden Park had originally been opened in 1903 by the Lord Provost of Glasgow, who was also chairman of Rangers. His name? Sir John Ure Primrose, my great uncle.

2
Jock and Billy, the heroes

'Have no fear for me in the wind and the rain
For I am one with the sky and racing clouds forever.'

Unknown

The smile on my mum's face changed into a look of deep sadness. Involuntary tears began to fill her eyes and roll gently down her face. It was not a moment to utter words of consolation. She simply needed time to take in the number, rank and name on the cross in front of her. It read '*1108051 Sergeant J.P. Wilson. Pilot. Royal Air Force. 27th February 1942. Age 19.*'

J.P. was John Primrose, better known as Jock, the eldest son of my dad and mum, my brother. After a sensitive period of time, my wife Megs gently invited our three children, John, Anna and Robert, to join their grandmother in saying the Lord's Prayer. Aware of their nan's tears, they nodded a silent agreement. By the end of the prayer, Mum had not just recovered her composure, but the smile, which throughout her life rarely ever left her face, had returned. Robert's action in placing an elasticated plant pot holder on his head had the desired effect on all of us. At four years of age, he was unaware of the significance of the moment; this was the first time his grandmother had set eyes on Jock's grave.

The plant itself was carefully inserted into earth of this little corner of France, which had become a British Second World

War cemetery. My mum's great wish to visit the last resting place of her first born had been fulfilled.

One year later, the sad but enriching scene was repeated as Mum looked for the first time upon her second son's grave. The tears were as instinctive, the recovery of composure took slightly longer. This time there were no children present, no impromptu breaking of the ice by Robert.

'1452338 Sergeant W.P. Wilson. Air Gunner. Royal Air Force. 16th December 1943. Age 20' – the headstone of William Primrose Wilson, known as Billy, was identical to Jock's in almost every detail, except this was a corner of a different foreign field, just inside the German border neighbouring Holland. Reichswald Forest War Cemetery is the last resting place of 7,416 Commonwealth servicemen of the Second World War.

My two eldest brothers were heroes. All those men and women who fought for their country's freedom were heroes whether they survived or not. At the time of Jock's death I was just four months old. When Billy was shot down and killed I had just enjoyed my second birthday. I have no recollection of either of them, but throughout my life they have been an inspirational driving force. I have always known that whatever I did with my life, I could never match the courage of Jock and Billy. Being prepared to pay the ultimate price in order that others can enjoy their lives in a free country has no comparable achievement.

It intrigues me to know what they were like, what it meant to them to fly, the joy, despair and desperate fear they possibly experienced in the cockpit of a tiny Spitfire and the rear turret of a lumbering Lancaster bomber. The effect of their lives and deaths on my parents and the surviving three brothers and sister was very individual.

In Jock's last letter to my mum and dad he wrote, 'Many years ago I felt the urge to fly. Since I have begun, the effect has been like a drug. I could never give it up now. It is an essential part of my very existence.'

The time span of Jock's flying career from his first training flight in a Miles Master to his death in a Spitfire is staggeringly brief. His pilot's log book, meticulously maintained, gives 10 December 1940 as the date he took to a cockpit with a Flying Officer Smith as his instructor. He was eighteen years and seven months old.

The aircraft was a Blackburn B2 and the sequence of training set in stone for all aspiring fighter pilots:

  1 Air experience
 1a Familiarity with cockpit outlay
  2 Effect of controls
  3 Taxiing
  4 Straight and level flight
  5 Climbing, gliding and stalling
  6 Medium turns
  7 Taking off into wind
  8 Powered approach and landing
  9 Gliding approach and landing
10 Spinning
11 First solo
12 Sideslipping
13 Precautionary landing
14 Low flying
15 Steep turns
16 Climbing turns
17 Forced landing
18 Action in event of fire
18a Abandoning an aircraft
19 Instrument flying
20 Taking off and landing out of wind
21 Re-starting the engine in flight
22 Aerobatics

*   *   *

On the seventeenth day of initial training, Jock flew solo for the first time, after less than ten hours familiarity with the cockpit. He then moved on to a DH82 Tiger Moth for a further seven weeks of tests and examinations before having his log book stamped as follows:

Flying time, Dual 22 hours 15 mins. Solo 23 hours 25 mins
Instrument flying 4 hours 55 mins
Proficiency as a pilot – Average
February 26th 1941

Almost immediately the sequence of instruction was repeated in a Miles Master 1 aircraft, culminating in eight solo flights in a Hawker Hurricane 1.

So after five short months, a total of seventy-six hours and forty minutes on all courses and types of aircraft, Sergeant J.P. Wilson received a special nineteenth birthday present – a grubby typed piece of paper permitting him to fly the fighter plane with which he had fallen in love and upon which he had set his heart, the legendary Vickers Supermarine Spitfire.

Slimly built with a beautifully proportioned body and graceful curves just where they should be, it was impossible for any young pilot not to be captivated by the sheer beauty of the Spitfire.

I wondered whether the legend would live up to reality. It did and more. There is a rightness about the aircraft that gives an instant feeling of being part of the machine.

In the air the grace of the aircraft is matched by the way it handles. In a dogfight I always felt that my Spitfire and I were as one.

Three pilots' graphic descriptions of Reginald J. Mitchell's inspired design. Between 1938 and 1948, a total of 20,351 were produced. Undoubtedly, the Spitfire played a huge part in ensuring that the war in the air against Germany ended in victory.

My brother Jock's part in that victory began with his posting to 65 (East India) Squadron, operating from Kirton-in-Lindsey, Lincolnshire, and equipped with Spitfire IIs. Throughout late July and early August the nineteen-year-old baby of the squadron began to learn his trade. Formation practice, camera gun practice, cloud flying, sector reconnaissance and wing formation exercises were followed by his first operational mission, which took place on 12 August. Flying a Spitfire IIA, Jock took part in an offensive sweep over the Dutch coast off Rotterdam. He was airborne for one hour and fifty minutes and no enemy activity was observed. It is quite clear from Jock's log book that he was rarely involved in the sort of dogfights that made heroes of Johnny Johnson and Douglas Bader.

In fact, records show that Jock rarely fired his guns in combat against enemy aeroplanes. He regularly opened up on ground targets but only occasionally fired upon the Luftwaffe in the air. Only when you understand the role and types of missions given to pilots such as Jock do you realise that, as in any job, there are unsung heroes, of which he was one.

Throughout 1941 and into 1942, Fighter Command was flexing its muscles in continuous air operations, particularly over occupied France, aimed at drawing the German fighter units into combat and hopefully draining their resources. The largest of these missions bore the names of Rodeo and Circus operations. Rodeos were fighter sweeps consisting of one or two wings of thirty-six aircraft apiece. Once the few Luftwaffe squadrons in France began to ignore these operations, the RAF added a handful of bombers, protected by large numbers of Spitfires and Hurricanes. Some of the fighter support would sweep ahead of the bombers, the remainder would remain close as high escorts. Clearly Jock took part in many such missions, and reports occasional incidents: 'Attacked by Messerschmitt 109 diving out of cloud cover. Slight flak from coast.' The worst of these came on 21 August after an offensive sweep over France: 'Squadron attacked by 109s out of sun. Sergeants Kay and Baxter missing.'

If Jock was reminded then of his own mortality, he never said as much to his nearest and dearest. A letter written just in case he failed to return was already in the possession of his squadron leader.

It's impossible, hard as I have tried, to put myself in my brother's shoes. Imagination and a degree of knowledge is one thing; the reality of close combat and fighting to the death is another. However, it is fascinating to read vivid descriptions of what was expected of a pilot in charge of these sleek pieces of machinery, just 29ft 11ins in length and with a wing span of 36ft 10ins. Powered by one Rolls-Royce Merlin engine, the Spitfire had a range of 395 miles and a maximum speed of 362 miles per hour.

All our pilots were instructed identically in the art of engagement. In Richard Hillary's book *The Last Enemy*, he describes how

we learned of the advantage of height and of attacking from out of the sun; of the German's willingness to fight with height and odds in their favour and their disinclination to mix it on less favourable terms; of the vulnerability of the Messerschmitt 109 when attacked from the rear and its standardised method of evasion when so attacked – a half roll, followed by a vertical dive right down to the ground. As the Messerschmitt pilots had to sit on their petrol tanks, it is perhaps hard to blame them. We learned of the necessity to work as a Squadron and to understand thoroughly every command of the Squadron Leader whether given by mouth or gesture. We learned that we should never follow a plane down after it had been hit, for it weakened the effectiveness of the Squadron and further was likely to result in an attack from the rear. If we were outnumbered and the formation broken, we should attempt to keep in pairs and never for more than two seconds fly on a straight course.

Operating in pairs was to become a major role mission for Jock when his time at Kirton-in-Lindsey came to an end in early September 1941, the month before I was born. The intensity of action during his time with 65 (East India) Squadron was amazing. Between 27 July and 7 September, Jock often flew three times a day, occasionally four times, and there was barely a day's respite or leave.

Jock's last flight with 65(East India) Squadron was on 7 September, his first at his new posting one day later. In that time he had travelled from Kirton-in-Lindsey to North Weald, Essex, to join 222 (Natal) Squadron. There was an immediate bonus. Instead of the Spitfire II he had flown previously, he now enjoyed the more up-to-date Spitfire VBs armed with 20mm cannon instead of the outmoded eight .303 machine guns of the Mark II plane. Jock quickly gained a special friend at 222 Squadron. Pat Rusk was both his pal and partner when it came to the type of dangerous activity in which they were to specialise.

'Rhubarbs' were readily acknowledged as the most lethal of missions. They involved flying at low levels, and were usually carried out in cloudy weather conditions by pairs of fighters. The objective was to shoot up targets of opportunity as they swept over the landscape of occupied Europe. RAF fighter pilots hated Rhubarbs above all other tasks. Vulnerable to light flak and even rifle bullets, the planes were at such low level that pilots rarely had time to bale out when hit, a variety of improvised crash landings being the only method of survival.

Hundreds of allied pilots died in these varied, unsound and perilous activities.

In between the Rhubarb sorties, 222 Squadron was also involved in a variety of missions escorting Blenheim bombers or fighter sweeps around France. Jock's log entries became increasingly matter of fact as his experience mounted: 'Attacked by numerous ME 109s in usual manner. Intense flak no problem. No bombers lost.' The Rhubarb flights were always reports of a different nature: 'Rhubarb to Furnes with Sgt Rusk. Hit French coast at Gravelines. Attacked by accurate flak. Still flew inland, then dived down and attacked aerodrome. My port wing hit by flak.'

I'm glad the damage on that particular mission was not more serious. The date was 18 October 1941. A week later, Jock was given a few days' leave. Back in Chesterfield, Mum and Dad, brothers Billy, Don and Hugh and my sister Jean were thrilled to see him. It was an emotional time for everyone but especially for my mum. At any moment she was expected to give birth to her sixth infant.

Jock brought with him two colleagues from his squadron. Their names were Tilston and Souter. As usual, Mum provided a terrific supper before excusing herself on the grounds of tiredness. The truth was that she had gone into labour. My sister Jean was sent to stay overnight with neighbours and the three pilots bedded down in the dining room on camp beds. Just imagine their faces the next morning when Mum's nurse woke them up by showing them the new born, all 10lbs of me.

Jean remembers Tilston and Souter's suggestion that apart from being called Robert, my other Christian names should be their surnames to mark their presence at such an event. Now there's a thought – Robert Tilston Souter Wilson. Would that not have been preferable to Robert Primrose?

The same day I was born, Jock returned to North Weald, and with the intensity of warfare came increased concerns at home. The most dramatic of the log book accounts over the next month stated, 'with Pat Rusk I carried out Rhubarb attacks with cannon and m/g on hangars, gun positions on a tower and on alcohol factory. Direct hits on all three at Berke-sur-mere. Destroyed two goods trains.'

Christmas days during wartime were evidently not memorable for a large exchange of gifts. There were always stockings hung up, but Santa's visit came and went with an orange, apple, book and maybe one toy. Hugh in particular recalls a Dinky lorry and trailer as being the 'special' present at this time. Christmas 1941, though, had something much better and more significant for the Wilsons than any number of parcels. It was the one and only time that the entire family were together – Jock, Billy, Don, Jean, Hugh and 'wee Robin', as I was known in my early years. Hindsight is a wonderful thing but how I wish Mum and Dad had taken a photograph of us all together that day. Plenty of shots exist showing the first five children together but not all six of us; 25 December 1941 was to be Jock's last Christmas day with his family.

His world was shattered on 27 January when his best mate in the squadron was killed. Jock's entry in the log book reads: 'Sgt Pat Rusk killed when his aeroplane came to pieces at 10,000 feet a mile from 'drome. Reason unknown.' His diary expressed his inner feelings: 'A most disastrous and black day. According to reports, dived, pulled out and the aeroplane came to pieces. Wrote to his people immediately. I did not fly.'

Around the time he lost his pal, an official British war photographer took a picture of Jock in the cockpit of one of the unit's Spitfires. He is shown fastening his flying helmet. He sent a copy to Billy inscribed 'To my brother and best friend Bill. With all the very best of good wishes' and it served as inspiration.

Jock's last leave with his family came in early February. On the twenty-seventh, exactly a month after Pat Rusk's death, he took off from North Weald in Spitfire VB Srl No AB869 for a Rhubarb mission. His partner was a Sergeant Batman. They lifted off from British soil at 11.38 a.m. on a very dull day with low cloud and headed across the Channel for Calais' Marck airfield. Thirty minutes later, just off the French coast near Calais, both aircraft were visible on the radar screens. In the next twenty minutes both aircraft plots disappeared from view.

Heavy flak had met the pair and in the low cloud Sergeant Batman slightly misjudged his height over the sea. The tips of his airscrew blades clipped the water. Immediately, his engine temperature rose and he called up Jock on the radio transmitter to say he was returning to base. Batman's engine failed off Dover but he managed to bale out into the sea and was safely recovered by an RAF launch. Later he explained that he had become separated from Sergeant Wilson in heavy cloud over the target area. The last words he heard from Jock were, 'Target sighted, about to attack.'

Such positive words, but sadly they were to be Jock's last. At about 12.30 hours Sergeant Pilot John Primrose Wilson was hit by enemy ack-ack fire and crashed in the town of Marck. He died nine weeks before his twentieth birthday. He had been a qualified pilot for exactly one year and one day. By a strange irony, Mum's brother, Walter Primrose, had been killed in action on 27 February while flying during the First World War.

Eventually, my mum and dad learned that Jock had initially been buried close to the crash site. Only at the end of the war were his remains exhumed and re-interred at the Commonwealth War Grave Cemetry at Pihen Les Guines, Pas de Calais, Row C, Grave 1, but the facts about Jock's last moments and resting place came to light much later, and the family held out great hope that he might just have survived being shot down. Both Jock and Billy ordered their parents never to give up hope.

With Dad at work, it fell upon Mum to receive the initial phone call about Jock's failure to return to base at North Weald. Jean was at school but recalls how she arrived back at Threepwood to find Mum waiting at the gate. One look was enough for it to sink in that there was bad news about Jock. Mum tried to be as optimistic as she could and held on to the possibility that Jock had survived or been taken prisoner. There were tears from Mum, lots of them, but Jean remembers the stoic stance of our military trained father. I have little doubt that privately he shed many a tear, but such weakness was not for public or family consumption.

One week after Jock's last flight, the local Chesterfield newspaper, the *Derbyshire Times*, included in its Friday, 6 March edition news of the Borough Engineer and Surveyor's son. Headlined 'Reported Missing', it appears to all intents and purposes an obituary in waiting: 'He was head boy of Chesterfield Grammar School, he attained great distinction in the field of sport, he was secretary to the School Rugby Football Club, he was a prominent athlete.'

Only in late September did Mum and Dad finally accept that Jock was never coming home. A communication from the Air Ministry stated that 'In view of the lapse of time and the complete absence of any further news regarding your son, it must be regretfully concluded that he has lost his life.'

More than five years later, on 20 August 1947, a beautifully handwritten letter from the Air Ministry informed my parents that the RAF's Missing Research and Enquiry Services in France had confirmed that Jock's aircraft crashed in Marck, four miles east of Calais. So many unanswered questions remained for the family but of one thing we were sure. Jock died a happy, contented and fulfilled man. The reason why is explicit from his last letter:

Dearest Mum and Dad

When one is flying in the RAF in wartime, particularly on active service, sometimes exceptionally active, one does not have to be much of a realist to come to the conclusion that there is always present the possibility that I might meet with an accident or be unfortunate enough to be shot down. It is for this reason that I am writing you this letter.

Many of the boys before me have written such letters and I share one thing in common with the majority of them – I have no premonition that anything will happen. In fact, if the truth be known, I cannot imagine such a thing despite the fact that I am hardly known as 'Lucky Jock'.

My wish is to comfort you and reassure you as much as is possible. If I am posted 'missing', always remember there is the chance, however slight, that I am OK.

If I am killed, what a harsh word that seems, please believe me when I say that I shall have died neither afraid nor unhappy. For as much as anyone else I have always been a firm believer in the saying 'What has to be will be'. How then could I be afraid?

In my short span of years I have achieved almost all that I ever set out to gain. I won my wings, certainly the greatest ambition of my life so far. Many years ago I felt the urge to fly. Since I have begun, the effect has been like a drug. I could never give it up now, it is an essential part of my very existence.

Also have I not had the honour of belonging to one of the finest and certainly the happiest families in the country? For this latter privilege I thank you, for it was you two whose devotion to your family made it so. Indeed I have had everything of importance to be thankful for and nothing of importance to complain about. From your example and my experience I have built myself a number of high ideals up to which I have striven hard to live.

There is little else to say except that if it can in any way be said that I have helped Britain by my service in the air, then I feel I can go feeling happy about it.

Thanks to my Scots instincts I have continually been aware of my inborn love of this country of ours. No effort can be too great to preserve its absolute freedom.

And so cheerio. Please give my love to the best sister and four finest brothers any person could ever have.

All look after yourselves. Ever smiling. As always, your loving son

Jock

PS Concerning my belongings, I would like all that I have to be split up amongst the family. I wish you to have the wings on my tunic in particular, after all, I valued them above anything and any amount of money. To me, they represent the ideals I believed in apart from them being a symbol that I flew.

Jock

How lucky Mum and Dad were to have had such a son. How fortunate Billy, Don, Jean, Hugh and I were to have had Jock as our brother. Jean, who clearly loved everything about Jock, describes him as 'a strong but gentle giant of about six feet one inch. He always had time for anyone, always wanted to please, was never argumentative and had a lovely nature. He was never embarrassed at holding his little sister's hand. Jock, like Dad, was studious and clever. Both found pure and applied mathematics a stimulating challenge. He was head boy of Chesterfield Grammar School and loved his sports, athletics and rugby in particular. With really craggy rugged looks and the Wilson smiley eyes, it would be difficult to find a more balanced or engaging person.'

Over the years my own dreams and thoughts have brought him close to me and I cherish the thought that he held me in

21

his arms a few times during the first four months of my life. It was a time of war but a time when Jock was at one with himself and his beloved Spitfire.

High Flight

Oh I have slipped the surly bonds of earth
And danced the skies on laughter-silvered wings;
Sunward I've climbed and joined the tumbling mirth
Of sun-split clouds – and done a hundred things
You have not dreamed of – wheeled and soared and swung
High in the sunlit silence. Hov'ring there
I've chased the shouting wind along, and flung
My eager craft through footless halls of air
Up, up the long delirious, burning blue, I've topped the
   wind swept heights with easy grace
Where never lark, or even eagle flew – And while with silent
   lifting mind I've trod
The high untrespassed sanctity of space
Put out my hand and touched the face of God.

This poem was written by nineteen-year-old Pilot Officer John Gillespie Magee of No. 412 Squadron RCAF who was killed on active service 11 December 1941. It has been ranked with Rupert Brook's 'The Soldier' and was posted in all Commonwealth Air Schools.

Jock's life came to an end as Billy's ambition to fly had just begun. On 15 February 1941, two weeks before his mentor was killed, Billy had enrolled in the Air Training Corps, 331 Chesterfield Squadron. A local friend of Billy's, Douglas Robinson, recalls that evening at the drill hall on Boythorpe Road. The two young men hit it off immediately, after Billy had introduced himself in typical friendly style.

'After the news of Jock, all Billy really had on his mind was to get into uniform and try to avenge the death of his brother,' says Douglas Robinson. 'It was a difficult time because he was inconsolable. He became someone who had the woes of the whole world on his shoulders.'

The effect of Jock's death on Billy was devastating but he was determined to follow his brother's brand of courage and leadership.

'He was fired by a mixture of inspiration and anger at the loss of his brother. Billy didn't have Jock's placid nature,' says Jean. 'He had a temper and was quick to explode. Even with Dad he would argue and have a fracas. Mum was always helping to make the peace.

'He had a really complex personality. He'd inherited the Primrose family's artistic streak, both with his sketching and handwriting, which contained sweeping loops and turns. He could also play the piano by ear and his musical talent incorporated great promise as a drummer. Billy's idols were the great Gene Krupa and Buddy Rich. He even gave a solo concert at Chesterfield's Regal Cinema. He was six foot two and, although losing his hair prematurely, very good looking.'

Billy's character was in many ways very different from Jock's, but one thing they did share was athletic prowess. In fact, the love of sport is transparent in all six of us, inherited from our dad who was a good footballer, even better cricketer and a fabulous golfer. Goodness only knows how many trophies have been won by the Wilson clan over the years. I do know that both the quality and importance of trophies in schooling has changed from Jock, Billy and Don's early years. Beautifully inscribed and made of high-quality silver, copper or brass, they put most of today's plastic awards to shame and remain worthy keepsakes. At the Chesterfield School sports day in 1940, Jock, Billy and Don's combined haul was eight silver cups and fifteen plaques.

A mixture of the right genes and a good competitive spirit gave Jock and Billy the competency needed to fight for king

and country, but their roles in aerial combat were opposite –
not by choice because Billy would have loved to have followed
Jock's lead as a fighter pilot. His difficulty with rudimentary
mathematics and the lack of time available to become more
proficient in the subject led directly to Billy becoming an air
gunner with Bomber Command.

Being 'Tail End Charlie', as rear gunners were affectionately
named, did not appeal to the vast majority of RAF trainees or
volunteers. It was by far the loneliest and most dangerous crew
position. Training procedure was as standard and demanding
for Billy as Jock's experience in a Spitfire. The period of the
course was a year and for the final month Billy was in Southern
Rhodesia with 24 CAOS. Training a whole crew could not be
undertaken in the same way as a solo flyer. There could be no
speeded-up course when seven lives were at stake. Crews had
to become not just proficient, they needed to gel as a team and
understand each other's jobs. If they became great pals, it was
a bonus.

Like Jock, Billy was to experience five different aircraft
– Anson, Airspeed Oxford, Wellington, Stirling and finally
Lancaster bombers. Although he was always part of a team,
the position at the rear of the Lancaster meant he was very much
in a world of his own. What a world! Enclosed in a small perspex
capsule, totally isolated from the other crew, it was a case of
understanding hydraulics, pyrotechnics and above all control of
the Fraser Nash turret with its four Browning machine guns.

Magazines of ammunition were fed up in metal channels from
containers, which were a considerable distance away on either
side of the fuselage. The rock-hard parachute pack was used
by most rear gunners as a seat, which was preferable to the
tiny rectangle that was provided for that purpose. In the rear
turret there was usually a strong smell of fuel oil, and Lancasters
were not pressurised so rear gunners needed a constant supply
of oxygen.

An important commodity for all rear gunners, of course, was a head for heights. All that lay between the occupant and the vastness of space was a layer of perspex. Outside temperatures could be as low as 30°F. A good flying suit and gloves were necessary as were the escape kits zipped into the suit pocket. The kits contained European currencies, maps, compass and condensed Horlicks tablets.

It's hard to believe any rear gunner enjoyed his job outside the camaraderie it created. The responsibility didn't begin and end with the firing of guns at enemy fighter planes. A rear gunner's vigilance could save an aircraft and his fellow crew by an early warning to his captain to take evasive action.

Apart from the intense loneliness of the position, journeys out and back provided far too much thinking time and for the emotionally driven Billy those long hours must have been tortuous.

From 5 May 1943 until the middle of December, he had several bases – Horwood, Newmarket, Waterbeach, Wratting Common and Tuddenham. Throughout much of this time, whatever the type of aircraft, the name of the pilot was usually Geoff Tyler. He was Australian and became one of Billy's closest friends. The crew of any bomber entrusted their lives to the skill of their pilot. In warfare, though, skill alone was not always enough, fate and luck played a huge part as well.

If the Spitfire is held responsible for victory in the fighter war, the Avro Lancaster is synonymous with the success of the bombing campaign. The pilots of these aircraft had to know their own job inside out as well as the duties of the rest of the crew.

The pilot's seat was raised and padded and fitted with arm-rests. Apart from when over enemy territory, Geoff Tyler would fly the aircraft with the left hand, using the right hand for other instruments and setting the gyro. The flight engineer would be in the adjoining seat watching the response of the four Merlin engines. Elsewhere, concentrating on their own jobs, were a bomb aimer, navigator and wireless operator. To complete the seven-man crew, there was one individual in the mid turret and finally the rear gunner in the back. But in all, forty skilled men and women were needed to keep one Lancaster operational.

The duration of Billy's flights was very different from Jock's, and major operations were nearly always flown at night. Lasting between four and eight hours, targets included Mannheim, Montlucon, Modane, Hanover, Bremen, Kassel and Berlin.

Everyone who flew experienced stark terror at times, as well as elation and relief. Billy considered Geoff Tyler to be an outstanding skipper simply because he never transmitted his own fears to the rest of the crew. My brother wrote about the 'horrible and ghastly things seen and the real meaning of the words life and death'. He was referring to the terrifying sights he witnessed during missions – Lancasters hit by enemy fire, bursting into flames, battling to remain on an even keel despite their mortal wounds; tiny figures falling out of aircraft not knowing whether their parachutes would open or not and the flaming wreckage littering the foreign landscape below. For Billy and all rear gunners, such horrors were observed from a grandstand view. Intelligent men quickly realised that sooner of later they might not return. On some nights when Bomber Command was out in force as many as ninety aircraft would be lost. Fifty-six squadrons were equipped with Lancasters. The odds of surviving a tour of thirty operations were 3–1.

Geoff Tyler and his crew had returned from seventeen operational flights, surviving the intense searchlights fastened upon them, opening the bomb doors and releasing the 14,000lbs of destruction. Each time, the huge 29 ton aircraft had struggled to escape the enemy retaliation before cruising home at 216 miles per hour.

On 16 December 1943, Lancaster Mk III Srl No. JB543–J,

one of 7,377 Lancasters to be built, took off from RAF Oakington in Cambridgeshire at 16.21 hours. The crew consisted of P/0 G. Tyler, Skipper; F/Sgt A. Smillie, Navigator; Sgt A. A. Tucker, Flight Engineer; Sgt C. R. Underhill, Wireless Operator; Sgt D. Woolford, Bomb Aimer; F/Sgt R. R. Macmillan, Air Gunner; and Sgt W. P. Wilson, Rear Gunner. As on all previous take-offs, Bill would have turned his guns so they didn't face backwards towards the next aircraft preparing to take off, which they did at intervals of thirty seconds. Billy's plane was in 7 Squadron, part of 8 Group, the Pathfinder Force, comprising 483 Lancasters and fifteen Mosquitoes. The target was Berlin, and primarily the Berlin railway station.

At 18.23 hours, a German night fighter engaged and shot down Lancaster JB543. It crashed at Wilsum, a small German town ten kilometres north west of Neuerhaus, close to the Dutch border. Initially, all seven members of the crew were listed as 'missing presumed lost', but subsequently it was discovered that two members of the crew had been able to bale out. Sergeant Woolford and F/Sgt Smillie were captured by the Germans and became prisoners of war.

After the war, my father tried, without success, to make contact with them. Letters were sent but without a response. It might simply have been a case of the letters not reaching the right destination, although my dad came to believe that perhaps the details of the Lancaster's last moments were too painful for either survivor to relay. Whatever the truth, the news of Billy's failure to return to his base came as a desperate blow. For twenty-two months Mum and Dad had slowly come to terms with Jock's death. Now the pain had to be endured for a second time and, in a way, the news of Billy's failure to return from the mission was harder to bear.

On this occasion the bad news was hand delivered. Hugh, not quite four years old, heard the knock on the front door and, with a family friend's help, opened it to receive a telegram.

Hugh remembers clearly Mum appearing and quickly taking in the dreadful truth. Her response was anticipated and in order to leave her to her sobbing, Hugh was whisked away to another part of Threepwood. Don and Jean were just as devastated and Dad again somehow controlled his feelings while wee Robin, now two, remained unaware of events.

Just two weeks before Billy died, the entire crew had been guests in Chesterfield when Mum and Dad threw a twenty-first birthday party for Geoff Tyler. A precious photograph remains showing the crew with Jean performing a trumpet solo. It had been Billy's idea to celebrate Geoff Tyler's coming of age in Chesterfield. To Mum and Dad, the six other members of that Lancaster crew were like extra sons and to Jean, who was only fourteen years of age, they were mature men. Thought had even been given to Geoff's entry to the party with the playing of a newly acquired twelve-inch recording of the RAF march.

There is no doubt whatever that Geoff enjoyed his surprise, his last letter to his parents, written on the eve of his final flight, describing the event.

Mrs Wilson was waiting to meet me and take me home. When I arrived I got the usual marvellous greeting. I always feel so welcome, everyone seems to be so glad to see me. The rest of the crew were there when I arrived. The party opened with a beautiful spread. They must have been saving some of the rationed goods for weeks. For sweet we actually had a few remaining tins of fruit salad Mrs Wilson saved from pre-war days for an occasion like this. We were all standing around just talking when suddenly the lights went out and lo and behold, in rolled a trolley and on the top was a cake about six pounds in weight I'd say. Around the edge were twenty-one candles lighting up an aircraft in the centre. I drew in a deep breath, expelling about half of the air in the room and in one mighty blow blew every one out.

I hope you receive the piece of cake sent by Mrs Wilson. I

endeavoured to make a speech but you can imagine what a flop that was.

Geoff's Mum and Dad received my mother's account of the event together with the piece of cake.

I wish you could have seen them all, such grand boys and all so fond of each other. They have such a sincere admiration for Geoff their skipper. My husband and I are very fond of Geoff, as are all our family.

Geoff looks very handsome and smart in his officer's uniform. I know you must be very proud of him. As Geoff will have told you, he and his crew are now with the Pathfinder Force and they hope to get their Pathfinder Wings in a few weeks' time.

I pray that our sons will come safely through this war.

Geoff Tyler and Billy didn't make it and nor did thousands of other young men in the prime of their life. Of the 72,786 killed and 6,538 missing from the RAF during the Second World War, 55,573 were from Bomber Command alone; 8,325 aircraft failed to return.

After Billy was lost, the RAF returned his notebook to Mum and Dad. In it they found this poem:

Have no fear for me when I fly by night
For I may wander freely mid the stars
And taste the wild intoxication of heaven.
Have no fear for me in the wind and the rain
For I am one with the sky and racing clouds forever.
I know that in an hour begrudged of time
My spirit whirling through the sky may
Come to rest upon the edge of darkness.
But waking I shall discover the brightness of eternity.
So in the beauty of the Universe shall I take delight
And in destruction, death and sorrow
Shall find my freedom.

My brothers Jock and Billy may have touched my life only briefly but their impact upon me has been constant and inspirational.

Jock's last letter to Mum and Dad was one designed to comfort. The one they received from Billy helped them in that way too, but its content also struck at the enemies of peace, happiness and freedom and illustrated why evil should never win.

My dearest Mum and Dad

Things are moving fast and I'm writing this letter for the same reason as dear old Jocky wrote the last one we received from him.

In the past few weeks I have taken part in seven of the devastating attacks made on the enemy by the RAF. I have, as each operation has passed, realised there is an ever-increasing possibility of my not returning. I would be a fool to suppose that I was not to share the possible fate of every crew who do these trips. But like Jocky, my dear mother and father, I have every faith that I shall see the ultimate conclusion of this most damnable war, and that world which we all look forward to, a better and cleaner world, fit for such truly wonderful children as my brothers and sister to grow up in.

Do not in any way grieve if you should hear I am missing. Remember again the words that Jocky wrote and which, if I am reported missing, equally apply to myself – 'there is always the chance I may escape'. I have given many hours of my spare time making out an escape plan and feel confident that I could manage it. So I ask you to share my confidence and look forward to the day we meet again. About the war there is really little I can say, but believe me I am proud to be wearing RAF blue and to be serving, in the air as Jocky did, this wonderful cause we are fighting for. It was Jock's wonderful example that gave me the necessary courage to do my job of rear gunner. I am no hero, but if it may be said that in some small way I have helped to keep up the wonderful and well-deserved reputation of the Primrose Wilsons then I shall ever be happy.

I have seen some horrible and ghastly things happen, seen the real meaning of the words life and death. But what is more I have seen some wonderful acts of courage, sacrifice and loyalty, and it has been an honour to fly with my crew, especially my skipper Geoff, whose praises I cannot sing too high and also to go into battle with all the other crews. But perhaps the greatest service the RAF has done to me is that at last I have found that for which I have searched all my life, a cause and a job in which I can lose myself and to which I can give every ounce of my strength and my mind. I have mentally and spiritually conquered my fear of death and now my prayer is that God will send you, who are no doubt having to suffer more than I in your worry, his strength and peace.

There is little else to say except to send you all my very deepest love and my thanks for just being my mother and father and family.

So for the present and until we meet again, even though it may not be on this earth, I say cheerio to my most beloved brothers, Hugh who's my main joy in life, wee Robin, my only but adorable sister Jeannie, and Don. May he ever be as fine as he is now, and of course yourself my darling mother and very wonderful father.

May God bless you all always with many smiles. I am ever and always, Your very loving son – Billy.

3
A crooked spire

'Whichever way you turn your eye
It always seems to be awry
Pray, can you tell the reason why?
The only reason known of weight
Is that the thing was never straight.'

Anon

To their eternal credit, my mum and dad never gave any immediate indication to anyone with whom they came into contact that they had suffered such grievous loss within their family. 'We have six children' was always the reply to questions about their sons and daughter. They spoke as if Jock and Billy were simply away at work. It was an attitude and stance that, much later in my life, I came to understand only too well.

Life does have to go on. People, however sympathetic, get on with their own everyday existence. Grief and how you deal with it is intensely personal. As a result of Mum and Dad's fortitude and courage, the Wilson family household in Chesterfield always radiated fun and laughter. If one of us put on a miserable face, Mum would ask who this strange person was. She had a name for him – Johnny Baggely. Grumpy looks were simply not permitted. If the moodiness persisted beyond a few minutes, woe betide my father's patience. We all knew the limits.

I was privileged to be born into this family – and to live

in Threepwood. By any standards it was big – detached, five bedrooms, huge lounge, separate dining room and airy kitchen and utility room. It was an impressive abode, but other features were more important as far as I was concerned.

The back lawn was one of my two favourite spots at 204 Ashgate Road. At any one time that patch of immaculately groomed turf represented Lord's, Wimbledon or Wembley Stadium. Test matches, tennis finals and international soccer matches were played out there, a fierce competitive spirit was nurtured at the same time, and dreams and fantasy slowly turned to reality during my first fifteen years.

If the back lawn was too wet or the grass too long, I was usually to be found in my other favourite place, on a sloping driveway in front of the double garage doors. They were wooden and, from the time I began to love football, were the target for thousands of shots I aimed at them. Before the famous goalkeeping jersey was given to me on Christmas Day 1949, I would kick a ball against the doors, varying the pace and angles while learning to control and master any size of ball. After Christmas 1949, I was smitten by the goalkeeping bug, and with a mixture of kicking and throwing, I'd practise catching and parrying the balls that rebounded in my direction. I spent hours there by myself and, unwittingly, developed basic techniques and ball-handling confidence.

Lost in my own little world, a style began to evolve as I imagined myself to be goalkeeping legends Jimmy Cowan, Frank Swift, Jack Kelsey, Bert Williams or even Ray Middleton. Ray who? Well, Ray Middleton was the keeper for our local team Chesterfield who were then a very decent Second Division side. He made more than 300 consecutive appearances for them in a career that had begun just before the Second World War. For a time, Dad used to get tickets for the games at Saltergate and although the team had some really good outfield players including Stan and George Milburn,

Gordon Dale and George Smith, I only really had eyes for Ray Middleton.

He was a solid and consistent keeper, so much so that he made four appearances for the England 'B' team. I sort of hero-worshipped him although this also had something to do with Ray being a local magistrate serving on the same bench as Mum. When he was transferred to Derby County in 1951 he often picked me up and took me with him to games at the Baseball Ground. I sensed his anxiety pre-match and listened intently to the post-match verdict on the journeys home. The sights and smells whetted my appetite. The inside of the game looked as attractive as the outside.

Ray Middleton was one of several famous keepers who were either born in Chesterfield or represented the local team. When people ask me about my birthplace and what it is famous for, I reply, 'A crooked spire, George Stephenson and goalkeepers.'

Let me start with the last one because to me it is the most important. Even before Middleton there was Sam Hardy. Born in 1883, his playing career began at Chesterfield and he went on to make around 600 appearances at his four clubs, the others being Liverpool, Aston Villa and Nottingham Forest. A league championship medal, two FA Cup winners' medals and twenty-one England caps bore testimony to his greatness. Since Hardy and Middleton, there has been Gordon Banks, John Lukic, whom I was to get to know so well in later times, John Osborne, a schoolboy team-mate, Steve Ogrizovic, Alan Stevenson, Steve Hardwick and me. All were to enjoy successful Football League careers, and two or three found the international spotlight, notably England's only World Cup winning number one, Gordon Banks.

Banksy, as he became known throughout the game, was born near Sheffield but began his illustrious career playing in goal for Chesterfield FC Youth team and went on to the first eleven. From the outset he was clearly a special talent. I would stand behind his goal for both halves of a game – there was no segregation or crowd problems in those days – and I thought he was brilliant with a tendency to be slightly flashy. When our career paths crossed, he laughed at this interpretation of his game. In his prime he could never be accused of anything but marvellous consistency.

The truth is that Gordon was born with the most natural spring in his step, so lithe and supple. Every movement was poetry in motion and I coveted the qualities that he possessed. Chesterfield adopted Gordon Banks as one of their own sons and as he performed miracles at Leicester City, Stoke City and under the England crossbar, the town deservedly took some of the credit.

Crossbars and goalposts always have to be perfectly proportioned and predictably straight, which is more than can be said of Chesterfield's famous crooked spire, which has become both a symbol and landmark for this historic market town. The Church of St Mary's and All Saints stands in the heart of the town, and its eight-sided spire, distinctive in its imperfection, is absurdly crooked. Twisted and warped, it leans 8ft 7¾ins to the south, 9ft 5⅜ ins to the south west and 3ft 9ins to the west.

The phenomenon is steeped in superstition, the oldest of the legends accusing the devil of spitefully sitting atop the weather vane and allowing his massive weight to crush the spire.

Probably much nearer to the truth, and the accepted version of the curiosity, is that in an early experiment in the construction of a perpendicular spiral, unseasoned wood was covered with lead, and the wood duly sagged under the weight. Apart from its eventual value as a tourist attraction, St Mary's Church was purely a place of worship.

Of greater value to Chesterfield was the arrival in 1838 of the father of the steam railways, George Stephenson. The man who invented the famous 'Rocket' became the most distinguished and influential resident, and his last great work in building the North Midland Railway created the vehicle that allowed local rich seams of coal and other mineral deposits to be exploited. Stephenson lived in Tapton House, and died there in 1848. Both Tapton and the crooked spire were to play a part in my growing up but that was all in the future.

The first eighteen years of my life were spent happily in Chesterfield. The town displayed two faces. One was dour and industrial while the other was gentle and green. A sign welcomed travellers to 'The Centre of Industrial England', but it was also the gateway to the Peak District, leading to the fell walks of Monsall, Lathkill and Dovedale and the splendour of Chatsworth House.

Dad loved the Derbyshire countryside almost as much as his beloved Scotland. It had a huge bearing on his decision to settle in Chesterfield as assistant in the town surveyor's department in June 1914. On his return from the Great War he became deputy Borough Engineer and Surveyor before a six-year spell in Widnes. After his return as the number one official he went on to serve Chesterfield for forty-five years.

He and Mum were never rich in monetary terms but neither were they hard up. He had a good job and made sure the family were never short of anything of importance. Mum's dowry had enabled them to purchase such an imposing home, and because of his position as Borough Engineer and Surveyor, we were considered by others to be wealthy.

The admission book from my first school illustrates the diversity of fathers' occupations. Bricklayer, joiner, electrician, works foreman, bus driver, clerk, lathe operator, wagon repairer and miner are all listed alongside the names of parents of the new enrolment on 13 January 1947 for Old Hall Road School.

A twelve-minute walk from our house, the primary school provided me with the springboard I needed to further my love of the world's greatest game. Jack Hemmings was the teacher in charge of football. He was a great enthusiast, cared for his charges, believed in strong discipline and was a qualified referee. His recollections of the young Wilson are of a 'little boy not too keen at first to keep goal because there wasn't enough activity for him. Centre-half or midfield was the preference for a couple of years. He was always taking knocks, which often produced tears, so I remember telling him if he ever wanted to be a real player, he'd have to get up and get on with it.'

It's a pretty accurate assessment, especially the tears. One way or another, I have always cried too easily. Over-protected in the family circle, I rarely got into the same scraps or fisticuffs as my schoolmates. I wasn't hard or strong enough. Worse, I never could accept defeat easily as a kid. It's been hard enough as an adult but at primary school or in the back garden it was all-embracing. 'Super game' or 'rotten game' was the simplistic response I took to winning or losing.

I believe my brother Hugh and his friends played a huge part in helping to nurture and sharpen the competitive spirit burning within me. Being almost three years older, he was always that little bit bigger, better and stronger than me. I hated losing to him at tennis, cricket or anything else. The more I lost, the more I hated it, particularly when football was the sport of the day.

Hugh and his pals used to stick me in goal and then try to break the back of the net, except there was no net. I'd love to know how many miles I trekked retrieving a football. It proved to be the perfect grounding for the future. Slowly but surely the age gap didn't appear as great. On the way up, Hugh was always there with me. His stake in my success as a footballer is profound. At the moment of my greatest achievement with Arsenal, collecting an FA Cup medal to complete the 1970–71 double, Hugh's face was the first one I spotted in the crowd that lined the downward steps of Wembley's presentation area. He deserved the gold medal I proudly held as much as I did. Super game!

That medal came some twenty years after my first triumph as the goalkeeper for Old Hall Road Primary School when we won the local schools tournament. The journey had begun.

Sport dominated my early life as much as it has since. Several sports came fairly easily to me. Finals of Chesterfield Tennis Championships were won and lost and for a time I thought it would be better to pursue a career in tennis, simply because you performed alone. There were no team-mates to blame in defeat, only yourself.

The same could be said of athletics. I enjoyed increasing success as a long jumper and as a runner in the 440 yards. School, town and county championship wins meant I represented Derbyshire in the All England Athletics Championships in Southampton. Being humbled now and again does no one any harm and humbled I was. Drawn in the outside lane of an early heat in the first event of the first day, I was in the lead for all of two hundred yards. Then the stagger began to unfold. First one, then another and another until R. Wilson (Derbyshire) came in last place. Two full days of competition and lonely digs ended any great ambition of an appearance in the Olympic Games, as an athlete at least. Rotten game!

Mum and Dad's patience was tested to the full especially when, in my teens, the moodiness of adolescence added to the long faces and door slammings. Johnny Baggely wasn't allowed in the house. On two occasions Dad had enough and Mum was unable to dissuade him from exacting the ultimate punishment of a strapping. It hurt but did no harm. It was deserved.

The military man and the minister's daughter were a wonderful partnership and perfect foil for each other. Dad's organisation and intelligence was a perfect balance for Mum's common sense and loving nature. Every day was a joy, every holiday an absolute treasure. Anderby Creek near Skegness, Prestatyn in North Wales, and Scotland of course, were the main destinations of the family holidays. The alarm clock would be set for

3.30 a.m. We would leave home by 4.15 and be well into our holidays by lunchtime – such was the military precision with which Dad planned his and Mum's well-deserved breaks. Every family photograph reflects the pleasure we enjoyed as a family. Jock and Billy expressed their thoughts about their parents and family in their last letters, and I would endorse the sentiments expressed. Our gratitude was magnified after Mum and Dad survived a dreadful car crash in 1950.

Occasionally they would take a break by themselves, always in Scotland, returning to either Ayrshire where my Dad's roots lay, or to the fair city of Perth where Mum's brother, Sir John Ure Primrose, was the Lord Provost for nine years.

They had pulled into a lay-by to take in the beauty of the Scottish countryside. Mum and Dad were in the front, Dad's sister Winifred was in the rear. An oncoming car, driven by a lady doctor, who later admitted to have been glancing at a map, went out of control. My parents sat transfixed as the vehicle careered across the road and hit them with great force, spinning their car like a top across the road.

Auntie Winnie, who was a large lady, was hurled out of the car and thrown some distance, sustaining a variety of injuries. Mum's injuries were less severe, although a huge cut on her head left her hair matted with blood. Dad was lucky to come away with a damaged leg and severely bruised chest. The great thing was they lived to tell the tale.

The drama was thankfully short-lived. Don and his fiancée Mary, my sister Jean, who was nursing, plus family friends, all pulled together to ensure that Hugh and I remained partly unaware of just what a close call my parents and Auntie Winnie had experienced.

Donald Primrose Wilson was born on 7 June 1927. He was a character 'in extremis'. I used to call him Walter Mitty because his engaging personality often included touches of fantasy. At the height of my success with Arsenal he rarely asked me about my work on a football field; instead, he had visions of glamour and a showbiz life. Hard as I tried, I could never convince Don that we didn't spend each and every night at film premieres or in the company of glamorous ladies.

Of the six of us, Don had the worst deal. Losing Jock and Billy catapulted him into the role of eldest son. It was so hard for him. He never enjoyed the opportunities provided by good schooling, the best teachers having left and gone to war, to be replaced by supply teachers, many of them unqualified. Problems in one particular subject were so severe that in seeking outside help for Don, Mum and Dad were advised to let his teacher know he would benefit simply by more encouragement and kindness. The supply teacher duly got the gist of it, marking Don's next work '0/10. Much better effort'.

I loved that story and never forgot its significance in my own days as a schoolteacher. Don had a love of big bands, Frank Sinatra and farming. He and Mary had their own smallholding above Ashover in Derbyshire although eventually the demands took their toll and he left the land to work for Tarmac.

Catherine Jean Primrose Wilson was the only one of the six not born in Chesterfield. My sister's arrival, on 10 June 1929, came during Dad's spell as Borough Engineer and Surveyor of Widnes. It's a family joke that my sharp goalkeeping reactions come from Jean. In her early teens she would help Mum in changing my nappy. On one occasion I seemed to be unduly disturbed and all attempts at stopping my crying failed until Jean checked the new nappy. Without going into too intimate detail, she found the pin had embraced not just the towelling but also my manhood. So to Jean I owe the anxious, agitated appearance I adopted within the penalty area. The experience was at least good training for Jean when she went on to pursue a successful career in nursing.

Hugh and I were always competing against one another and if it wasn't Dad encouraging us it was our babysitters. Joe and

Myrtle Sanderson looked after us on the evenings our parents spent at the local Caledonian Society, at council events or with their friends. Joe and Mrs Joe, as we knew them, would set up an imaginary boxing ring in the dining room, stools placed in each corner, and proper gloves provided. Rocky Marciano, Sugar Ray Robinson, Floyd Patterson and two British fighters, Don Cockell and a local Chesterfield fighter Bruce Woodcock, were the legends we had been brought up on. Our fights were meant to be tame and friendly but when the occasional straight right or left connected all hell would break loose.

Loving sport as passionately as I did was not conducive to good schoolwork. When it came to the 'three Rs', I was good at reading, average at writing and absolutely hopeless at arithmetic. I was also distracted by Elizabeth Pogson. She was slim, pretty and my first girlfriend. At ten and eleven years of age, such liaisons are always special. When we passed our eleven-plus exams we both were placed at Tapton House Grammar School.

George Stephenson's old home had been turned into a mixed secondary school. Dad was less than enamoured at the examining body's choice for me. My four brothers all went to Chesterfield Grammar School. It was an all-boys establishment and Jock had been head boy there. From day one, my parents sought to have me transferred from Tapton to the family preference, but it took two years.

During that time, my footballing ambitions continued to flourish to the extent that, in the 1955–56 season, I was selected for the Chesterfield Boys Under-15 team a year ahead of my time. Playing at football league grounds was both exciting and nerve-racking, but I was in a good team and we made the last eight of the English Schools Shield Competition before losing 3–0 at Brighton's Goldstone ground.

Our left-half was John Osborne from Staveley Netherthorpe School. He was a good player for one so tall and gangly, and he had a strong personality. We were to meet again as professional players, and his position was a total surprise. He was the opposing goalkeeper, playing for West Bromwich Albion, after taking up goalkeeping in his late teens. Not only did he make 250 league appearances for the Baggies, but John remains forever in the record books as Albion's FA Cup winning keeper when Jeff Astle's goal beat Everton in the 1968 final.

I can't honestly say I was a confident keeper in my first year in the Chesterfield Boys team but I must have done enough to catch the eye because I was chosen to play in a junior international trial. As a result, I travelled as reserve keeper for the England Under-14 team when we drew 1–1 with Ireland at Carrow Road, Norwich. Barry Smart from West Suffolk got the nod for the No. 1 jersey and he was to remain my main rival a year later. At this stage, I was more delighted than disappointed at my progress.

Talking of stages, for a short time an acting career became a faint possibility. Thanks to Phyl Wildin, an amazingly talented lady, Tapton House had earned a fine reputation for amateur dramatics. During my first year, Miss Wildin gave me the male lead role in 'The Princess and the Woodcutter'. In true Hollywood style I fell for my leading lady. Where I held ambitions of being a footballer, she only ever wanted to act. Her name was Margaret Miles. That she didn't fulfil her ambition to go on the professional stage is entirely my fault, only because she decided to remain my real-life leading lady.

Our early love affair was conducted through long walks in the company of one of our classmates, Billy Tart. Very romantic! It began when we were twelve and has continued, with the exception of a two-year spell between thirteen and fifteen, to this very day.

My time at Tapton drew to a close after two years and a second starring role, in Shakespeare's 'As You Like It'. I was love lost in that production as well, playing Silvius and pleading

'Sweet Phoebe, do not scorn me. Say that you love me not but do not scorn me.' These are the only words I can remember but boy, did I deliver them with great melancholy.

Within months I was rehearsing for another of Shakespeare's classics, but at a different school where the roles of women were taken by boys. 'King Henry IV Part One' was my debut play at Chesterfield Grammar School. Dad and Mum's persistence had been worthwhile, the family tradition upheld. Again I can recall just one line, the last when Harry Hotspur dies with the words 'No Percy, thou art dust and food for w-o-r-m-s', delivered with a stuttering that would have left Olivier or Branagh in hysterics.

By now I knew tights were not for me. Great legs that I possessed, they were far better suited to football shorts. My new school sustained the dreams I had always held. The physical education teacher was a touch formal but a brilliant organiser of fixtures and unfailingly loyal in his support of his most talented players. To Gordon Jephcote I owe a huge debt. He made me believe that the talent I had was out of the ordinary. He pushed me into situations that shyness on my part had previously prohibited, and in arranging thirty-six games every season, he made sure that I was never short of match practice.

Very quickly, I was again representing Chesterfield Boys Under-15 team. The hours spent in front of the garage doors paid huge dividends. Where I was once anxious I became certain, where negative thoughts had prevailed I was filled with self-assurance. I knew I was good. How good was altogether another thing, but the write-ups were encouraging and indicative of a style that came to serve me so well in years to come – 'Fast feet and very brave, keeper Wilson shows distinct promise' reported the *Derbyshire Times* after Chesterfield Boys beat Grimsby in the divisional final of the 1956–57 English Schools Shield.

There was a similarly complimentary write-up in the next tie, but it didn't make up for a 3–1 defeat by Manchester Boys who knocked us out in the First Round Proper. Manchester's third goal was scored by a skinny little guy who had run the game from the inside-right position, as we knew it in those days. Afterwards I studied the programme and found his name – Norbert Stiles, St Patrick's School. What a player I thought; he's got a real chance. Norbert did take his chance and became world famous as Nobby Stiles, the toothless hero who jigged his way around Wembley Stadium after England became champions of the world in 1966.

The summer of '66 was still ten years away, and forty-five days after our first meeting, Nobby and I shared the same dressing room as the North met the South at Cadburys Bournville Lane ground in Birmingham. It was a trial match for the 1956–57 England Under-15 team. The North put three goals past Barry Smart in the South goal. I kept a clean sheet and felt I'd played well. Selections for the final trial seemed to agree with my assessment for the England team versus the Rest included No. 1 R. Wilson, Chesterfield, No. 8 N. Stiles, Manchester.

It was a massive moment for me. I had got there with a mixture of hard work, blind ambition and, above all, thanks to the support of my parents. New boots, and only the best, had always been forthcoming, usually from Archers, an amazing sports shop opposite Sheffield United's ground at Bramall Lane. Mum or Dad or both came to every game of importance. Constructive criticism was my father's role, whereas my mother focused on a pat on the back or a consoling word or two, notably, 'Don't worry, dearie, it will all turn out for the best.'

The city and venue for my biggest game was hugely significant. The ground was Old Trafford, home of the Busby Babes, a side every boy of my age wanted to play for. I was no exception and I knew Matt Busby and his staff would be watching. Manchester was the home of my goalkeeping idol, Bert Trautmann, a former German prisoner of war who played for City, the other team in town.

Dad did not share my enthusiasm for either my idol or my ambition. The years 1956 and 1957 were to play an extraordinary part in my life. They were dramatic years for me in every respect, a time when Chesterfield and all it meant to me took second place, a time when the city of Manchester helped shape a boy into a man.

4

Manchester, mentor, Munich

'Macte nova virtute, puer, sic itur ad astra.'
Good luck to your young ambition, lad,
that is the way to the stars.

Virgil

It was truly a heady, intoxicating football cocktail that I con-
sumed between May 1956 and February 1958. In those twenty-
two months, I was captivated by events surrounding the city of
Manchester. The brilliance, both collective and individual, of
its two famous football teams, United and City, excited and
enthralled the nation, not just me, but I had more than a passing
interest. The reds were the team I had a chance to join, the blues
possessed the goalkeeper I idolised. Events were to embrace me.

When I walked on to the Old Trafford pitch on Saturday,
2 March 1957, playing in goal for England versus the Rest,
I knew Manchester United were not just hosting the England
Under-15 trial but were watching.

Joe Armstrong, their famous chief scout, was a small, delight-
ful man, a retired civil servant. It was he, as much as anyone,
who had brought the best young talent in Britain to the theatre
of dreams, and given manager Matt Busby the chance to create
one of the most exciting teams ever seen at club level. Roger
Byrne, Tommy Taylor, Duncan Edwards and the rest had

already been crowned the 1956 champions and were to retain the title the following year. Where so many First Division teams contained older players, the Babes intrigued a nation with its youthfulness.

Gordon Jephcote, my sportsmaster, and other Chesterfield School officials, had already whispered to me that Manchester United had been asking questions about the curly haired keeper, but, as so often happens in football, immediate ambitions were dashed. It wasn't that I played badly – not for the first or last time, my trademark save, diving at opponents' feet, ended in injury and I failed to return for the second half. Miserable is not the accurate word to describe my feelings as I sat out the second forty-five minutes. Not even the awesome surroundings of Old Trafford offered consolation.

When, a week later, the England team was announced to play Eire at Plymouth, the name Barry Smart appeared in goal. Bobby Wilson was reserve. Worse was to come in the aftermath of the 9–1 win at Home Park. The chairman of the English Schools Football Association, Eric Hayhow, first congratulated the squad on their performance and then led on to the arrangements for the next fixture, which was to be against Wales at Wembley Stadium. Imagine what being involved in that game meant to a fifteen year old. Every detail of the occasion was unveiled to an increasingly excited group of players, when the chairman unexpectedly said, 'I'm afraid one of you is going to be disappointed to miss Wembley, but the selectors have decided that another boy did well in the trials and he's going to take your place Bobby.'

Did he mean Bobby Tambling, our brilliant No. 9, who was to go on to make a name for himself at Chelsea and Crystal Palace? No, he was not looking at the boy from Havant, he was looking straight at me.

'I hope you understand, Bobby?' he said. I think I nodded. I hope I nodded. Knowing me, I doubt that I nodded. Tears weren't far away as I dashed away and stumbled through corridors to find my room. Totally inconsolable my world had fallen apart. In my place as reserve for the Wembley game was Bob Charles from Southampton.

A knock on my door revealed the team trainer, Trevor Churchill. Once a keeper himself, he understood my hurt, cared enough to share it and made it quite clear that I would not only be back, but would play at least twice for England before the end of the season. It helped a little, but not much.

Coming second or third has had to become an acquired taste for the competitor I have always been. At that moment, the taste was particularly bitter. My heart had been set on being involved at Wembley, the stadium where every footballer in the world wanted to play at least once. To me, Wembley already conjured up images that have lasted a lifetime – the Matthews Final of 1953, the 6–3 annihilation of England the same year by Ferenc Puskas and Hungary, and, top of the list, the moment my mentor and hero, Bert Trautmann, played on with a broken neck to help ensure Manchester City won the 1956 FA Cup final.

Choosing an idol is invaluable. It can help speed the learning process by providing unlimited inspiration; allied with natural talent and determination, that can produce an unstoppable force. I chose well. Bert Trautmann was one of the greatest goalkeepers of all time. Many other keepers hero-worshipped him, including Gordon Banks. Bert had a presence and style unlike any other I had seen at the time, and one area of his game was uncannily similar to the one I was developing. It was an ability to dive headlong at opponents' feet. It's dangerous and most textbooks, although stopping short of calling it stupid, still suggest it is unnecessary. Such advice usually comes from individuals who have never played in goal and faced an onrushing forward, sensed the momentary loss of control of the ball and seized that moment to save a certain goal.

Diving headfirst will always get keepers to the ball quicker than diving to the side to block. If it saves a near certain goal, the risk is justified.

Bert nearly lost his life diving at feet, but on the day he broke his neck, his save single-handedly ensured FA Cup glory for Manchester City. Having Bert as an idol held an additional problem for me. My father was, understandably, less than enthusiastic about my choice. The Great War and the loss of Jock and Billy in the Second World War had scarred him for life when it came to acceptance of the Germans. Mum could acknowledge that war was war, that young men and women from both sides were victims of their country's cause, just or otherwise. Forgiveness for my dad was not an option. He never sat me down and told me I shouldn't idolise Bert Trautmann, but one day he made his feelings clear.

Those tears that accompanied my non-selection for England Schoolboys at Wembley had been replaced by the joy of a third international selection. Northern Ireland and Scotland had been defeated during my first two appearances. Now I was standing on the platform at Chesterfield railway station heading for the Neckar Stadium in Stuttgart, opponents Germany.

'Play well. Just do your best,' was Mum's fond farewell. Dad's was even briefer and very much to the point.

'Win,' he said, and repeated, 'Win!' His face was set, his fingernails dug into my arms and hurt, physically.

It is a poignant and sad memory for in that moment I instinctively understood how much Germany had taken away from him and why he found it so difficult to accept my love of Bert Trautmann. As I journeyed south to Harwich and across the water to the Hook of Holland, I thought about my idol's fame. I looked at both sides of the debate and, without ever detracting from the pain that my parents suffered during wartime, the admiration I had for Bert somehow increased rather than diminished.

If my own father, such a proud and lovely gentleman, felt so strongly, so too must thousands of football fans throughout Britain. The hostility and abuse that Trautmann endured in his early career would surely have shattered the confidence and belief of a weaker man. Yet at this very moment in 1957, Bernhard Carl Trautmann, former member of the Hitler Youth Movement and Nazi paratrooper, had won over a nation. He was the reigning Footballer of the Year in England.

The honour reflected massive credit on the man and the background from which he came. It was a story that fascinated me and provided valuable lessons. The first foreigner to receive the award, the first goalkeeper, Bert took his place in line behind the illustrious previous winners Matthews, Carey, Mercer, Johnston, Wright, Lofthouse, Finney and Revie. This moment, the pinnacle of his fame, had all begun in a German prisoner-of-war camp at Northwich in Cheshire.

Football was the favourite pastime but it wasn't until he moved to another camp at Ashton-in-Makerfield that his career in goal started. Released in March 1948, he chose to stay and play for St Helens rather than be repatriated. Two years later, Manchester City, looking for a replacement for the great Frank Swift, signed Trautmann. Initially, Bert understudied Ronnie Powell, who was soon to be transferred, ironically, to Chesterfield, where I would regularly watch him in action.

The signing of Bert Trautmann by City so soon after the agonies of the war created bedlam. He received protest letters, abusive phone calls, and particularly vitriolic attacks on his name and nationality from the Jewish community, still reeling from the inhumanity of the Germans between 1939 and 1945. A wise Rabbi, Dr Altmann, saved the situation from developing.

'Despite the terrible cruelties we suffered, we should not try to punish an individual German who is unconnected with these crimes, out of hatred,' was the Rabbi's message. 'If this

...therine Wingate Primrose – my mum – on ...wedding day.

Dad – William Smith Wilson, Highland Light Infantry.

...e man after whom I was named, my ...ndfather, the Reverend Robert Primrose – ...all accounts, a spellbinding preacher.

My brothers and sister – Jock with Jean, Billy with Hugh, and Don. I had not yet put in an appearance.

On the back lawn at Threepwood, below the bedroom where I was born two years earlier. Billy (*back row, second left*), Don (*back row, far right*), Hugh (*little boy on left*) and Jean celebrate pilot Geoff Tyler's (*back row, far left*) birthday, together with two more pals from the Lancaster crew. Two weeks later, all but two of the crew were killed. I'm at the front, too young to know much about it.

Handwritten on aircraft: *To my brother and best friend, Primrose and Bill. at Balfour the very best of good wishes.*

John Primrose Wilson – Jock sent this photograph of himself in his beloved Spitfire to Billy.

William Primrose Wilson – Billy standing by the Lancaster in which he was the rear gunner.

Mum visiting Jock's grave for the first time. Robert, who relieved the moment by putting a plant holder on his head, Anna and John look on.

An early double – Old Hall Road Primary School team with a proud goalkeeper.

The game my dad wouldn't watch – tipping over during the England schoolboys Under-15 international versus Scotland at Hillsborough.

e Mayor of Chesterfield, Alderman W.
eston, presents my England schoolboy cap,
57. Dad (*centre*) was there to witness it.

Victory in the 440 yards, Chesterfield and
District championships, aged seventeen.

Chesterfield Grammar School production –
nry IV Part One. What a Harry Hotspur!

Megs as St Joan – seventeen-year-old
leading lady.

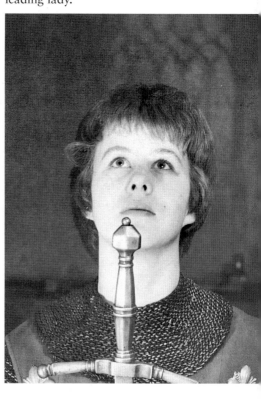

Off to college, Megs north to Bretton Hall, me south to Loughborough.

I was proud of this save, as Loughborough Colleges beat mighty Bishop Auckland 3–1 en route to the quarter-finals of the 1960–61 FA Amateur Cup.

Billy Wright conducts a training session with Tony Burns and me prior to the pre-season game in Hamburg, August 1963.

an and Dennis had a miracle escape when a Handley Page Victor bomber flattened their rmhouse in Stubton.

ving at the feet of Hamburg's Uwe Seeler, the famous West German international, August 63.

Rutherford School celebrates the selection of 'Sir' for the Arsenal first team.

I made my league debut against Nottingham Forest in October 1963 while still an amateur.

footballer is a decent fellow, there is no harm. Each case must be judged on its merits.'

Bert's appreciation of this gesture, written in a newspaper article, was similar to the appreciation he felt for an altogether more succinct letter he received direct from an impatient City fan: 'I don't give a fuck what you are or where you come from as long as you can play and put some life into this fucking City team. Best of luck and take no fucking notice of these miserable bastards.'

Bert Trautmann's professional career was under way. Within weeks his illustrious predecessor had given his seal of approval. 'Good lad, Bert, you'll do for me,' was Frank Swift's assessment. More than 600 appearances later, one evening in April 1964, a combined Manchester City/United team met an international eleven in front of almost 50,000 fans at Maine Road. Bert Trautmann's testimonial game paid tribute to a magnificent goalkeeper and equally outstanding human being. Fans were weeping unashamedly as Bert waved goodbye. In the fourteen years he played for City, Bert Trautmann won the admiration of all football fans, and with his sportsmanship and daring style, did more than any German politician to help bring together two nations so divided by wartime experiences.

To me, he was the best goalkeeper of his time, and because of his influence upon me, he remains probably my favourite. When I stood behind his goal, as a teenager, I knew I would rarely see his like again. His presence, his skill and his will to win were obvious, but the party piece that made him different was almost too quick for the senses to take in. Diving headlong at a forward's feet became a flurry of action with Bert invariably emerging clutching the ball. I don't remember ever applauding as I stood in the crowds at Maine Road – I was star-struck, hopelessly star-struck – but it was a skill I could replicate, of that I was certain. The embryonic Trautmann in the body of Bob Wilson was beginning to grow and when City reached two successive FA Cup finals, in 1955 and 1956, the German had no bigger fan.

City lost 3–1 to Newcastle in the 1955 final and despite some breathtaking saves, Trautmann made an error when he let Bobby Mitchell squeeze one between the near post and himself. As a fourteen year old, I should have studied the mistake more carefully because sixteen years later I was to make a near identical blunder in the 1971 FA Cup final. No one blamed Bert Trautmann in 1955, especially his father who was overcome by the post-match reception his son received.

'I have seen the British people as they really are and I am so proud and thankful. You must never forget them, Bert, or what they have done for you.' In a whisper, he added, 'You know, Bert, Hitler never had a reception quite like this.'

One year later, on the same Wembley stage, Bert Trautmann repeated his brilliant saves without any error and by his courage in diving at the feet of Birmingham City's Peter Murphy, made a save that kept Manchester City's 3–1 lead intact. For the last twenty minutes, the goalkeeper was in absolute agony. Watching from afar in Chesterfield, I was suffering for and with him. The final whistle and most of what ensued was a blur for Bert. He grasped his neck all the time while he collected his precious winner's medal from the Queen, only later complaining that 'my neck's giving me Old Harry'.

The X-rays confirmed the worst possible news. With his neck broken and encased in plaster, it was seven months before my idol played again. It didn't matter because what I had witnessed inspired me not just for the moment, but forever. Twenty-five years after Bert Trautmann broke his neck, he and I were both back at Wembley Stadium for the 1981 FA Cup final in which Manchester City met Tottenham Hotspur. The event was of secondary importance to me because I knew I was going to meet the man in person for the first time, just prior to kick-off.

On the television gantry, high above the Wembley pitch, I

was there as a BBC reporter, my own football career having ended in 1974. I was as nervous as if I had been going to play in that day's final. Suddenly, he was there, tall and blond and wearing the biggest smile you could imagine as he spotted me. I shouldn't have worried that he wouldn't know who I was or about what embarrassing words I might utter. Bert never gave me a chance to make a fool of myself. He stuck out a huge hand and said, 'Hello Bob. I know, I was your idol. Thank you. I'm glad.'

As journalist Frank McGhee put it, he was 'a man who insisted on keeping his German nationality because he felt that what a man is, is more important than where he was born.' I only wish my dad had been with me.

Back in March 1957, almost every bit of disappointment I had previously felt at being left out of the Wembley game evaporated as the news of my selection to play in goal for England hit the local newspapers and was confirmed by letter. Trevor Churchill's predictions had materialised. The next international was to be played on Friday, 5 April 1957 in Belfast, Northern Ireland the opponents. I was the only change from the side that had played at Wembley. After two wins, the pressure was on me.

Travelling overnight by boat across the Irish Sea on the Thursday is certainly not the ideal preparation for an international to be played the following evening, but that's exactly what happened. We disembarked, somewhat dishevelled, at Donegal Quay at 8.30 a.m. on Friday morning and were taken to our hotel, the Kensington in Fisherwick Place. After settling in, a training session of sorts took place on the playing field of Queen's University, followed by a grand luncheon at 1.00 p.m. Between 2.30 and 3.30, the Rt Hon. H. Midgley MP, Minister for Education, Northern Ireland, received the England team at Stormont, Ireland's Houses of Parliament. The evening meal was at 6.00 and a private bus took the players to Grosvenor Park, home of Distillery FC at 7.00. Kick-off was at 8.00.

You might describe our preparation as being inadequate. Still, what mattered was how England's debut boy played in goal. The programme read, 'Robert Wilson (Chesterfield School) goalkeeper. Height 6 ft. Weight 11st 2lbs. Regular keeper for Chesterfield Schools and Derbyshire for two seasons. Quick, agile and has excellent positional sense. Kept wicket for Derbyshire Boys at cricket last season. Idolises and imitates Bert Trautmann. Fearless at opponent's feet.'

The opposing centre-half had a friendly face. He came from Bangor and his name was Terry Neill. Later, he was to be a team-mate, a room-mate and, as manager of Arsenal, a boss. He brought me back to Highbury as the goalkeeping coach.

It was the opening match of the Victory Shield competition, the first schoolboy international to be played under floodlights. England were the better team and won comfortably enough in the end, but I was grateful to the Chesterfield Boys' Secretary A.D. Wilson, who accompanied me on the trip, for sending a telegram to my folks stating, 'Won three nil. Bob brilliant!'

It wasn't that good a display but it was from that performance that Manchester United confirmed their interest in me and Nobby Stiles. United's first-team coach, Bert Whalley, was watching me for the third time and reported back to Joe Armstrong. The little scout approached my father directly. Dad was thrilled at my progress and performances but remained decidedly cool towards United's enquiry.

I arrived back in Chesterfield with a new possession to treasure. My England Schoolboys' cap, with its tarnished gold tassel and edging, remains on display alongside my Scotland cap. It's a unique pairing but many unpredictable years and an historic international rule change separate the two seasons that those caps embrace.

Dad faced a bit of a dilemma when I kept my place for the next

Victory Shield game. It was to be played just twelve miles from Chesterfield at Hillsborough, the home of Sheffield Wednesday. That was the easy part for Dad. It was the opponents that created the problem. Scotland meant so much to him and he'd never really envisaged his goalkeeping son being good enough to play at international level, let alone for 'the auld enemy' England. But the rules in 1957 were clear. You could only play for the country in which you were born, and in my case that was England.

Dad didn't let on about his intentions on matchday. I expected him to be there because he was clearly delighted that I was doing so well. Come Easter Tuesday, 23 April 1957, the Wilson clan gathered expectantly to watch their Bobby; all, that is, except Dad who preferred to support from a distance. With hindsight, I think it would have been too much of a double-edged sword for him, with his son keeping another clean sheet but Scotland going down 3–0 despite playing the better football. Four days after Hillsborough, England Boys wrapped up the Victory Shield competition by beating Wales again, this time at Swansea. Bob Charles was given his cap in goal and I was reserve.

A month later, my departure for the friendly in Germany led to my Dad's emotional and emphatic demand, 'Win!' This, the first international to be played on foreign soil by an England Schoolboy side, did meet with his strong approval, 3–1 to England the scoreline. I nearly got carried off. Diving at feet, I was winded quite badly and, while trying to recover, was simply picked up and plonked on a stretcher. My German was limited to *Ja* and *Nein*, so yelling and gesticulating, I threw myself off the stretcher. Feeling somewhat foolish, I returned to my goal with a mixture of applause and laughter ringing in my ears.

The experience of playing in the Neckar Stadium was enhanced by the fact that our game acted as a curtain-raiser to a full international between Germany and Scotland. The Scottish senior players were brilliant with us and I chatted with and got the autographs of keeper Tommy Younger, centre-half George Young, Blackpool's little striker Jackie Mudie and one Tommy Docherty of Preston North End. What a strange thread it is that seems to weave the different stages of my footballing life. Nobby Stiles, Terry Neill, Bert Trautmann and Tommy Docherty were all there at the beginning of my career and again much later on. I'm certain that on that day in May 1957, Tommy Docherty never dreamt he would eventually be manager of Scotland; less possible still was the thought that I would be his first selection as goalkeeper.

On our return to England, the schoolboy team shook hands and wished each other well. All but one of the squad immediately became apprentice professionals. The exception was me, but not of my choosing. Real success for the fourteen youngsters was limited. I know Cliff Jackson played for, among others, Crystal Palace and Torquay United, and Derek Woodley for Gillingham. The careers of most hit a brick wall. Just three made the big time – Bobby Tambling, Nobby Stiles and, after an unusual route to the top, me.

I had a foot on the first rung of the ladder to being a professional footballer. Any mention of it to my parents was met with both encouragement and a warning. I was now certain I had been blessed with a special talent – the best team in the land in 1957 were knocking on the door to confirm it – but Manchester United and football as a career held no real security, not in relation to a job that guaranteed both a present and a future. I only half listened to my mum and dad and didn't realise that they were preparing me for a hammer blow that was to come crashing down in less than twelve months' time.

Before it fell, they seemed to go along with United's advances and allowed me to travel to Manchester between July and December 1957 to play for one of United's junior sides. Every time the train pulled in, Joe Armstrong was there to meet me, usually with Nobby Stiles in tow. It was one of the touches that made Manchester United the club it is. Most of the junior games were one-sided and we'd win 6–0 or 8–1. The highlight always was being taken back to Old Trafford from United's training grounds. I would walk out into the vast stadium and marvel at the row upon row of red seats. Crowds of 50,000 plus came to worship here.

Central to the Reds' success were Matt Busby and his assistant Jimmy Murphy. To be in their company was as difficult for a fifteen year old as it was special. I tried to listen hard and understand what they told me, Busby in the gentle Scottish brogue that was familiar to me from my parents, Murphy with an emotionally charged Welsh accent straight from the Rhondda. Certain things that Matt Busby said to me made such an impression that they stuck. I guess he was simply selling himself and the club he loved but he talked about the part I would play in his plan.

'This isn't just about the current team. What we have in mind is a succession of Busby Babes, four, five or six teams. Above all,' he stressed, 'you must want to come here. I don't want you if you have any fears or doubts. To be a United player, you must have skill, flair and character, and the greatest of these is character.'

Very few youngsters have ever turned Manchester United down but the records show that I did reject the chance to join the best team of its time, one of the most charismatic ever. I'll never forget the night my parents and I were invited by Matt Busby to Old Trafford to watch the 1957 Charity Shield. Manchester United, as champions, met Aston Villa, who had controversially beaten the Babes in the FA Cup final, Peter McParland scoring both Villa goals and inflicting serious injury upon United keeper Ray Wood with a shoulder charge that nowadays would earn a straight red card.

Having been deprived of the famous League and FA Cup double in such a manner, there was an electric atmosphere at

Old Trafford. I knew why we were there. United were expecting to cross the t's and dot the i's on a schoolboy contract that would tie me to Manchester United. The United coach Bert Whalley took me to one side as Matt Busby turned on his immense charm with my parents. Bert asked me how well I had thought the Villa keeper Nigel Sims had played. I told him he was one of the three best around at that moment and that he'd confirmed it during the game, saving Villa from a bigger thrashing than the 4–0 they received.

Bert Whalley knew how to impress a fifteen year-old youngster.

'There's no reason why you shouldn't be out there one day,' he said. 'You could be twice the goalkeeper he is.'

He needn't have been so over the top. In my head I was already a Manchester United player. When Matt Busby took my dad into his office separately, I assumed it was to discuss the small print and how I could make the most of my schooling. On his return, there was no clue to what had been agreed. Matt Busby put his arm round me and wished me well. Bert Whalley, who was a big man, gave me a bear hug and bade me farewell with the words, 'Don't forget how good you can be, son.'

The suspense was awful but within minutes of getting back in our car and setting off on the drive back to Chesterfield, Dad relayed to me his private meeting with the United manager.

'Matt Busby asked whether you would be prepared to join the club on schoolboy forms. I told him no. Football and Manchester United can wait until you get some decent qualifications behind you.'

His voice was gentle but firm. It was a good thing that it was night-time. The darkness hid the miserable face and the tears. It never occurred to me to argue or to question my father's decision, nor has it done since, but I have always wondered. It has become the great imponderable of my life. Ten years on from that moment, I was still battling to find first-team football.

Twenty-six years of age was late to become a regular choice. If I had gone to Old Trafford at fifteen, would I have become a Busby Babe by nineteen or twenty, shared in their triumphs, perhaps even made an earlier appearance in international football? Would I have become a better goalkeeper? Or would I have been stamped 'reject' and dumped along with the hundreds of young footballers who suffer such a fate?

My father was right, of course; at least, in 1957 his decision was sensible. He was determined none of his children should have a wasted career, and football, he believed, could be just that. The maximum wage was £20 per week, the professional game offered me no security and I had nothing else to fall back on. It was time to swallow my pride and buckle down to school work and the best education possible. It was difficult, sad in its way, but at least Bert Whalley's words couldn't be taken away from me – 'Don't forget how good you can be, son.'

They were great words, made more meaningful because they were the last I would ever hear from Bert, one of twenty-three people to perish six months later in the snow and slush at the end of a Munich runway. In my short time, playing in the United junior sides, I had been introduced to the stars who made up the Busby Babes. I just remember how relaxed they were, how confident they appeared and how friendly. I followed their every move and every game, and when their special brand of football began to terrorise the best teams in Europe, cheered from afar. I may have been made to wait a little longer to be a Red Devil, but the dream never wavered, especially in the months immediately following Dad's decision. The events surrounding United in the first week of February 1958 made sure that my time as a United schoolboy would never be forgotten.

On Saturday, 1 February, United played Arsenal at Highbury in a classic game that both clubs' fans still talk about. The final score was Arsenal 4 Manchester United 5. The United side read as follows:

Gregg, Foulkes, Byrne, Colman, Jones, Edwards, Morgans, Charlton, Taylor, Viollet, Scanlon.

Rested in preparation for the European Cup tie against Red Star Belgrade four days later were Blanchflower, Berry, Pegg and Whelan. I had met them all. It was one of the most memorable games in the history of the Football League, between the team I had a tenuous connection with in 1958 and one that was to give me a permanent place in the record books in years to come.

If that Highbury game was illuminating, what happened five days later plunged British sport into total darkness. Its impact on me remains as vivid now as it was on the afternoon of 6 February. Just back from school, Mum called me in from my daily goalkeeping practice against the garage doors. She made me listen to the radio and the news that was filtering through and being repeated by the BBC: 'The aircraft carrying the Manchester United football team home after their thrilling 3–3 draw against Red Star Belgrade, has crashed during take-off at Munich airport. No further details are available but it would seem casualties have been sustained. We will bring you further reports when we can.'

For the next few hours I was glued to the radio. Every bulletin painted a more horrific picture. The final death toll of twenty-three was from a passenger list of forty-three. Eight of the Busby Babes died on impact or, in Duncan Edwards' case, after a sixteen-day fight for life. Duncan's progress from schoolboy to England star made him a particular hero of all schoolboys of my age. He was only a handful of years older than me, but already potentially one of England's greatest players. His death affected me greatly. So, too, did the heroics of goalkeeper Harry Gregg, who risked life and limb to go back into the wreckage to save lives. The battle for life, and eventual return to health, of Matt Busby remain etched in my memory.

Bert Whalley was not so fortunate, nor was the legendary Frank Swift whose goalkeeping for Manchester City and England had been an inspiration. He was on the plane as a journalist. I still remember both men fondly. There is little doubt in my mind that the amazing charisma that surrounds Manchester United Football Club stems directly from the emotional outpouring that followed the Munich air crash. I was a name on the books of the club at that time and I will always carry both a permanent scar and a feeling of pride as a result of the memories I have retained.

Staying on at Chesterfield School, and then going on to Loughborough College, meant my association with Manchester United was at an end although four years later, during an injury crisis at Old Trafford, I received a call asking if I could play for the reserves. By then, another big club held my registration, but United clearly had not forgotten the boy from Chesterfield. Neither had Nobby Stiles when, in the 1968–69 season, after I'd at long last established my place in the Arsenal first team, he reintroduced me to Sir Matt Busby.

'You remember Bob Wilson, Boss, don't you?' he said. Not surprisingly, the great man didn't, until Nobby and I between us reminded him of 1957.

The fickle finger of fate was never so apparent as at that moment. Bob Wilson and Arsenal were in the ascendancy, heading for glory. The great Manchester United were in freefall.

5

Schoolboy to schoolteacher

'Knowledge is gained by learning
Trust by doubt
Skill by practice
And love by love'

Thomas Szasz

Falling in love was the main reason my last three years at school were so enjoyable, and it was equally embracing during my three years at Britain's best institute of sport. Margaret Miles was the daughter of Chesterfield's most popular newsagent, Stanley Miles, and his wife Kathleen, the sister of one of my brother Hugh's class-mates, Peter Miles, the Princess to my Woodcutter.

After our early friendship, romance blossomed at the time my affair with Manchester United came to an end. Hugh brought her to my attention with youthful zest. 'Hey, have you seen Pete Miles' sister recently? If you haven't, you should!' My brother has always been an amazing enthusiast, so I thought, if she's become that special I'd better find out for myself.

I discovered that it was her practice to go to church every Sunday evening. St Mary's was the place of worship. As I remember, it was a cold wait under the crooked spire, and when the service came to an end I had the problem of recognition. At twelve, Margaret Miles had short hair. How was I to know the young lady with a truly spectacular ponytail was the same one I had sat behind in the class at Tapton?

When no one else emerged from the famous landmark, I decided ponytail had to be the one. I ran after her but the attempt to make it a casual chance encounter was ruined by the obvious state I was in. I was out of breath and desperately nervous. The distance from St Mary's to the Miles' home in Cobden Road was about a twenty-minute walk. In that time, nerves evaporated, old memories were revived and the journey went by far too quickly. No definite future meeting was arranged, just a promise to get in touch.

School life returned to the more mundane after the Manchester experiences. Sport continued to keep me fit and, to a lesser degree, occupied, but it seemed to me that the big moment had been lost. The dream would have to remain just a dream. 'Find a job you love and you'll never have to work a day in your life' is a truism, but whatever job I set my sights upon, it was not a decision made from the heart. It was bound to be second best or so I thought. That might have been so had one of my parents' suggestions materialised. Dad's brother Archie was a well-known police officer.

'It's a highly honourable profession and the Metropolitan Police has wonderful sports facilities so you can carry on with your goalkeeping and football' was how it was sold to me, and leaflets were forthcoming. A second option was more appealing – 'What about Loughborough College in Leicestershire? It's one of the best sports colleges in the country and learning to teach all your favourite sports would be perfect for you.'

I thought hard about the two options and decided Lough-borough would suit my temperament best. To get a place would demand more study than I had previously been prepared to do. I needed five O and two A levels. Four Os were already in the bank so I immediately underwent a crash course in Religious Instruction, and within a couple of months or so got a fifth

O level of which the Reverend Robert Primrose would have heartily approved. As for the As, I chose to study history and geography in the sixth form.

Football success continued to come my way, even though my drive and dedication were tempered now with other equally challenging interests, especially Miss Miles.

The FA Schools Week, held at St John's College, Oxford University, was memorable. Playing as well as I had ever played, the A team drew 2–2 for the first time ever with the Universities Athletic Union XI, and then dramatically beat the famous amateur side Pegasus 3–1. The latter game took place at Iffley Road running ground, where in 1954 Roger Bannister became the first man to break four minutes for the mile.

I stood comparison with the England international amateur keeper Mike Pinner, and my performance led to an immediate interest from the England selectors. They were all present three days later when I kept goal for England Grammar Schools at the ground of Dulwich Hamlet FC. We won 4–3. The team was coached by Norman Creek, coach and manager to the national amateur side, and he made it quite clear that my performances had put me in line for both the international squad and the Great Britain Olympic team. He hoped to make the 1960 Olympics in Rome.

Suddenly life was a total joy again. My football fortunes had been revived and, better still, Margaret Miles had become my girlfriend. The way it happened was interesting. One of my best school friends was Roger Pexton. With his parents away for an evening, we planned a foursome. He knew how I had taken a shine to Margaret, and he liked Elizabeth, the same Liz who had been my girl at junior school. As you can appreciate, it was a little awkward, but a success. Youthful romance took over and Margaret Miles, whose nicknames had been Maggie and Maggots, became Megs, only to me at that time I might add, but I preferred it. She liked my choice and Megs she remains.

She preferred to call me Bob and that became the last of the many versions of Robert that I had endured from birth – Rob, Robbie, Robin, Bobby and Bob.

Megs and I began to spend every spare moment in each other's company. The two families knew and liked each other. It was impossible not to like Kath and Stan Miles. He was one of the funniest men I've ever known; she had a great way of keeping his humour in check. Their home became my second home. Their attic window gave a grandstand view of Chesterfield FC's Recreation Ground. Its position was perfect, at an angle, high above Saltergate, which was the ground's more popular name.

The view of the pitch also included a bird's eye view of the men's toilet in the corner of the ground, a roofless building about 12ft square, big enough to house thirty relieved gents around the edges. The lads who spotted me while otherwise engaged didn't mind my presence above them, but when Megs brought a cup of tea and sat with me, she got an occasional fist waved in her direction. I promise it was only a fist.

Life was near perfect. Megs' uncles all loved and played football and so she understood the game and, from day one of our liaison, what football meant to me. She accepted my absences like a true footballing widow and those times became increasingly regular and important.

Olympic trials were well under way. The biggest occasion by far was the game at Villa Park on Wednesday, 22 April 1959. The Probables met the Possibles and in direct opposition were R.P. Wilson (Chesterfield Grammar School) and A.K. Waiters (Loughborough College). Tony Waiters had already built himself a fine reputation. He was a fantastic physical specimen and everyone knew that he had already signed amateur forms for Blackpool while a Loughborough student.

The incentive was not lost on me. If he could break into the professional game from the Loughborough College team, surely so could I. The hope was that Tony would vacate the college position sooner rather than later because I had just been accepted, subject to exam results, for Loughborough. It never became an issue. Tony left to join Blackpool as I arrived for the start of my teacher's training course.

He went on to play memorably at Bloomfield Road where he won five full England honours between 1964 and 1965. In one of those two years, playing for Blackpool at Highbury, he made a diving save at the feet of Arsenal's England right-back, Don Howe. The ensuing collision resulted in a compound fracture of Howe's right leg. It was sickening and the reason I use the word is because I both saw it and heard it. By 1964, Don was a favourite colleague of mine at Arsenal. The injury ended his playing career but not our friendship. He became my favourite coach.

The result of the Olympic trial game at Villa Park went my way, the Possibles beating the Probables 2–1. I loved all seventy-eight minutes of it, enjoying a mixture of luck and skill, which was to serve me so well. As for the last twelve minutes, I was back in the dressing room, carried off after diving into some flying boots and injuring my leg.

Such was my crazy style, the England team manager, Norman Creek eventually went on record stating I was too fearless and injury prone. I think he'd simply read the match report in *The Times*, which stated 'The Chesterfield Grammar School keeper was fearless to the point of self-destruction.'

Initially, it didn't stop my selection as one of thirty potential Olympic Games players invited to Bisham Abbey at Marlow in Buckinghamshire. The lovely Abbey is where England teams in all sports prepare. It was a huge honour and most of the best amateur players of the time were present, including Roy Sleap, Mike Greenwood, Robin Trimby and Laurie Brown, the big Geordie who played for both Arsenal and Spurs.

Keepers named were Tony Waiters, Malcolm Shaw and me; no Mike Pinner, whose place was more or less guaranteed. The best I could hope for was selection as one of the reserve keepers, but the possibility of making the qualifying stages for the Rome Olympics increased when Tony Waiters suddenly announced he was turning professional.

Before any possibility became reality, all hopes came to an abrupt and worrying end. Playing for the school against Swanwick Hall Grammar School on a memorably cold wet day, I took a blow to the chest, which my desperate save had invited. For once I couldn't catch my breath. Whenever injury occurs you usually instinctively know how serious it is. This time I was in big trouble. My rib-cage felt as if it had caved in. Sharp movements were excruciatingly painful; standing still was difficult enough. The X-rays revealed three broken ribs and a punctured lung.

I was detained in Chesterfield Royal Hospital and for twenty-four hours had special care. The seriousness was reflected, perhaps even exaggerated, in the two local papers but both said I was 'fairly comfortable'. From my ward window at the front of the hospital, I still managed to sneak a wave to Megs as she passed in the morning on her way to Tapton School. Olympic selection was out of the question. Norman Creek had been proved right . . . for now.

Three months later, and with a lot of tender loving care behind me, I was back with the most unusual contraption strapped to the front and side of my damaged chest. Mum's ingenuity knew no bounds. The foam rubber protection worked well, although spectators and officials alike thought I'd put on a bit of weight on the top of my body.

I saw out my school career captaining both the Chesterfield and Derbyshire football and cricket elevens. That and the greater interest in my studies led to the school headmaster, William Glister, inviting me to be vice captain of Chesterfield Grammar School. The invitation came behind closed doors, in his study. Praising me for my sporting success and leadership of the school teams, he reminded me that I was accepting a position of importance and second only to the one my brother Jock had held when he was head boy in 1940. Kindness was tempered with a request – 'Would you please refrain from walking hand in hand with your girlfriend on the way to school?'

I shyly but reluctantly agreed to his request. By now all sorts of promises about the future had been exchanged between the Princess and the goalkeeping Woodcutter. Affection between us knew no bounds. She watched me play in goal; I followed her on to the local stage when her acting career blossomed, in order to be close. Still seventeen, Megs, who had taken many of the lead roles in the school plays, was cast by the local amateur dramatic society in the title role of George Bernard Shaw's 'Saint Joan'. It was a massive challenge for her and a salute to the talent she had. She received deserved rave reviews for her performance as the spirited French girl who followed her voices to triumph and the stake.

The story of Joan of Arc was performed at the local Civic Theatre and professionals would have struggled to match the youthful intensity she produced. She was outstanding and the helmeted soldier in Act 2 and hooded monk in the final act who stood and sat by her on stage knew it, blinkered as he was. I have no doubt that her star would have continued to be in the ascendancy to this day, such was her acting ability, but her parents, like mine advised her against going on the stage. Instead, they persuaded her to become a teacher.

As she went north to Bretton Hall in Yorkshire, a music, art and drama college, I went south. I was eighteen and had the academic qualifications needed at that time to gain entry to Loughborough College. There was a practical exam to be passed first, which included juggling a football. Never before or since have I been as confident of success as I was with that test.

As I arrived at Loughborough, changes were taking place in the teachers' training programme. The two-year qualification course became three years from September 1960, when my course began. The third year incorporated the Specialist Diploma of Loughborough College, which, at the time, was the closest you could get to a degree in physical education. One thing had long been established by then. Loughborough and Carnegie College in Leeds were the most sought-after institutions for sporting prowess and excellence.

Any misgivings I had at leaving home quickly dissipated. I found I was designated to be leader of our group, much to the chagrin of two or three young men who had arrived from public school. I knew they were initially wary of the Chesterfield Grammar Schoolboy with the ostentatious England Schoolboy badge on his tracksuit. It didn't last long. One thing I inherited from my mum was a smile and friendly disposition that most people have warmed to. The same guys who were unsure became close friends and, in some cases, lifetime buddies.

Loughborough College in 1960 bore only a passing resemblance to the University that exists there today and remains supreme in its sporting excellence. It has become very scientific in its approach to sport, and academic studies take precedence over the practical.

In 1960, our lives as students seemed to be dominated by practice and more practice. The aim was simple – to produce the best possible teachers of physical education. The Loughborough way then was to make sure students experienced at first hand what eventually they were trying to pass on to their pupils. We had six or seven lectures a day, the majority taking us from sport to sport – from athletics track to rugby field to swimming pool to gymnasium to hockey field to boxing ring to soccer pitch or some similar rotation. Interwoven with the practical was the study of a second subject, in my case history. Without exception, the lecturers at Loughborough were top men in their field. I can't speak too highly of their abilities and the influence they had upon me.

I had a wonderful time at Loughborough. We were students,

responsible to no one but ourselves. We had no money, were permanently broke, but we were at what we considered to be the leading PE college. The confidence was good for me. I had never been naturally confident but my love of all sport and a growing awareness that I had a natural ability and the personality to transmit my knowledge were important in my twenties and a passion for me in later years.

Teaching practice was the way our abilities were judged. Purely by chance, students would be placed in a variety of schools in the Leicestershire, Nottinghamshire and Derbyshire areas. In the main, I was lucky to find myself at pretty civilised schools but some found themselves bang in the middle of a blackboard jungle. Experiences varied greatly. One of Group PIB's greatest characters was Roger Wrightson, a county-class cricketer. He found himself at a school notorious for its indiscipline. Under observation from a college lecturer, Roger found control of his class impossible. Paper darts were flying back and forth, the kids were running riot. So the Loughborough tutor signalled Roger to step aside while he took over. No improvement in control was forthcoming. The tutor called Roger over and said, 'Come on, Mr Wrightson, let's get the hell out of here.'

Another of our year was being observed while he was teaching his pupils how to throw the javelin. The class, divided into two groups, were lined up facing each other, spears at the ready. The tutor rectified the error with great haste.

The role of the teacher in society may well have changed from the days when he and the minister were arguably the two most respected members of any local community. But educating and education should always have priority status in any civilisation.

During my three years at Loughborough, there were never enough hours in any day. Work had to be balanced with a frantic social life and my constant and unswerving ambition to make the most of my footballing talent. In my first year the College produced a football first eleven that matched the very best amateur teams of that era. Our coach, Allen Wade, was truly outstanding and eventually was head-hunted by the Football Association as Director of Coaching. The season's performances took us almost all the way to Wembley and the FA Amateur Cup final.

We were certainly one of the purest amateur teams ever, paying five shillings every time we played, buying our own kit, doing our own laundering and contributing to our expenses for away travel. Our side had a perfect mix of fresh-faced but talented lads straight out of school and more mature players who had arrived direct from national service. Progress was uneventful until the fourth qualifying round, when a local side, Moor Green, were the visitors to our humble ground. In a game not enjoyed by either defence, we won 10–5. Victory took us to the first-round proper, which brought a Bradford-based team, Salts, to Leicestershire. A close match was predicted, but we won 6–1. Loughborough College had never reached the first round before, let alone the last thirty-two. The draw for round two attracted national interest. It was the equivalent of Farnborough meeting mighty Arsenal in the FA Cup.

Bishop Auckland's reputation was well deserved after sweeping all before them in amateur circles during the fifties. Two of their players were famous. Harry Sharratt, the keeper, played for Blackpool, Nottingham Forest and Oldham Athletic and was Great Britain's number one at the 1956 Olympics in Melbourne. Their striker, Seamus O'Connell, was a star as well. He had played on the professional stage for Middlesbrough and then scored seven goals in ten appearances for Chelsea in their 1954–55 league championship season. An England Amateur, O'Connell had won an Amateur Cup winner's medal with Bishop Auckland in 1955.

The fame of the club from the north east of England had

been further enhanced by an amazing FA Cup record, with memorable encounters against Preston, Burnley, Wolves and Sheffield United. In the 1954–55 FA Cup, they knocked out Crystal Palace and Ipswich Town before losing to York City.

The upstarts of Loughborough College were not given a chance, but interest was at fever pitch. When Bishop arrived and saw our ground with no grandstand, they must have thought they had arrived at an outpost of the Empire. We had been obliged to fence off the playing area to comply with Amateur Cup rules and the few seats provided were for local dignitaries. The playing surface itself was perfection and it was influential in the outcome. There was no score at half-time but by the end we had run them off the park and won 3–1. The reputation of Loughborough College as a sporting institution increased and in *The Times*, eighteen column inches were given to the great journalist Geoffrey Green who produced a beautifully descriptive piece, which captured the event and the Loughborough way of life between 1960 and 1963.

There is nothing like a change to blow away the cobwebs: there is nothing so bracing as something fresh and vigorous. A visit to Loughborough on Saturday in fact, was a tonic: as much for the famous victory over those giants of the North, Bishop Auckland, that put the young Colleges team into the third round and last sixteen of the FA Amateur Cup for the first time in their brief history in this competition, as for the spirit and setting in which it was achieved.

Here in stark reality was David against Goliath. Here was an outcome to satisfy the enemies of power, as the little man for a change came smiling through. Now the Colleges, fired by a new spirit, ask only one thing, that the wheel of fortune turns their way in today's draw and offers them either Corinthian Casuals or Pegasus. They dearly would like to show one or other a thing or two. They could too.

Bishop Auckland have an unchallenged record of eighteen

Amateur Cup finals; they have won the trophy ten times; they possess a well-appointed stadium which can hold 17,000; they claim a host of followers, most of whom, festooned and vociferous, made the 300 mile round journey for this occasion which no doubt gave them the right to let off some pithy northern comments, especially about the referee, as the tide for once turned against them. Perhaps it was the simple setting itself that made them ill at ease.

There were ropes around the touchlines and not even a duck-board to safeguard boots from damp and mud. Across the 100 acres of playing fields other activities were in progress. Elsewhere the colleges' rugby football 'types' were battling it out with the young medicos of Middlesex Hospital, the thwack of hockey sticks resounded in another direction, there were chaps in the indoor swimming pool, chaps playing badminton, chaps on the trampoline in the gymnasium. In fact chaps everywhere indulging in their particular branch of physical education.

Yet this day the real heart of the Colleges beat on the open field hiding coyly behind white and billowing awnings. A grassy bank to one side held most of the 2000 spectators, strung out around the ropes. Among the expectant, noisy students in their coloured scarves were dotted proud locals, all united by a single hope. A wind whistled and the sun glinted between the flying clouds: on the horizon rose the outlines of a new student village of technology. This was the simple anvil on which was hammered out a victory that makes the Colleges a new force in the amateur field. It was like some super house match and Lord Kinnaird of old would have loved it, even if modern streamlined Bishop Auckland did not. Nor was there any doubt about the result!

The Loughborough team was R. Wilson, J. Detchon, J. Henderson, T. Casey, T. Goodwin, R. Ralfs, J. Raybould, A. Bradshaw, K. Bowron, B. Moore, A. Brimacombe.

He was a prophet because we did indeed draw Corinthian-Casuals in the next round. Laden again with the best amateur players of the time, including John Swannell, Robin Trimby, Mike Smith and Doug Insole, the Casuals went the way of Bishop Auckland, beaten 2–1.

Plaudits at our achievements were tempered by jealousy. We were praised for 'taking over the mantle of Pegasus as the leaders in pure soccer amateurism' but then challenged by many clubs. Led by Maidstone Secretary Dick Pritchard, we were described as 'having too big an advantage, being physical education students, and not competing in any recognised amateur league'. Most observers were on the college's side. 'Petulant childishness' was an accurate headline in Loughborough's favour. Our critics didn't have to worry for much longer. Two of the team were injured as we lined up for the quarter-final with Hitchin Town and ten minutes into the big match, I broke three ribs diving at the feet of Dennis Randall, their fine striker. Hitchin were a terrific side and may well have trounced us whether I had left for hospital before the final whistle or not; 5–1 was a cruel end to a famous adventure for a bunch of PE students.

The enforced rest from football at least enabled me to socialise more, and trips to Bretton Hall and Megs became more frequent. I often arrived in Yorkshire in a style that reflected the beauty of the historic parkside house. Nigel Seale, my closest friend, had been given a vintage 1930 Riley for his twenty-first birthday. Arriving without incident was rare and we learned how to use chewing gum to seal a leaky radiator, and a college scarf to re-attach an exhaust pipe.

The relationship between Megs and me was developing and before our teacher training came to an end, I had decided to ask her dad whether there would be any objections to our becoming engaged. The only questions Stan Miles asked centred on what job I intended to apply for. Pop Miles knew I still regarded teaching as a means to an end. He also knew that my desire to become a footballer, far from being dampened, had been warmed by events that unfolded before and after the Amateur Cup success in my opening year at Loughborough.

Several professional clubs came 'sniffing' around the matches in which I appeared, whether it be for the College, the English Universities or the England Amateur squad, for which I had been a reserve to Mike Pinner in an international at High Wycombe against France. Facing many of the best Midlands professional clubs – Derby, Nottingham Forest, Leicester and Aston Villa – helped me measure my progress. Playing a 'blinder' when we faced Wolves led to an invitation to Molineux. Stan Cullis was the legendary manager of a club that had excited the land with the first televised floodlit games against foreign opposition, Spartak Moscow and Honved. Mr Cullis had an intensity that was hypnotic and I quickly agreed to sign amateur forms for Wolverhampton Wanderers and play whenever college commitments permitted.

For about two years, I would occasionally take time away from my college work to catch a train, or more likely hitch a lift on the roadside or travel on the back of a motorbike, in order to play for Wolves reserves or third team. I was treated royally, given generous expenses, which helped improve my time at Loughborough, and was allowed to rub shoulders with the Wolves stars of the time. Keeper Malcolm Finlayson, Ron Flowers and Peter Broadbent were special heroes. I would stay in digs one hundred yards from Molineux where the mother of a former Wolves player, Bill Shorthouse, looked after promising youngsters. One of my room-mates was Peter Knowles, a fabulous talent who was later famously to prefer the life of a Jehovah's Witness to football stardom.

There was no such dilemma for me. I now knew that I was going to become a professional footballer, once I had passed my Loughborough final exams. The only doubt was whether I would choose Wolves. What I had to consider was exactly where I would complete the compulsory one year of teaching after college. PE was taught in all schools but there was less choice for Megs since drama was a relatively new subject on the curriculum and viewed with great scepticism. Jobs were limited and we would be forced to go where there was work.

Stan Cullis was fair but firm when I was asked to declare my intentions to some of the Wolves directors, a nerve-racking experience for a student. The chairman, Stanley Baker, understood the reasons for my reticence on moving to Wolverhampton but John Ireland, who was to be his successor, was far less understanding. He accused me of dithering because of the interest of other clubs and directly accused me of wanting money to sign. His manner soured my taste for Wolves so I put a decision on hold and simply carried on doing my best for Stan Cullis and the Wanderers.

I was on my way to play for Wolves on the afternoon of 23 March 1962 when I learned of another remarkable catastrophe involving my family. Slipping away from Friday afternoon lectures, I'd caught a train to Birmingham *en route* to Wolverhampton and an overnight stay prior to a reserve match at Burnley. At New Street station I had a forty-minute wait for a connecting train to Wolverhampton. To help make the time go quickly I bought a local evening paper. Almost immediately my eye caught a headline in the stop-press column: V Bomber Crash. I read on and froze – 'Experimental Victor bomber crashed on farmhouse in Stubton, Lincolnshire. Four dead.'

The tiny village of Stubton was one I knew well. My sister Jean and her husband Dennis lived there on The Home Farm, the only farmhouse in Stubton. My mind was racing. 'Oh God, not again,' I thought, remembering Jock and Billy. Surely my parents had suffered enough. At that moment I simply visualised the scene and the dead whom I presumed to be Jean, Dennis and their home helps, fifty-two year old Annie Gibson and her twenty-two year old niece Cecily. Uncharacteristically, I headed immediately for the railway bar. I couldn't really afford the brandy I gulped down. Plucking up courage and shaking with fear I rang home to Chesterfield. Dad answered and as soon as I heard his voice, uncertain and cracked, I knew the report had indeed referred to Jean and Dennis's home.

As soon as he recognised my voice he was sensible enough to say, 'They're not dead.' He had been trying to contact me all afternoon, the rest of the family having been available and informed. He relayed the gist of what had happened and told me it would be better to carry on and play for Wolves as there was nothing I could do to help. The story of Jean and Dennis's survival mixed tragedy with miracle and remains a tale that almost defies belief.

It was unusual for Jean and Dennis to follow their lunch with a quick coffee. It was around two o'clock when they first became aware of a jet engine. With RAF Cranwell close to where they lived, they were used to such sounds, but one big bang followed almost immediately by a second was out of the ordinary. Jean ran to the bay windows of the lounge and Dennis headed rapidly for the front door. Their actions saved their lives.

At that moment, 65 tons of Handley Page Victor bomber more or less pancaked on top of the charming seventeenth-century farmstead. Jean instinctively covered her head with her hands for protection as the pressure blew her clean through the windows many yards from the stricken aircraft. She has no recollection of going through the glass or of the pain from her left leg which had been gashed to the bone. Somehow she was conscious and her concern was Dennis. She spotted movement near where the front door should have been, but where now the massive bomber was sitting, reasonably intact, smouldering dangerously.

Jean, despite her injuries, clambered over the wall at the bottom of the garden and saw farm foreman John Scrimshire running up the road from his house close by. 'Get Dennis' was Jean's plea and John's loyalty took him straight into the rubble. Dennis was covered almost up to his neck but was also conscious as the foreman arrived. By obeying Dennis's instruction to pull him and not carry him, John put a critical few yards between them and the plane. As they reached the sunken garden, its small wall protected them from the plane which was now exploding and bursting into flame, destroying all of what remained of itself and The Home Farm.

For both Jean and Dennis it was a miraculous escape, although both had sustained awful injuries, Dennis especially. About one minute only elapsed from impact to the igniting of the kerosene fuel. Jean, whose appearance was unrecognisable beneath the grit, dirt and blistered, kerosene-soaked skin, was concerned for Mrs Gibson and Cecily, pleading for someone to get them out. An ambulance arrived on the scene very quickly, answering the Mayday call put out by the crew of the plane.

The aircraft, XL 159, had taken off from Boscombe Down, and was undertaking a variety of stalling tests. The Victor went into a stable stall followed by a flat spin and the test pilot and his RAF co-pilot were unable to prevent the bomber from hitting the barn behind the house, which partly halted it and turned it to pancake on to the farmhouse.

Both pilots ejected and survived albeit with badly damaged backs. Only one of the three other men on the plane survived. He managed to overcome the 'g' forces at the fourth attempt and at 10,000 feet parachuted clear. The two other crewmen were killed. So too were Mrs Gibson and Cecily, their bodies being recovered the following day.

So many imponderables were left hanging. Ten minutes earlier, Jean and Dennis's youngest daughter Joanna had been at home having lunch before going back to school; ten minutes after the crash, Jean and Dennis would have been elsewhere; if the impact had been ten yards to the left, they would most certainly have died; one hundred yards to the right and a local boys school could have been obliterated; had the plane not caught the edge of the barn, the whole village could have been wiped out.

It was a cold bright day and the smoke could be seen for miles around. Jean was thankful Dennis was alive and although moaning in obvious pain, the words he spoke reflected his gentle nature born out of his Quaker upbringing.

'Don't blame anyone. No one's to blame. Don't worry, we're building a new house.' He was referring to the half-built home he and Jean had designed and started to build just a mile down the road.

Staying conscious was a big factor in Dennis surviving the fractures of his lower vertebrae, pelvis and head of the femur. His big boots and heavy farming clothes helped lessen the injuries. Jean's main injury was the eight-inch gaping wound to her leg, which she would be lucky not to lose.

Initially, they were taken to RAF Cranwell before being transferred to Nocton Hall hospital. It was there, the next day, that the family were allowed in to see Jean. For a week, Dennis remained in a critical condition, the fractures turning the skin on his entire body black and blue. He remained in hospital for almost three months, but he lived and so did Jean. Their story provided the miracle. For Cecily and 'dear Gibbo', as the family called her, and for the two airmen, it was a tragic end.

The experience reshaped Jean's whole outlook on life. She recalls, 'It changed forever any silly ideas and thoughts about materialistic items. They are of no real importance. Life and living it everyday is the only important aspect. Dennis should have died that day and possibly me as well. Instead, we were given an extra forty years together.' Dennis died in the autumn of 2002, a year after they celebrated their golden wedding anniversary.

Jean's attitude to life is admirable but the immediate fallout from the crash was, nevertheless, traumatic. Think of every item you possess, every item from treasured gifts to insignificant but essential utensils. Jean and Dennis lost just about everything and had to prepare such a list for insurance purposes. Shap, the Jack Russell terrier, survived, found wandering in the rubble after being blown out of the house behind Jean. Their two gundogs died of shock a day after the crash. The family car remained intact being at a local garage for repairs, but from inside the farmhouse only a couple of spoons, an ashtray and an old blunderbuss were recovered. John Scrimshire's bravery was rewarded with the British Empire Medal.

Even now it is difficult for me to comprehend all that happened on that March afternoon in 1962. In a daze, I duly caught my train to Wolverhampton and next day played for Wolves reserves at Burnley. We all wore black armbands. There had been a pit disaster.

The crash and all its implications made the whole Wilson family appreciate what a tenuous hold we all have on life, even without war, and how fate can destroy or create in equal measure. It made me realise how thankful I should be for all I had so far enjoyed. There was so much to look forward to. Megs and I got engaged at Christmas and decided that July 1964 would be a wonderful time for a wedding.

The latter part of my days at Loughborough were as brilliant as the early ones. Three years of the best football, the best tutoring and best friendships had produced promising teachers. Right to the end, we absorbed new ideas alongside tried and tested methods. When fibre-glass suddenly revolutionised pole vaulting, we were at the sharp end of the technology. Learning how to use pyjamas to survive in water by inflating them with air was more basic and amusing.

My knowledge and ability in all sports improved dramatically, especially athletics. That was thanks to my close friendship with athletes John Cooper and Robbie Brightwell. Robbie occupied the room next to me in the halls of residence. Whenever his fiancée, Ann Packer, visited at weekends, I would vacate my room and either head for Bretton Hall or find other accommodation. Occasional items of ladies clothing left behind drew interesting looks from our cleaning lady.

My college group, P1B, was acknowledged as a collection of the brilliant, the zany and the downright different, but we had a togetherness that other groups envied. Somehow we all negotiated our final year and final exams, being required to write three dissertations, one for each subject. Unsurprisingly, I chose 'Goalkeeping' as the title of my PE thesis. 'The Roman Gladiatorial Games' and 'Quaker Education' satisfied my history and education tutors.

Loughborough friendships remain among my closest and I take great pride in the wonderful successes that have been achieved in diverse fields by Michael Turvey, now a distinguished professor and senior research scientist in Connecticut, and Nigel Seale, head of the famous actors' directory, 'Spotlight'. Our regular reunions are emotional and, for our wives, dreadfully predictable. 'Do you remember when . . .' has become a stock phrase, usually preceding tales of daring and followed by howls of laughter. Without Loughborough it is doubtful whether Bob Wilson would eventually have enjoyed such success as a footballer, let alone spent twenty-eight years in the perilous occupation of television presentation. It gave me far more than a Teacher's Training Certificate and a Diploma of Loughborough College, First Class Honours. It made me grow up, helped me set standards, and I believe it created the most natural Bob Wilson – not the footballer or the TV presenter, but the teacher and coach.

I wasn't able to appreciate the fact back in 1963 when I was about to leave Loughborough because I was too engrossed in deciding which football club I would like to join. Wolves were no longer the only interested party. Also on the table was an interest from within some marble halls in North London.

6
The marble halls

'Success is how high you bounce when you hit rock bottom.'

General George Patton

Nobody suggested it was going to be easy, no one made promises, but I never envisaged the struggle for success that filled the five years immediately after Loughborough. Everything on the horizon had appeared so rosy. Marriage was only twelve months away. I had applied for two London teaching posts and been offered both. Two great football clubs were just as keen to take me on.

The choice of school was without complication. Rutherford School was a modern comprehensive situated in Paddington, within convenient striking distance of the football club that had most appealed to me since they had made their interest known. I was aware of Arsenal's history and reputation long before their physiotherapist, Bertie Mee, made contact. Bertie had been physio at two of the FA Schools weeks I had attended at Oxford and Cambridge. Somewhere along the way he had mentioned me to the Gunners' hierarchy and tabs were kept on my progress. They weren't deterred by the fact that I'd signed forms with Wolves and were just one of six or seven clubs that contacted me. I was a strict amateur and could still choose where and for whom I wanted to play, or so I thought.

In my last year at Loughborough I was invited to go down to Highbury and meet the manager, Billy Wright. I shall never forget that first visit in February 1963. I was twenty-one and close to the end of my college education. Although I owned an old Ford Prefect, which I bought for £50, I didn't trust its reliability, so I borrowed a sparkling Triumph Herald belonging to a fellow student and skipped lectures. After getting lost around Islington, I eventually found my way to Avenell Road, N5.

As I approached the historic art-deco exterior of the East Stand, the history student in me marvelled at the architecture. It was like no other football stand I'd ever seen, not even Old Trafford. Entering the marble halls, I came face to face with the bronze bust of Herbert Chapman who had done so much to take Arsenal FC from being a 'bit part player' to one that set standards for everyone else. It wasn't just the three championships he had won at his previous club, Huddersfield, before setting up a repeat at Arsenal that made him such a great manager. It was his foresight in demanding a ground that would be the envy of the football world, including marble reception areas and huge dressing rooms with underfloor heating. He required standards of dress and behaviour in the players that were still in place on that February morning as I was met by one of the most famous faces in football.

Billy Wright was an England legend. Heroic skipper of his country and Wolverhampton Wanderers, the club he was now trying to dissuade me from joining, Billy was a lovely man but not cut out to be a football manager. His charm lay in his friendly smile and cheerful approach to everyone eager to meet him and shake his hand. My tour of Highbury began in the marble halls before proceeding upstairs for a look at the packed trophy cabinets and directors' boardroom. A huge silver shield on the wall was the legacy of Arsenal's three successive championship triumphs between 1933 and 1935. The route he took was clever and designed to impress.

Back downstairs I was shown the dressing rooms and the

two huge hot and cold plunge baths. The medical area and equipment were equally impressive and he explained that X-ray facilities were present at every game. 'If you have to break a leg, break it at Highbury,' he told me with a laugh. It was ironic that Billy actually broke my left ankle in a training accident at Highbury when there was no X-ray unit on site.

Finally, we left the home dressing room, walked down the narrow corridor and then, before reaching the marble halls again, turned right. Now we were into the tunnel where another right turn led directly to daylight and the pitch. By now I was beginning to have doubts that I would be good enough to walk the way of so many household names. Almost immediately, as we stepped on to the pitch my fears evaporated.

What I saw inspired and sent shivers down my spine. This wasn't a football stadium; it was a cathedral. I found it difficult to listen to the England legend. I was lost in my own thoughts. I could feel the excitement running through my body. If they wanted me badly enough, why not give it a go? I always set my sights too high. Arsenal as a club had, since Chapman, always been acknowledged as one of the best.

My mind was made up by the time I set off back to Loughborough. On the way I was encouraged that the three professional clubs for which I had special feelings as a boy were all playing a part of my life – Manchester United, Wolves and Arsenal. I hadn't reckoned on any ugly reaction from Wolves when I told them I would not be joining them during or after my teaching year. Wolves reacted angrily. They immediately challenged me and claimed I was their player. I pointed out that I had only ever been asked to sign forms requiring me to play in the Central and Midland Intermediate Leagues. A lengthy legal battle developed, which was a great pity because I had enjoyed playing for their second and third teams and loved my head to head talks with Stan Cullis about football and education.

My father was incensed by the club's attitude and immediately threatened to take Wolves and the Football League to court. This dragged the formidable league secretary Alan Hardaker into the dispute and he was particularly objectionable and stubborn. Replies to my dad's questions were, in the main, monosyllabic. Accusations by the League that I had been 'tapped' by other clubs ignored the fact that I had never actually been advised by Wolves that the form I signed before my occasional visits to Molineux was in any way a legal document binding me to Wolverhampton Wanderers FC indefinitely.

In the whole of my time at Loughborough, a dozen clubs approached me one way or another. Dad asked Mr Hardaker what steps the league management took to ensure that professional clubs acquainted a minor's father of the commitment undertaken if his son signs a form without consent. Hardaker's response was as blunt, blinkered and negative as ever.

Dear Sir, I am in receipt of your letter, the contents of which I note. I do not wish to enter into a lengthy argument regarding the recent judgement, but I am afraid that your interpretation of it is not quite correct.

The Football Association's secretary, Dennis Follows, one-time secretary to our Universities Athletic Union team, was dragged into the bitter exchange of letters. Over eight months, stalemate developed. I guess I should have been flattered that Wolves protected my registration so jealously. I had given them my services as a goalkeeper free and didn't even play regularly. The ruling seemed to make nonsense of the distinction between true amateur and professional.

While this was going on, my priority had been to secure a teaching post where I could complete my probationary year, preferably near to where Megs could find a suitable post in drama. It was seemingly of no consequence.

I had accepted the post of assistant physical education teacher at Rutherford School and was enjoying my time as a PE teacher. The head of the department was a guy called Tom Hughes who was experienced and very organised. Headmaster Raymond Long's school contained a real mixture of society. Located less than a mile from Marble Arch and half a mile from Paddington Station, the school attracted both the well off and the disadvantaged. The new PE man attracted great attention from the pupils, attached as he was to Arsenal as an amateur goalkeeper. While the contractual arguments rumbled on, I wasn't prevented from training or playing at Highbury as an amateur. The issue centred only on any possible professional contract I might eventually consider.

Settling to life in London was not a problem because I had so much work on. Planning my first term's work at Rutherford was a priority but throughout the summer I had taken part in Arsenal's pre-season training at London Colney, near St Albans. The setting in the Hertfordshire countryside was idyllic, the workload an eye opener, even for a fit PE teacher. To say I had been received by the Arsenal players with some scepticism is a gross understatement. Being an amateur was difficult enough for them to accept, but the sight of a college scarf and duffle coat on colder days created very obvious nods and winks in the dressing room.

Professional footballers have to adhere to strict club rules but when it comes to accepting new faces in a squad, they always return to their own private union standards. Any group of players at any football club will have leaders and followers. Players are notorious for their mickey taking and I was naive and terribly gullible. They are also wary of anyone who doesn't conform to the norm. I was immediately aware that I had to prove myself worthy to be considered one of them. The game of football has changed in so many ways since 1963, but in one area it will remain the same. Footballers aren't really bothered that you may be a loner, an eccentric or even an amateur. The only question that has to be faced, answered and proved is, 'Can you play?' For great footballers, approval can be instant. For players like me, acceptance can be lengthy and a demonstration of skill and character can be demanded. I believe the general rule applies to most jobs but not as dramatically as in the world of sport.

Inclusion in the pre-season first-team photo didn't help my cause. Every second Arsenal player seemed to be a keeper. Jack McClelland stood beside me in the picture but Ian McKechnie, Tony Burns and Ian Black were left out, and not best pleased about it. The senior players of the group were George Eastham, Vic Groves, Billy McCullough, Geoff Strong and Joe Baker. I had met just two of the eighteen players before – Laurie Brown from the Olympic trials and Terry Neill when making my debut for England Schoolboys in Belfast. In truth, I sensed I was out of my depth, that I wasn't yet worthy of consideration for a first-team place and that I was serving a late crash course apprenticeship.

It didn't deter me. I just smiled a lot. Being an Arsenal player and being part of the club was enough for now. Fate, though, takes its own route. Jack McClelland got injured and Billy Wright and his coach Les Shannon chose me and Tony Burns to go on the pre-season tour two weeks after my arrival. The main fixture was in Hamburg's impressive stadium against a team captained by Uwe Seeler. Walking out behind our captain George Eastham and the great German star in itself fulfilled a dream. If I was never to play another game, I had achieved more than I truly expected.

The game was quicker than anything I'd ever experienced previously, and the noise from a 30,000 crowd was deafening. Geoff Strong and Alan Skirton scored two first-half goals and those plus a couple of decent saves by me increased the self-belief. Hamburg pulled one back from Dorfel and two minutes from time, I was beaten by an extraordinary overhead kick from Bahre. At the final whistle, Uwe Seeler ran towards me and shook my hand. My night was complete.

Billy Wright and the team added genuine congratulations. The 2–2 draw was a surprise to us all. The first hurdle had been negotiated; I was up and running. I always thought football was the greatest game on earth. At that moment, I knew it was true.

I was under no illusions, though, and didn't expect to make my First Division debut on our return to England. Jack McClelland was fit again and took back the green jersey as the new season opened. I concentrated on gaining the respect of the lads in the reserves or third team while knuckling down to my probationary year as a sportsmaster at Rutherford School. Life was very exciting. I loved my teaching and adored my football. Megs completed my happiness.

I lived in digs in Boundary Road near Turnpike Lane, the home of George and Eileen Rowe. Eileen's cooking was both simple and plentiful – huge plates of eggs, steak, chicken or lamb accompanied by a mountain of chips! Dietary restrictions were not in place in 1963. Had Arsene Wenger been around then, he would have been left speechless. I shared a bedroom with a young Arsenal centre-half, Gordon Ferry. He was a good player, had a dry humour and put me straight whenever my 'amateurism' surfaced. 'Get rid of the college scarf and duffle coat,' he told me. Certain pieces of advice I would accept; getting rid of Loughborough wasn't one of them.

My daily schedule was not like his or any other Arsenal player's. By the time Gordon got up at 8.30 a.m., I would be approaching Rutherford School in central London. My alarm was set for 6.45, Eileen would have breakfast ready by 7.10 and by 7.40 I would be on the underground. Six stops took me past Arsenal to King's Cross St Pancras and four more took me to Edgware Road. Another five minutes' walking and I was at the school gates in Penfold Street.

Lessons had been prepared the night before and teaching began after assembly at nine. Mornings found me either in the gymnasium or a classroom although the number of history lessons I taught was small in comparison to PE. There were no playing fields at or near the school so every afternoon we would travel some six or eight miles by school bus to a field near Edgware. Then it was back to school and a debrief with Tom Hughes before catching the tube to Highbury's indoor gym. There and on the adjoining pitch, three evenings a week, I would change from teacher to pupil.

There were no goalkeeping coaches but I was thankful an old Arsenal favourite, who had become reserve-team coach, took a special interest in me. Although a hard midfielder, Alex Forbes had a good understanding of angles. He would draw a semicircle from the goalline outside the six-yard box to just beyond seven yards and then move me constantly around it. When Alex stopped I had to stop. He would be checking my position and deciding whether I had judged my angle correctly. His advice was invaluable and I would include his angling theories twenty-five years later in my own goalkeeping clinics.

At around nine o'clock at night, I would make my way back to Turnpike Lane, tuck in to Eileen's chips, prepare next day's lessons and, at around midnight, collapse into bed. The nightly calls to Chesterfield, where Megs had secured her first teaching post and lived with her parents, was money well spent. We exchanged talk of our daily experiences and plans for our wedding which would take place at the end of the summer term.

As an amateur player at Arsenal, I was paid expenses, and the salary I drew as a schoolteacher was not much more than that. Even with a London allowance, my weekly pay was only £12 while Megs received less living in Chesterfield. Our combined monthly total of £90 wasn't going to buy much in terms of bricks and mortar and how we were going to make ends meet became the priority. The more we talked about it, the more we were convinced that my turning professional was the best solution.

Events were about to take a remarkable turn. Arsenal's season had begun badly with three of the first four games lost, one at Leicester with a scoreline of 7–2. Things had picked up a little by the end of October, but Jack McClelland was injured again. Billy Wright had taken exception to the fact that Ian McKecknie was overweight, and so fifteen games into the 1963–64 season and five days before my twenty-second birthday, a dramatic phone call to Rutherford School from the club told me I would be making my First Division debut the following day against Nottingham Forest at Highbury.

The story was too good for Fleet Street to ignore. Photographers invaded Rutherford School. Reporters tried to ambush me at lunchtime, after school and on my return to Boundary Road. 'Arsenal Call Up Amateur Schoolmaster' was the favoured headline. It was a big story. The copy made a play of the fact that I was the first amateur keeper to play for Arsenal since Dutchman Gerry Keizer in the 1930s and the first amateur since Albert Gudmundsson, an Icelandic inside-forward who made several appearances just after the Second World War.

There was one major problem. So unexpected and late was the call-up that I couldn't possibly change my commitment to referee a school game on Rutherford's home ground, Wormwood Scrubs, on the morning of the game. I just daren't tell Arsenal and, besides, I felt it would serve as a good warm-up.

Saturday, 26 October 1963 was the biggest day of my life so far. I left my digs at 7.00 a.m. and blew the kick-off whistle at 10.00. Edgar Pierce, a supply teacher who had become a good friend, offered to help me out and refereed the second half while I encouraged from the touchline. The Rutherford team won and, with time running out, I changed at midday before travelling to Highbury where I arrived an hour and a half before kick-off.

Every way I turned someone slapped me on the back and offered encouragement. Telegrams were piled by my kit from the family, Rutherford School and my Loughborough tutors and friends, including Robbie Brightwell and Ann Packer. The one from Megs read, 'Good luck, play well, keep them out. Have a good game.' That greeting was to become an essential superstition later in my career.

Megs came down for the game in the company of another of my athletics pals, John Cooper, who was now on the verge of selection for the British Olympic team. My nerves were stretched to breaking point and weren't helped by the team's obvious concern at my selection. Only the Scottish striker, Joe Baker, recognised fully my anguish and went out of his way to try to help me. I had hoped Billy Wright would find the right words but, hard as he tried, that was not his forte. 'Bob, we want you to play today like no one has seen you play before. We want you to play well.' The moment was too delicate a one to laugh, but I knew what he meant. It certainly wasn't Churchillian. Billy was always so full of good intentions. As a manager, he deserved a better reward for his goodness.

During one of several visits to the loo, I heard the bell signalling the imminent kick-off. Lots of good lucks and back slapping bolstered the fear which by now tore at my stomach. George Eastham gestured for me to follow him out. George was a great inside-forward and became famous in 1961 for taking his former club Newcastle to court on a 'restraint of trade' charge for refusing him a transfer. He won. It followed the abolition of the £20 a week maximum wage, championed by Jimmy Hill and the players' union, the PFA. George was outwardly the calmest, coolest member of the team I played in that day. The team sheet read thus:

R. Wilson, Magill, McCullough, Brown, Ure, Barnwell, MacLeod,

Strong, Baker, Eastham, Anderson. The initial in front of my name signified my amateur status.

A crowd of 40,000 gave a loyal welcome to the team and collectively a curious glance towards the new goalkeeper. In almost every way it was to become a dream debut. We were four up inside thirty-five minutes, but the trouble with the Arsenal team of this era was that it was quite capable of then letting in five. A good goal from Forest's Dick Le Flem five minutes before the interval led to terrific pressure, which required two smart saves by me, the second from Quigley as spectacular as I had ever made. 'To have reached it was an achievement. To have caught it was Yashin class,' said the *Daily Mail*. 'Telescopic reach' was the *Sunday Mirror*'s verdict. Forest scored a second early in the second half through Frank Wignall, but we hung on to win 4–2.

Getting cramp with fifteen minutes to go and needing the attention of physio Bertie Mee surprised and annoyed Billy Wright. I didn't let on that six hours earlier I had been refereeing a school game. What surprised me about my debut was that despite my early nerves, I had relished almost every moment. It was like nothing I had ever experienced before. I loved the atmosphere, loved the challenge and truly had a feeling that, given a bit of luck and a following wind, I could perhaps one day soon make the position my own. Strange how the mind can play tricks.

The game against Forest was indeed the first of more than 300 first-team appearances I was to make for Arsenal. It wasn't as quick as I'd thought and sooner became later, much, much later. Between that memorable day and 16 March 1968, some four years four and a half months later, my total number of First Division games for Arsenal FC totalled nine.

That total and period of time would have tested the strongest character. I survived because, firstly, I loved playing for Arsenal;

secondly, I never lost belief in my ability; thirdly, and most important, having a new wife and family quickly became far more important than success or stardom. At a quarter to five on that Saturday in 1963, all I knew was that I had fulfilled another ambition by playing in the top division of English football. It was a defining moment for me and the memory remains the more special because of the historic fact that I remain the last amateur ever to play for Arsenal at that level.

After the game, Megs and I motored back to Chesterfield. For twenty-four hours, wedding plans and time together were more important than football. I was back in London late the next night and on Monday morning another week's teaching took precedence again. Sir's time in the first-team spotlight lasted exactly three weeks and comprised six first-team appearances, five in the First Division and one in an Inter Cities Fairs Cup tie against FC Liege. Two wins, 3 draws and 1 defeat deserved a mark of 7 out of 12.

The week after the Forest game, we drew 2–2 at Bramall Lane against league leaders Sheffield United. Birmingham City were then beaten 4–1 at Highbury where four days later we drew with West Ham 3–3. Up to this game life was good, but the ten days following the West Ham game were utterly miserable.

On the Monday any chance of at last winning an England Amateur Cap evaporated when the selectors named Malcolm Shaw as replacement for Mike Pinner, who had just become a part-time professional at Leyton Orient. They also made it clear that they thought I would follow suit at the end of the season and so immediately ruled me out of the possibility of selection for the Tokyo Olympic squad. They never asked but simply presumed.

The week ended with Arsenal and me playing badly at Stamford Bridge against Chelsea. We lost 3–1. Three days later newspaper headlines carried the news that Billy Wright had signed a new goalkeeper: '£16,000 paid to Liverpool for Jim Furnell'. Worse, the story talked of the 'unsettled Arsenal players having dressing-room discussions about union members playing top grade soccer with an amateur, who can't join training sessions because he is a schoolmaster.'

I had clearly failed to win the Arsenal lads over. It wasn't just about being an amateur. They didn't believe I could play. Without that group acceptance, any footballer must struggle. I hit rock bottom.

Between them, Billy Wright, Bertie Mee and club secretary Bob Wall, quickly tried to cushion the succession of blows. All talks centred on the possibility of my signing forms that would make me a part-time professional straightaway, with my salary backdated once I had finished my probationary year's teaching in July. With the amateur selectors having made their views clear, the offer was too attractive to turn down, especially the salary – £30 per week plus bonuses of £4 for a win and £2 for a draw. It would help towards the wedding pot.

So it was that Arsenal finally settled the dispute with Stan Cullis and Wolves. Rather than fight a lengthy and expensive test case in a court of law, which we felt confident we would win, they agreed a first-ever transfer fee for an amateur footballer. The sum was around £6,500, the national publicity unique. The dispute had dragged on for a year and Wolves must have thought they'd done pretty well out of the deal. For the rest of the 1963–64 season I played reserve-team football, twenty games in all that did nothing to further my career but a lot for my determination. At the same time, I was grateful to one big match on the horizon, which I was looking forward to eagerly and which would give my life a new dimension and direction.

'Well-known footballer marries teacher' was the *Derbyshire Times* story after Megs and I were married at Holy Trinity Church, Chesterfield, on Saturday, 25 July 1964. I had said my farewells to everyone at Rutherford School on the previous Thursday, my probationary year fulfilled and fulfilling.

Raymond Long and Tom Hughes gave me the last day of term off. They wished me well for my continuing careers, which had now changed in priority – part-time teacher, full-time footballer. The wedding was no celebrity bash, no Posh and Becks; there was no *Hello* or *OK* magazine type coverage. Such was the low profile of bride and groom and the way of life then, that the newspaper actually printed the address of our first home, 50 Tenniswood Road, Enfield. It didn't worry us in the least. Our wedding day would remain as one of the most memorable days of our life. The wildness of the Derbyshire countryside in Chatsworth Park provided an appropriate backcloth for the Princess and the Woodcutter. We were both twenty-two years old.

The newlyweds climbed into their battered little red Austin Healey Sprite and roared off to Devon via Stratford upon Avon. Football and teaching were the last things on our mind. The little open-topped sportscar had been purchased for £250 thanks to a loan from the Arsenal bank manager, who was frankly amazed at the small amount I wanted to borrow. Within two weeks I needed a further £68 for a replacement engine and towing costs when the con rod went straight through the side of the engine while driving on the M1. The bill for seven days in room 14 at the Portledge Hotel, all inclusive, came to £63 7s 5d.

From the Devon coast it was exciting to be heading back, not to Derbyshire but to London and our first home in Enfield. The house was new and one we could afford only because Arsenal owned it. It was a small semi-detached house with a combined dining room-living room and two bedrooms. We paid Arsenal a rent of £2 10s a week. At the other end of our four-house block, in number 56, was Freddie Clarke, Arsenal's Irish full-back, and his new wife Greta. Our personal life was perfect, Megs teaching at a school just around the corner; but from 3 August 1964 to 12 March 1968, Bob Wilson dived into near obscurity as a keeper with Arsenal.

It began well enough. On the day I reported back for training, Don Howe, newly signed from West Bromwich Albion and whom I'd never met before, ran all of fifty yards to say hello. The rest of the Arsenal squad followed his gesture and congratulated me on both marriage and becoming a full-time professional. I had missed ten days of pre-season training but it didn't really matter.

Life as a full-time professional footballer must be as good as it gets. Blessed with a natural ability, he is lucky enough to have his talent nurtured and then gets paid for playing a game. Of course, the level at which he plays acts as a barometer to his enjoyment, but he gets to exercise in the open air, keeps his body perfectly honed and fit and gets to kick a football around.

Not once did I think the daily routine was a chore or a proper job. I loved keeping goal and appreciated the life I had chosen. My problems revolved simply around the management's lack of belief in me. Three or four months into the 1964–65 season, I had a twenty-four carat row with Billy Wright. I was the regular reserve keeper up to the middle of November. We then played amateur club Hendon at Highbury in the London Challenge Cup; 2–0 up in ten minutes, we contrived to lose 3–2. The team had been unprofessional and it was a collective bad night.

Two days later on Friday morning, when the teamsheets for the following day were posted, I found I'd been dropped to the third team, the only player to have been found guilty of underachieving. Immediately, I joined the queue outside the door of physiotherapist Bertie Mee, where Billy used to wait for 'unhappy' players. At first we spoke about the Hendon game man to man. When, fairly forcibly, I challenged his reason for dropping me, he went out and called for his entire coaching and medical staff to come into what was a tiny room. Suddenly it was like an inquisition. I stood, back against the door, looking straight towards the big mirror on the facing wall. Billy stood beside the mirror and, lining each wall, were coaches Les Shannon, Dennis Evans, Ernie Collet and physios Bertie Mee and Bert Owen. Alf Fields, a great Arsenal servant as player, coach and general help around the dressing room, was the last one to enter.

Billy took charge, relayed my version of events and then gave his own before inviting his staff to comment. Les agreed with the manager; so too did Ernie and Dennis. Bertie and Bert took my side as best they could by staying silent. Alf Fields said the whole team deserved to be dropped. Still I continued to argue and Billy became as agitated as I was. He then accused me of looking at myself in the mirror and the red mist descended! Speechless and close to tears, I reached for the door and slammed it shut as I made my exit. I quickly gathered my belongings from my peg in the dressing room and literally charged towards the marble halls. Alf Fields was already there and pulled me towards the little bench seat in the corner of the hall.

'Alf, he can stuff his fucking third team, I'm off,' I raged.

Without trying to be condescending, Alf Fields made his point.

'You can walk out of this club but it'll be the same anywhere else. Playing for Arsenal's third team is better than playing for most first teams. You set your sights on the best. This place is the best. I've told you already many times, you'll make it. You've got something that's different. I've hardly ever seen anyone plunge at feet like you. You'll be a fool to give it all up now.'

Alf took the wind out of my sails perfectly. I did my best to thank the tall handsome man who had won the British Empire Medal for bravery in Italy. On my way out I also took a long hard look at the bust of Herbert Chapman and the huge red cannon emblazoned on the marble beneath my feet. There and then, I resolved to show the manager that he was wrong.

Billy Wright was not the type of man who enjoyed rows and

I'm sure he disliked our shouting match as much as anyone. I learned later he'd sort of admired my spirit. The argument never clouded our relationship. It was all about his burning desire to succeed as a manager and an equal ambition of mine to be the best. Megs' response when I told her what had occurred was one of common sense – 'You're a professional now. They pay you money and you play.'

Being dropped to the third team was an ordeal. Bill Shankly once said there were two football teams in Liverpool – Liverpool's first team and Liverpool reserves. It was a good joke but couldn't be more off the mark. First-team and reserve football are as far apart as the poles. Playing for the 'stiffs', as the second team in any club is known, generates little interest, little crowds and little atmosphere. A crowd of one or two thousand inside Highbury produced a soulless echo that gave a ring of failure. Being a goalkeeper helped in a way because a shot was a shot and a save was a save, just as they were in the top team. My frustration wasn't helped by the first team's poor season. They finished thirteenth as Manchester United took the championship, and the goalkeeping jersey was shared by Tony Burns, who played in twenty-four games, and Jim Furnell, who played in eighteen.

End of season and pre-season tours always lifted my spirits and my hopes, as I would usually play a couple of games. Only once did I not want to travel and that was in the summer of 1965 when we were due to tour the West Indies. The reason for my reticence was that Megs was two weeks overdue with our first baby. Modern-day players would be encouraged to stay at home at such a time, but in 1965 there was no option.

Flying with the Arsenal then was different from other clubs. Long before the Munich tragedy, Arsenal players, directors and staff always travelled in two aircraft, and this tour was no different. We flew to New York, then to Jamaica, Puerto Rico, Curaçao, Aruba, Trinidad, and back to New York on a trip that lasted twenty-one days and included a riot. We played in a triangular tournament against Jamaica and Trinidad and, after we had struggled to beat Trinidad, the Jamaicans were convinced their local favourites would take the trophy. Two goals conceded by Jamaica in the first ten minutes, plus Joe Baker head-butting an opponent, were the signal for the first bottles to be thrown from the excitable crowd. The situation became rapidly worse, so the referee abandoned the game and we were locked tight in our dressing room for ages as objects crashed against walls and windows. Eventually we were smuggled back to our hotel.

News of the riot hit the papers back home just as Megs went into labour, giving birth to our first son, John. While she was battling the after-effects of the birth and feeling abandoned without her husband's support, I was being thrown into a swimming pool to help wet the baby's head in the Kingston sunshine, Joe Baker receiving the same treatment a few hours later for his firstborn.

We arrived home from the West Indies forty-eight hours before the start of the 1965–66 season. I hadn't slept during the long flight across the Atlantic, my stomach was queasy, and after landing at 6.00 a.m., I arrived home around breakfast time. Megs was waiting proudly to show me John, by now two weeks old. Everyone thinks that their children are the most beautiful in the world, and I was no exception. It's just that I had very tired eyes and my brain wasn't functioning as it should have done. I glanced at my first son and said to Megs, 'He's lovely darling, lovely. Just like a pickled walnut!' I would not recommend this kind of remark to someone who has been waiting to share the joy of parenthood for two weeks!

Being a dad excited me and helped my steely resolve. I'd played well in the West Indies, and both Billy Wright and Les Shannon had made encouraging noises about my form and fitness. They hinted I'd start the season against Stoke at

Highbury, but the day before the game they pulled me aside and said, 'We know you're playing great. You've done well but we've decided to go with Jim's experience.'

Jim Furnell was such a likeable man and, although we were rivals, we were also friends. For most goalkeepers, that is usually the case. After all, we are the only ones who fully understand and appreciate the problems associated with the job. An injury to Jim allowed me to play my first top division game since November 1963. We drew at Northampton and at Burnley and then it was hail and farewell for Wilson yet again.

Four months later, during which time Jim and Tony Burns shared the No. 1 jersey, and following nine games in which the Arsenal defence leaked twenty-seven goals, I was back with a promise. Billy Wright told me it was going to be the chance he knew I craved. It was Christmas. Sheffield Wednesday had beaten Arsenal 4–0 at Hillsborough on 28 December and the next day the return, for them and me, was at Highbury. I was required to make only one special save, diving at the feet of Johnny Fantham, as we won 5–2.

Playing in the Owls goal was England's Ron Springett. Countless times I had stood behind his net as schoolboy and college student. I used to take it in turns to travel the twelve miles from Chesterfield and learn by watching Ron at Hillsborough one week and Sheffield United's Alan Hodgkinson the next. What a Christmas present, to be back in the First Division, this time on merit.

The New Year promised so much and on the first day of 1966 I took my place in the Arsenal goal at Craven Cottage. At the other end was my old goalkeeping friend Jack McClelland, just as keen to prove Billy Wright wrong for selling him as I was keen to prove him right for selecting me. Ten minutes into the game I went up for a high ball with our centre-half Ian Ure and Fulham's Graham Leggatt. As I caught it at full stretch and fell to the floor, the two players crashed down on top of me, dislocating my right elbow. I didn't know it was a dislocation at the time, only that it was excruciating. I needed attention from Bertie Mee who realised it was serious. Bertie also knew how desperate I was to succeed.

'How bad is the pain?' he asked.

'It's fine,' I replied.

Amazing what an adrenaline rush and a stubborn refusal to admit defeat can do.

We lost 1–0 when Graham Leggat curled in Johnny Haynes' tapped free kick. Jack McClelland and I ensured the game didn't have another goal. Fulham's Johnny Haynes, George Cohen and Bobby Robson congratulated me on my performance and showed concern at my condition at the end of the game.

Within twenty-four hours my arm was swollen to twice its size and the bleed from the bruising totally discoloured the skin. Billy Wright was brilliant.

'Don't worry, Bob, the doc says you'll be back in three or four weeks' time,' he reassured me.

I didn't play again that season. Arsenal finished in fourteenth place, their worst position since 1930.

As England were about to become world champions in the summer of 1966, the Arsenal board dismissed Billy Wright. We had our ups and downs but Billy, to my mind, would always be the man who believed in me enough to bring me to Highbury and who persuaded me to turn professional. He was heartbroken at his sacking, and he was deemed a failure. As far as results and league position went, as far as bringing trophies back to Arsenal, that was the case; but the legacy he left was rich in promise and had a huge bearing, albeit four years later, on the club's greatest ever season to date.

I don't think there was one player on Arsenal's books at the time of Billy Wright's departure who didn't raise an eyebrow or express surprise when we each received a letter from the club secretary, Bob Wall. It stated that Billy Wright and Les Shannon had 'relinquished' their posts and then came the surprise: 'The directors have appointed Mr Bertie Mee as acting manager of the club and I am sure the directors and I can rely upon your wholehearted loyalty to the new manager.'

Loyalty to Arsenal was never a problem for me, but my enthusiasm was tested as never before. Misguidedly, I thought Bertie would give me an early opportunity in his team. I knew him better than I knew anyone on the entire staff. During the latter part of my amateur days, it was he who told me that the position would be up for grabs. He directly set up my initial visit to Highbury, and Bertie and his wife Doris twice entertained Megs and me at their home, discussing how we could blend football with our teaching careers.

I'll never forget complimenting him during dinner on the perfect temperature of the red wine.

'How do you get it like that, Bertie?' I asked.

With an impish seriousness, he got up from the dinner table replying, 'It's pretty difficult. You just have to make sure you don't leave it on the radiator too long.' With that he picked a second bottle from the radiator behind me and we all had a good laugh.

Maybe the Arsenal players should not have been so shocked at his appointment because an outstanding precedent had been set when Tom Whittaker relinquished the physio's role to become manager in 1947. One thing we knew was that there would no longer be room for either sloppy indiscipline or favouritism. His technical knowledge was limited, but his greatness came through his brilliant organisational talent and his ability to delegate.

This was apparent immediately with the appointment of Dave Sexton as coach. One of football's deepest thinkers, Dave's knowledge and quiet style reaped an immediate response within a bemused dressing room. The first change of playing staff was almost as big a shock as Bertie's appointment. George Eastham was sold to Stoke City, not because he lacked skill, but because the management didn't think he fancied a fight when the team were up against it.

Moving up seven places in the First Division from fourteenth to seventh suggested an improvement, although it had nothing to do with me. I never came remotely close to displacing Jim Furnell during that 1966–67 season. The thirty-five appearances I made in the 'stiffs' and the nine in first-team friendlies confirmed that I was now firmly established as the Arsenal reserve goalkeeper. The thought had now occurred to Megs and me that I really wasn't going to establish myself at the top level.

I was twenty-five years old and players who made it generally did so well before that age. Megs and I had a better income than teachers, but money had never been a main motivation for me. If I wasn't going to find success at Arsenal, I didn't fancy going anywhere. To alleviate the boredom in the afternoons following training, I decided to keep my hand in at teaching.

Holloway School was only two or three miles from Highbury and their playing fields were reasonably close to London Colney, our training ground. The games teacher, Alan Wright, was a fully qualified FA coach who had a multitude of contacts in football and showbusiness. He had been partly responsible for nurturing the talent of a young lad at the school called Charlie George.

Everyone knew he was special, not least Charlie himself. He was not just talented and cocky but funny with it. Charlie was always getting into trouble in the classroom, always a huge bundle of trouble to opponents on the football field. He loved Arsenal and Arsenal loved him. The club made sure they secured him on their books and rightly so. With Bob Wilson it was a gamble. With Charlie George it was a racing certainty he would succeed.

As Bertie Mee's first season in charge came to an end, I found myself facing a crossroads. The signpost pointed in two very clear directions. One way said education, the other football. The pull to be a really good teacher received an extra tug when I wrote to my former Head of PE Department at Loughborough enquiring whether I had enough experience and qualifications to apply for an advertised lecturer's post. Clinton Sayer's reply pointed out how keen the competition would be for the vacancy but that the job would go to the person whom the college believed to be the best candidate. He encouraged me to apply.

The other letter I wrote asking for advice went to the Football Association, where my old Loughborough coach Allen Wade was now Director of Coaching. The response was charming but blunt. In brief, Allen reminded me that I had already travelled a long and strange road into football but that I was a professional. 'You have a wife and family now,' he went on. 'They are your priority. I hope you are big enough to stop feeling sorry for yourself.'

It was the perfect kick up the pants. My life was nigh on perfect with a lovely wife, a home and now two beautiful children. John's sister Anna had arrived on 7 December 1966 and, unlike my absence at his birth, I was there for what must be the greatest of all experiences known to man and woman, the arrival of a new life.

My only frustration was making the decision about whether my obsession with goalkeeping took place on a small stage or a large one. The love of being in goal and making saves had never wavered and never would, and therefore I should make the most of the lifestyle that I had. The Loughborough College application remained as a keepsake. The crossroads were comfortably negotiated. Studying and working at the art of goalkeeping as a professional footballer was still the right road for me to follow.

7
You've got to be crazy

'All that I know most surely about morality
and the obligations of man I owe to football.'

Albert Camus,
philosopher and goalkeeper

Throughout the many twists and turns taken by my Primrose path, there has remained one constant – a love of goalkeepers and of the art of goalkeeping. You may raise a questioning eyebrow at Camus' statement; a 'crazy' assertion, you may well think, that football could provide a framework for life. Well, the state of mind of those daft enough to play in goal has always been questioned. Why would anybody want to risk the ridicule that is likely to be directed at some time towards anyone who has seriously attempted the old art of preventing a bladder of air from entering the net that surrounds two goalposts and a crossbar?

The area represents some 192 square feet. There are eight long yards between the posts, and an interminable eight feet between ground and crossbar. It's huge. In the world's most popular team game, the goalkeeping position is the most individual. The keeper is the one who has the ultimate responsibility of nullifying the prime objective of the game, to score goals.

'Felix throws out to Carlos Alberto . . . to Jairzinho. He's past Cooper . . . Pele's at the far post . . . Pele-e-e-e . . . Oh, what a save . . . Gordon Banks!' Close your eyes and, for those old enough to remember, it's still as clear as if it were yesterday. This was 7 June 1970 at the World Cup in Guadalajara, Mexico, reigning champions England versus competition favourites Brazil. The scoreline after ten minutes play was 0–0. More than three decades have elapsed since Gordon Banks' 'impossible play', as Pele described the England keeper's wonder save. It was a unique save.

People simply don't have an instant recall of the heroics of goalkeepers in the same way they remember goals and their scorers. After all, the greatest appeal of the 'beautiful game' is to see a ball hit the rigging. For one player however, that goalscoring moment signals failure, possible defeat, often humiliation, even despair. That is the goalkeeper's lot. He is a race apart, one of a breed who has to cope with the loneliness and peculiarities of the job, its single-minded confrontational face, the vulnerability, the obligatory presence and, of course, the humility and the camaraderie it exposes. Goalkeepers will always be the keenest of rivals but the greatest of friends. They might suggest that only they truly understand each other and the old art, but they would willingly invite anyone to have a less cynical insight into a position in a football team that is, quite frankly, full of contradictions.

So what are these peculiarities and complexities? The goal-keeper is the only person on the field of play allowed to handle the ball indefinitely, and who is required to dress differently from the rest. His is the first name on a teamsheet; he wears the No. 1 on his back. That in itself is suitably appropriate; number one has connotations of someone alone but it also suggests someone special, the first, the best.

One of the greatest joys of the role is that it has always catered for all types of personality and all shapes and sizes of physique. Skinny, tubby, tall or less tall, extrovert, introvert, it matters not; only that the individual who chooses to perform beneath a crossbar and between the posts can consistently stop a football from billowing the net, anyhow, anyway. Each and every part of the anatomy is a legal means of defence.

Saves may only be remembered occasionally, but the reputation of the greatest characters who made them will remain in perpetuity. A few of the early ones, whose antics set goalkeepers as a breed apart, fascinated me.

William 'Fatty' Foulke was, as his nickname suggests, overweight. At his slimmest he weighed in at around 22 stones. Towards the end of his career he was almost 26 stones. Standing 6ft 2ins tall, he 'filled' a goal better than any goalkeeper before of since. Ridiculous? Well, Billy Foulke became England's keeper and twice helped Sheffield United to win the FA Cup. Amazingly nimble, he could hold a ball easily in one giant hand, and the tale of a mis-punch that removed several teeth from an opponent only added to his reputation and presence.

It cost the equivalent of 7½ p to stand behind Billy's goal in 1899, and spectators would often be as entertained by his suspect temperament as his saves. Known as 'Little Willie' to his team-mates at Sheffield United, Chelsea and Bradford City, he once sat down at the dinner table early and, before his colleagues arrived, had eaten all the food intended for the whole team.

Where Fatty Foulke was the larger than life character in the early days, Albert Iremonger was the 'longest'. Goalkeeper for Notts County and Lincoln City from 1905–27, Iremonger at 6ft 6ins is believed to be one of the tallest ever to play regularly in league football. He didn't suffer from Foulke's dodgy temperament but he was a character with a sense of humour and a friendliness that endeared him to all who knew him. Iremonger thought nothing of abandoning his goalmouth and running as far as the halfway line to take throw-ins. Nottinghamshire folk tell the tale of the day he ran the length of the field only to belt a penalty kick against the bar. The rebound landed near the halfway line and, as he was trying to recover his ground, one kick from an opponent directed the ball towards Iremonger's unattended goal. The giant keeper caught up with the ball as it was approaching the line, thrashed out at it with his foot and volleyed it perfectly into the top corner of his own goal.

Albert was definitely the first of the great goalkeeping entertainers. Other names from the early twentieth century include Chesterfield's own Sam Hardy, who performed miracles at Liverpool and Aston Villa, and Harry Hibbs of Birmingham City who, like Hardy, built his reputation on a mastery of angles and anticipation.

Then there was the Greenock Morton and Scotland keeper Harry Rennie who, as a trained engineer, used his trade to enhance his positional play by spending hours making drawings of every conceivable position from which a ball could be struck at him. 'Master the theory of angles,' argued Rennie, 'and you master the men who score the goals.' Another practice of Rennie's was to spend half an hour every day diving full length on to rough boards 'just to harden myself up'.

A touch of madness or craziness has always been attributed to custodians but the memories they leave are such that Liverpool, no less, decided to use 'Goalkeeper' as their telegraphic address, an amazing tribute to three of their number ones, Sam Hardy, Ned Doig and Elisha Scott.

Legend has it that one day on Lime Street, Elisha Scott saw the great Everton striker Dixie Dean draw back his neck and, from across the street, head an imaginary ball. Just as swiftly, Elisha threw himself into the gutter to save. And what about the notable amateur keeper, J.F. Mitchell? He represented Preston North End and Manchester City, and played regularly in first-class football while wearing spectacles. He even went on to win one England cap in 1925.

Goalkeepers are notoriously superstitious. Dick Pym played in three FA Cup finals for Bolton – in 1923, 1926 and 1929 – and won all three. He attributed much of his success to always carrying a lump of coal to matches.

Nerves have affected pretty well every goalkeeper, but only the Welsh international Dr Leigh Richmond Roose, who played for Stoke, Everton and Sunderland, has ever admitted his fear so graphically. Filling in his expenses form as directed by the Football Association, he always began his list with what would seem an unusual item, that is unless you're a goalie – 'Use of toilet twice – two pence.'

These are just a few of the men who are still recalled many decades after they played in the most challenging position in any team. The examples quoted create a reasonable argument in favour of the belief that all goalkeepers are indeed a bit daft. Admittedly, there are times when it is difficult to produce a credible response. While studying the history of the position, I discovered a book from yesteryear entitled *Judgement and the Art of Goalkeeping*. In it, the author H.D. Davies states, 'It used to be accepted as axiomatic that goalkeepers were a "slate loose".' That opinion probably originated in the good old days of the Edwardian period, when 'rushing the goalkeeper' was a legitimate tactic during the taking of a corner kick and when goalkeepers often went into the net faster than the ball that followed. Happily, the legalities or otherwise of such tactics have become at best outlawed, or at worst more subtle these days.

Those goalkeepers who set the early examples are simply names in historical books but my earliest heroes all possessed a physique, mannerism, temperament or special style that matched the early breed.

Frank Swift was my earliest mentor and, at 6ft 3ins, was unusually tall for keepers in the late 1930s and forties. The England and Manchester City hero admitted to adding a touch of showmanship to a save occasionally – 'Oh well, I have to throw in a bit to please the crowd. After all, it's only a game.'

Frank's personality was immense, his attitude much loved, but the laid back look hid a sensitive soul. The nature of the keeper's role demands a bold outward bluff and Frank Swift hid his nerves behind a dazzling smile. His reaction as the final whistle blew in the 1934 FA Cup final illustrated perfectly the tension that can build inside a mind. Manchester City beat Portsmouth 2–1. During the last few minutes, Frank was mentally counting the clock down. The relief at the sound of the whistle released all the tension and Frank fainted in the back of the net.

Geoffrey Green wrote of big Swifty, 'Football is in his debt, both for the distinction of his goalkeeping and the rich vitality of his nature.' Frank Swift was one who inspired me as a little boy and his death in the Munich air disaster was a devastating blow. At the same end of Wembley that Swifty fainted, his successor Bert Trautmann broke his neck.

Others whom I followed avidly in *Charles Buchan's Football Monthly* as a youngster included Ted Sagar, Sam Bartram, Ted Ditchburn, Bert Williams, Gil Merrick, Jimmy Cowan, Ronnie Simpson and a predecessor of mine at Arsenal, Jack Kelsey. They were all part of a golden age of goalkeeping, an era when only one foreigner, Trautmann, stood on the goallines in British football.

I have to admit I never used to trust the consistency of foreigners. Italy's Aldo Olivieri and Giampiero Combi, Uruguay's Roque Maspoli and Ladislao Mazurkiewicz, Brazil's eccentric Felix, Hungary's Gyula Grosics and Yugoslavia's Vladimir Beara all fascinated me, were capable of thrilling me, but I didn't trust their flamboyant styles. Even some of the best 'modern' foreign keepers lacked the most important aspect, consistency. West Germany's Sepp Maier, Holland's Jan Jongbloed, Poland's Jan Tomaszewski and Dino Zoff of Italy are in the record books as World Cup winners, runners-up or third-place recipients. I have watched each of them at close quarters and while part of me queried their unorthodox methods, another part quickly appreciated that having a strange, sometimes bizarre technique doesn't matter as long as it works effectively.

In my developing years, only one other foreign keeper besides Trautmann was convincing to my eye. His nicknames included 'The Black Octopus', 'The Spider' and 'The Tiger'. Always dressed in black, Lev Yashin of the USSR was the European Footballer of the Year in 1963, the first keeper to win the coveted award. Europe acknowledged his greatness. At home he was made a member of the Order of Lenin and an Honoured Master of Sport.

Foreign keepers now dominate the top division of the British game. The influx of so many has created huge problems in the development of our own, and only rare genius or braver management will reverse the trend. Many years ago, Percy M. Young wrote in his book *The Appreciation of Football*:

> Foreign goalkeepers have a high degree of dramatic background which enables them to satisfy the deep-seated feelings for colour which an English environment so often denies to its natives.

The goalkeepers mentioned all made the biggest impact on me for their personalities and deeds on the field. Many others affected my thinking. Suffice to say they all became household names – Banks, Shilton, Jennings and Seaman the best of British, Schmeichel an adopted Dane. Each and every one of these had the ability to fill their goalmouth with a rare presence. Schmeichel and Shilton's way was very visual and audible; Banks, Jennings and Seaman were equally effective but in a much quieter manner. When anyone of these men walked into a room, they seemed to fill it with a special aura. Even though I describe them as the modern men, the ever-changing face of goalkeeping is perfectly illustrated within the years they graced the game and the goalmouths.

When Banks, Jennings and Shilton began their careers, they relied on bare hands to pluck the ball out of the dry air. In the wet, their cotton gloves were of highly debatable value.

Today, the gloves are rubber faced and perfectly tailored and help to produce extra belief and confidence. Their adhesive quality compares favourably with the gritty soil or chewing gum mixed with spit on naked palms that worked wonders for me.

Where the new gloves are helpful, the new ball is nothing short of a goalkeeping nightmare. No longer made of thick leather enclosing a heavy bladder, today's football has a thinner outer skin, different air pressure and is, when struck with any reasonable degree of power, totally unpredictable. Colourful and pretty in design, a football remains what it always has been – the goalkeeper's enemy; and neither will the objective ever alter – to make it as much of a friend as possible. Great outfield players could always make a football bend or curl by striking it with the inside or outside of the foot. Now, though, any one at any level, including someone like me with two artificial hips, can generate dip or swerve by kicking today's football with power.

In recent years, I was asked to help test a new Nike ball. After a few days the company's designer re-visited an angry group at the Arsenal training ground. He was informed by the goalkeepers that the lightness and movement through the air was reminiscent of a trick ball. Arguing forcibly, the designer told us that it was impossible for the ball to be unpredictable. 'It will always maintain its intended flight,' he said. There was only one way to disprove his theory. We put him in goal and for five minutes hit balls in his general direction. I've never known someone with such blind belief lose his tongue and his argument quite so quickly.

The game's governing bodies want more excitement and more goals to be scored. Unless the goalposts are widened, the crossbar raised or the keepers height restricted to 5ft 2ins, the only alternative they have is to redesign the balls. Consequently, all the books written about goalkeeping prior to the new technology are as good as redundant. 'You must always catch the ball this way or that way' they proclaim. Not so. Today, keepers have a fraction of a second to make a decision on how fast the ball is travelling at them. If the answer comes up 'fast' and registers alert signals, that ball has to be kept out by any means available. Catching or trying to catch could lead to disaster. Parrying the ball, hopefully away from the danger, is the top priority.

More than ever before, goalkeepers walk a tightrope. For eighty-nine minutes they can perform immaculately but an error in the last sixty seconds will completely obliterate all the previous good work. Strikers by comparison rarely suffer the abuse given to keepers. Pele, Cruyff, Bobby Charlton, George Best, Gary Lineker, Alan Shearer and the rest have all missed open goals, every one as crucial as a keeper's error. Such aberrations aren't often recalled, only the goals that were scored remain as a memory.

Napoleon once said of an up-and-coming officer, 'I don't want to know whether he's good. Is he lucky?' The same could be said of goalkeepers. The men who are based alone with their problems in front of a net have approached the task in a variety of ways. Some have paced up and down like caged lions, others have stood with hands on hips or arms folded. Whereas most of the early breed rarely deserted their goalline, the modern game invites, even demands, daring dashes from goal. Rule changes mean that today's number ones must be as adept at playing the ball with their feet as at handling. No longer can they pick up a back-pass and bounce a ball around a goalmouth wasting time as they go. A great first touch with the foot or an in-built timer, ticking off six seconds with the ball in the hands, has had to become an acquired skill.

For any one who has tasted success there have been untold hours, days, weeks, months and years of dedication and effort put in before gathering the rewards. In defeat, goalkeeper's faces reflect lonely rejection. Never seeking solace, mud-stained jerseys are removed with a mixture of anger and self-recrimination. In victory, there is rarely more than a look of great satisfaction or a clenched fist. It is dangerous, they know, to celebrate too wildly.

Mistakes and costly errors are never far away. All keepers make them; the best make the fewest. All feel privileged to have experienced the demanding role, to be the latest in a long and illustrious line undergoing this weird and wonderful examination of character. Before they realise it, or desire it, their goalkeeping careers will be over. Happily, little idiosyncrasies will not diminish with the telling or the passing of the years.

Maybe, just maybe, I have earned a place in goalkeeping history, simply because of my ability to dive headlong into oncoming boots and re-appear with the ball in my arms. The rest of my technique was normal, efficient and consistent, but my diving at feet was a diamond in my style and all keepers hope for at least one such jewel to dazzle onlookers.

Goalkeepers run great goalscorers close in the hero stakes. Great saves may be overlooked but the goalkeepers who made them are not forgotten.

> The unerring eye, the master touch
> More buoyant than the ball
> The fearless heart, the powerful clutch,
> The genius praised by all.
>
> The squirrel's swift leap, the falcon's flight
> The clear quick-thinking brain

Extract from T. Smith's poem in praise of John Thomson, Celtic goalkeeper, who lost his life in the name of goalkeeping on the field of play against Rangers, 5 September 1931.

July 1964 – our wedding day.

...eting Princess Margaret at Wembley
...ore the 1969 League Cup final.

George Graham about to enjoy a drink
of champagne from the European Fairs
Cup, which we won in 1970.

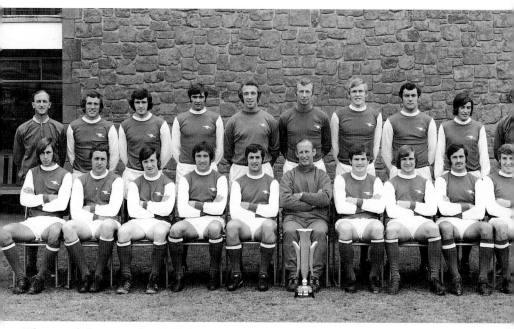

The squad that won the 1970 European Fairs Cup – and the double the next season.

I was part of the BBC team for the 1970 Mexico World Cup – and besieged by letters.

Anna, aged three, fills her dad's goalmouth Highbury.

y favourite save, versus George Best and Manchester United, August 1970, start of the
uble season.

Stoke City 2 Arsenal 2, FA Cup semi-final 1971. As the great Gordon Banks and I shake hands at the end of the game, the mental exhaustion is obvious.

ampions of England – the final whistle goes at White Hart Lane, 3 May 1971.

p of the Pops', May 1971 – a nervous group of footballers sing 'Good Old Arsenal',
ped by Pan's People.

Vital full-length save from Alec Lindsay – FA Cup final versus Liverpool, 8 May 1971.

The double is completed – Frank McLintock lifts the FA Cup.

e borough of Islington celebrates the achievement in traditional style.

e proudest moment – Arsenal's Player of the Year, 1970–71.

A fingertip save at Goodison versus Everton.

Forays into the advertising world were like going back to acting – model Viv Neves shows the Arsenal goalie how to pose.

Greatest of rivals, best of friends. The two managers to accomplish the double in the twentieth century were Bill Nicholson of Tottenham Hotspur in 1960-61 (*left*) and Bertie Mee of Arsenal in 1970-71.

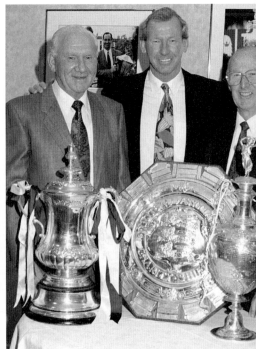

8
Success and stardom

'The main ingredient of stardom is the rest of the team.'

John Wooden

Success caught me by surprise. The 1967–68 football season had begun as predictably as the previous three. I was still the Arsenal reserve-team goalkeeper, Jim Furnell remained number one. Untypically for me, I was uncomplaining of my lot and, for perhaps the only time in my entire life, had virtually settled for being a second string.

We were reasonably comfortably off, but could only occasionally afford a special night out in London. The old Talk of the Town nightclub was a favoured haunt when we'd saved up enough to see great stars including Tony Bennett, Lena Horne and our favourite Johnny Mathis, who later became a good friend. On these nights out, we would sit excitedly with our college friends, worry about how much we were spending and sneak in a few half bottles of wine in the girls' handbags to keep expenditure down to a minimum. We would wait for the band to strike up before popping corks and supplementing our one bought bottle of Sauterne. They were very different days from now, when reserve-team goalies can earn a £4,000 draw bonus or £12,000 win bonus for simply sitting on the substitutes bench during one Champions League game.

Megs may look on this time, and my mood swings, in a different light, but I remember it as special, if not spectacular, and John and Anna were a joy to us. Remembering the warning my dad had always expressed about football and its unpredictable nature, I ensured there was a sound safety net if life at Arsenal ever turned sour. My part-time teaching at Holloway School increased, and during the summer of 1967 I went to Lilleshall in Shropshire to take my FA Full Coaching Award.

Two weeks of intense work, both practical and theory, gave me a completely new understanding of the game from which I earned a living. My teaching experience was a huge advantage when it came to organising my sessions whether they be 'defending in depth' or 'exploiting third man running'. The technical jargon was absorbed, digested and re-delivered packaged and stamped, part Loughborough, part Arsenal. I loved being a full-back, centre-half, striker, even a goalkeeper, and the outcome was a pass and another string to the bow. I now felt that when football failed me, I could be a successful teacher or football coach. What I didn't realise immediately was that the FA course had helped me fill the gaping hole left by my missing out on the normal apprenticeship served by footballers.

I arrived back at Highbury for pre-season training, a more complete player. It didn't show immediately. Bertie Mee and his excellent coach Dave Sexton seemed to be obsessed with their first team, and those on the fringes had to rely on the reserve-team coach to sustain their appetites and ambitions. In this respect I was again in luck. Don Howe, who had never fully regained the form he showed prior to the broken leg sustained in the collision with Blackpool's Tony Waiters, had taken charge of the Arsenal second team. He was knowledgeable, unbelievably enthusiastic and inspirational. Don had played in front of me, knew my strengths and weaknesses, and willingly answered my pleas for extra training aimed at specialised goalkeeping only. I grew in stature and increasingly believed I was the best goalkeeper at the club.

By December I was champing at the bit. The first team had won just eight of their first nineteen games, losing seven. A flu epidemic then hit the club, including Jim Furnell, and I was back in the big time – another chance, another appearance, except that you won't find any mention of it in the record books.

It was 9 December and Sheffield Wednesday arrived at the marble halls. After nine minutes of the game, Frank McLintock scored a great individual goal. Just before half-time, Wednesday's Jack Whitham struck a powerful drive and I was thrilled to hear the applause for my save, which ensured a 1–0 interval lead. Running out to the North Bank goal for the second half, I was amazed at the intensity of a sudden snowstorm. Highbury's famous undersoil heating was helping keep the pitch reasonably playable and I put my cap and gloves in the back of the net as referee Eric Jennings blew his whistle for the re-start of play.

A few minutes later I was desperately worried. I couldn't see further than the edge of my own eighteen-yard box and couldn't even hear the ref's whistle. Suddenly a policeman appeared beyond my post and, to my astonishment, shouted, 'Bob, what are you doing here? The ref's abandoned the game. The rest of the players are back in the dressing room!'

The snowstorm not only robbed me of a rare first-team appearance, it left me in deep depression. The game was declared null and void. Jim had recovered from flu by the next match and went on to complete more than a hundred consecutive first-team appearances.

To add to my woes, I lost Don Howe to the first team. Bertie Mee was unable to dissuade Dave Sexton from becoming manager of Chelsea and immediately promoted from within. My challenge, however, was not as difficult as Don's. The first-team dressing room rebelled openly at Don's appointment. They loved Dave Sexton's coaching methods and, in typical footballer style, gave Don a hard time.

It was the making of him. He took the players moans and groans for a week or so and then ripped into them in no uncertain terms. Extra running, extra training, extra anything was

Don's solution and it worked brilliantly. Although the league form was dreadful, just two wins in eleven games between my 'non appearance' and 23 March, a Cup run ended at Wembley. It indicated a stirring of success within the marble halls, which had been absent for too long.

On 2 March 1968, Arsenal FC appeared in England's most famous stadium. Their opponents in the Football League Cup final were Don Revie's Leeds United, a side on the brink of greatness. The day was exciting to a degree for me, but sitting in the stand was no substitute for the experience of playing. The days of five or six substitutes on the bench, hoping for a call to duty, were still a long way off.

The match was dreadful, uninspiring, a battle in the worst sense possible. A combination of Paul Madeley and Jack Charlton at best distracting Jim Furnell, at worst openly fouling the keeper, set up a glorious volley from Terry Cooper to win the League Cup. It was the only thing of beauty served up on the day.

One week later, I sat at Highbury in what is known as the Paddock, a group of seats, central and close to the pitch, from where the reserves and youth team watch matches. For me, a long-time reserve player, the paddock was an appropriate name, a bit like being put out to grass. By chance, the match programme for the FA Cup fifth-round tie against Birmingham City included a lengthy interview with me. It relayed my lack of first-team games, my loyalty to the club and my unlucky breaks, but ended with the question, 'Is goalkeeping a hard task master?' My reply read, 'It is, simply because you are not allowed to make a mistake.' Eighty-nine minutes after kick-off that observation was proved to be correct in dramatic style.

Arsenal led 1–0 and should have been out of sight, missing chance after chance. With the referee looking at his watch an innocuous looping header dropped into and out of Jim Furnell's fingers. Birmingham snatched the draw their dogged display had earned, if not deserved. At the final whistle I made my way swiftly out of the ground. I didn't speak to anyone. My stomach was churning. I just knew I would play in the replay. The chap up there who pulls the levers marked 'win' or 'lose' had decided in my favour.

Sunday proved to be a long day and Megs, John and Anna did their best to make life normal for me. My mind worked overtime, my destiny was again up for grabs. This time, hopefully, there would be no snowstorm, no dislocated elbow. I was twenty-six years old and that night, as on so many nights before and after, my prayers included the wish for a decent performance.

On Monday morning Bertie Mee told me I would be playing in the replay at St Andrew's the next night. Talking with Jim Furnell was difficult. I felt sorry for him and told him his mistake shouldn't have mattered if the team had just taken half of the chances they created. Jim, in return, wished me luck.

Fate and its fickle fingers didn't start and end with me simply facing Birmingham City. I knew their famous manager rather well from another life. The great Stanley Cullis had moved on from his beloved Wolves and was now in charge at St Andrews. Was this a good sign or a bad one, I pondered on the way to the match.

Outside the ground I gave two tickets to Dennis and John Roach, two friends whose furniture and carpet business had supplied virtually the whole of the Arsenal team. They said later I thrust the tickets into their hands and walked away as though I was going to the gallows.

Inside St Andrews, 51,586 fans created a fantastic atmosphere, and it took just thirty seconds for me to realise that Stan Cullis had given special orders to his team if engaging the Arsenal goalkeeper. City attacked from the opening whistle and a race for a loose ball gave me my first touch. As I grasped the ball cleanly, Birmingham's Fred Pickering hit me in a manner which these days would probably earn a straight red card. I actually used to enjoy being whacked early in a game. It ensured I was wide awake and it sharpened the reflexes. As bedlam broke out, Fred was well aware that he and Stan Cullis were testing my nerve.

Things went well for me but we lost and were knocked out of the FA Cup. Birmingham's opening goal is still remembered by their long-time fans, a spectacular and acrobatic volley from Barry Bridges that went in off the bar. Three minutes later Bobby Gould, recently signed from Coventry and my best pal at Arsenal, equalised from an acute angle. A third goal in a six-minute spell won the game for the home side; Geoff Vowden's run over half the length of the field set up Bridges' second. On the journey home, I was disappointed at the defeat, quietly elated by my performance.

Fans don't always see it the players' way. Out of the Cup, nowhere in the League, many Arsenal supporters wanted blood. Every second letter to newspapers began, 'Arsenal's first need is for a goalkeeper.'

There were thirteen league games remaining that season and every one was vital if I was to survive both the growing discontent of the fans and the manager's assessment. When Bertie Mee told me this was going to be my big chance, he implied that I would be given a decent run in goal. 'You've got six or eight,' he said. I thought months, he meant games.

If results had been the yardstick for the management, you would most likely never have heard of Bob Wilson again. Four days after being knocked out of the Cup, we lost at home to Wolves 2–0. It was one of five defeats in nine games. Only wins at Fulham and against Leicester City, plus a draw at Upton Park against West Ham, eased the tension and growing discontent that permeated Highbury. The one good aspect for goalkeepers playing in a side lacking confidence is that they have plenty of chance to show their ability. I made mistakes but far more saves, and felt that the team were comfortable with me. It was still touch and go but I'd survived Bertie's eight-game examination. Perhaps being selected for a ninth provided the psychological fillip I needed because we won the last five games of the season to finish in ninth place, some fourteen points behind champions Manchester City.

I had now completed five seasons as an Arsenal player and although the first of those was as an amateur schoolteacher, the total of twenty-four first-team appearances in major competitions was still a meagre return. One thing is for sure, there was absolutely no indication that the next six seasons would turn my life upside down and elevate my status from Arsenal 'leg end' to Arsenal 'legend'.

One week after the 1967–68 season ended, the Arsenal team were 6,000 miles away in Japan. These were the times when clubs undertook end of season and pre-season tours, occasionally as a goodwill gesture, usually for financial purposes. The duration of these trips varied between ten days and three weeks. Our Far East tour began in Tokyo at the Olympic Stadium. It was where my great Loughborough pal John Cooper won two silver medals, one in the 400 metres hurdles, the other alongside Robbie Brightwell in the 400 metres relay. Rob's fiancée Ann Packer became Britain's Olympic golden girl in Japan with victory in the women's 800 metres. I had watched from afar as their dedication to success reaped its reward. The Olympic Stadium in Tokyo was symbolic for me. This is where my success would begin in earnest, or so I thought. As a tribute to my three friends I ran one lap of the track and up the steps to where the Olympic flame had burned bright four years earlier.

The three games we played in Japan, two in the Olympic Stadium, one in Fukuoka, pitched us against Japan's national team. We won fairly comfortably but Japan surprised everyone at the Olympics in Mexico when they won the bronze medal. During our third encounter, in front of a record 70,000 crowd back in Tokyo, my suspect style of goalkeeping resulted in another serious collision and a break to the top left side of my collarbone. Reassurances from Bertie Mee and our physio

George Wright that I would be fit for the start of the next season helped ease the pain. I didn't play any further part in the tour, which took us via Hong Kong and Bangkok to Kuala Lumpur, but the sultry warmth seemed to help the healing process. After that, holidaying with the family relaxed me and put me in confident mood for what lay ahead.

I reported back for pre-season training, for the first time, as Arsenal's senior keeper. I realised the position was not yet secure, by any means, but I was raring to go, and my natural athleticism contributed to my growing belief as we concentrated, as always during the first few days of training, on building up running and stamina levels. Then it was time to return to goalkeeping practice.

Everything looked pretty sharp until I dived for the first time since Tokyo on my damaged left shoulder. As I hit the turf, the pain hit me – a lot of pain. So once more I was at the crossroads, facing absence through injury. Give the management half a chance to buy a new keeper and they most certainly would. When our specialist doctors informed me that the problem was localised and just needed more time to heal, I told them I didn't have time. We decided together that a cortisone injection prior to playing might get me through games. They didn't discuss it with the management because they understood my anxiety to start the season.

For the first three months of the 1968–69 season I had regular cortisone shots in my left shoulder before playing. Mobilizing my arm as best I could, I hoped that the adrenaline rush would overcome any pain. Talk of signing a new keeper continued but happily none was forthcoming.

We kicked off the new season at White Hart Lane and came away with a first victory over the old enemy for eleven seasons. Such was the excitement generated in games against Spurs that there was never a moment's concern with the damaged shoulder. The sight of my modern-day hero Pat Jennings between the posts at the other end inspired me, and a vital save from Jimmy Pearce will always remain in my memory bank.

In all ways it was a brilliant start but the Arsenal fans were not satisfied, forcing chairman Denis Hill-Wood to issue a statement prior to our first home game, against Leicester City. It said: 'We have made approaches for four top-class players and offered in each case a fee that would have been a British record. In each case, the club concerned said they did not want the money and would not part with the player.'

One of those players about whom Bertie Mee had made enquiries was Peter Shilton, whose displays of confident goal-keeping had prompted City to sell off the great Gordon Banks to Stoke. Leicester were our opponents for the first home game and 'Shilts' was in opposition. An emphatic 3–0 win was followed by a couple of draws and five straight wins, one of them against reigning champions Manchester City, which took us to the top of the First Division table.

We were unable to sustain the brilliant start, losing for the first time at Elland Road against Leeds United. Amazingly, though, the opening nine games were enough to silence all talk about Arsenal signing a new goalkeeper. It emphasises how goalkeepers, like goalscorers, play in a special position. The two roles are so dramatic and influence games to such a degree that you can be an unknown one moment and within weeks, if performing heroics, a star and public property.

I was not used to being in demand from newspapers, maga-zines and especially autograph hunters, but I relished the atten-tion. Autographs can mean so much, not just to youngsters, and I had promised myself that should the day arrive when my signature was wanted, it would always be a request granted.

Agents were a rarity in the late sixties but I received a couple of approaches based on my being a 'marketable commodity'. Ten games was not enough to warrant such attention. The first priority was to get a full season's appearances under my belt.

Second, Arsenal needed to win a trophy. Only then would I consider outside interests.

Bob McNab, Peter Storey and myself managed to play in all forty-two league games that season, as we finished fourth behind the champions Leeds. They conceded twenty-six goals; we let in just one more. In the FA Cup we again went out in the fifth round, losing 1–0 at the Hawthorns to the holders West Bromwich Albion.

In the League Cup, we made it all the way to Wembley, defeating Sunderland, Scunthorpe, Liverpool and Blackpool *en route*. In the two-leg semi-final we met Spurs. At Highbury, a giant kick out of my hands and into the night sky took the ball with one mighty bounce to John Radford who beat Pat Jennings.

The return at White Hart Lane produced the headlines 'London Cup Violence' and 'Vendettas'. For those watching, it was like sitting on the edge of a volcano. For those playing, it was unabashed hatred. Never before or since have I experienced the elbowing, disgraceful tackling and foul language that erupted out of the long-standing rivalry that was a north London derby. The stakes were too great – a Wembley place, local prestige and a passport to Europe. Twenty-two skilful footballers kicked lumps out of each other. In the modern game, only the two goalkeepers would have managed to avoid red cards; and yet today, those same players bump into each other occasionally, hold great respect for one another and laugh at how referee John Gow allowed the game to continue rather than abandoning play.

Experienced players, many of them internationals, lost their senses in the heat of the battle, Frank McLintock, Mike England, John Radford, Cyril Knowles and Terry Venables included. Only the two managers, Bertie Mee and the great Bill Nicholson, maintained any dignity with open condemnation of what had occurred. Bill is one of nature's gentlest creatures and he tried to defuse reaction to a style of play that was totally foreign to his and Spurs' philosophy. 'Our injuries are only in the heart,' he said. 'The game was too tense, too physical. It was like a series of explosions.' From Arsenal's point of view, we recovered from a Jimmy Greaves goal, which put the tie on level terms, and John Radford's late goal sent us to the twin towers.

First for me, though, was an X-ray following a wild tackle from Alan Gilzean in the last seconds, which was out of character. I never wore shin pads to protect my legs because I felt uncomfortable with them, and they made my legs feel too bulky. Alan caught me long after I'd gathered a shot and there was genuine fear that my leg was broken. Initial examination of the swelling took place in the Spurs medical room with Bill Nicholson the most concerned, but there was anything but sympathy from the Spurs lads as I made my way on crutches through their dressing room. A hospital visit later revealed nothing worse than severe bruising and with every day treatment for four days I was patched up and fit enough to appear against Everton the following Saturday.

It wasn't the only appearance I made that weekend. For the first time I was asked to be the guest on ITV's Sunday programme 'The Big Match', hosted by Brian Moore and Jimmy Hill. When the BBC's 'Sportsnight' programme then invited me to talk about the forthcoming international between England and Bulgaria, my profile was very much on the increase

Victory in that semi-final, although coming at price, was as sweet as it gets. With all the hard work done, Arsenal became certainties to win the League Cup final on 15 March against Swindon Town, leaders of the Third Division. However, Swindon were brilliant on the day, full of character and totally dismissive of their opponent's history and the reputations of the Arsenal players. Those features alone might well have been enough but they enjoyed a degree of luck as well.

During the ten days leading up to the final, a flu epidemic ravaged eight of the Arsenal team. We had played on 1 March and, with illness causing the cancellation of our next game, not again until the Wembley game fourteen days later. There was no question of asking for a postponement because of health problems but an appeal was made about the disgraceful state of the famous Wembley turf. Used for the International Horse of the Year Show, it had failed to recover. Three days before the League Cup final, England entertained France and gallons of water had to be pumped from the pitch. Torrential rain on Thursday and Friday produced desperate measures to allow the final to go ahead.

When we arrived, huge industrial blowers were having no effect. Psychologically, we feared the pitch would be a great leveller and we let it affect us. In the tunnel before the presentation of the teams to Princess Margaret, the Arsenal players were quiet and anxious. Alongside us the Swindon boys were laughing, shouting and making sure they were enjoying the day, whatever happened. Even the formalities of entering the arena and meeting royalty were subdued. My family were there in force because this was surely the fulfilment of a dream for me. Megs' anxiety didn't start and end with her nervous husband. She was eight months pregnant with Robert, our youngest child.

From the outset, Arsenal took the game to Swindon, as expected. Swindon defended with collective doggedness and their inspired goalkeeper, Peter Downsbrough, had one of the games of his life. After thirty-four minutes, his opposite number in the Arsenal goal conspired with Ian Ure to produce a terrible mix-up. The big Scot had the ball at his feet and decided to keep it there rather than answer my call for him to play it. As Swindon sensed a mistake in the making, Ian and I got too close to each other and, when the ball was played, it stuck in the mud and allowed Roger Smart to nip in and score.

Swindon kept the lead until four minutes from the end. Downsbrough's one mistake of the day was to leave his area and kick the ball to the oncoming Bobby Gould. My room-mate took advantage, levelled the scores and took a few minutes to be caught by his grateful, but exhausted, colleagues. Almost immediately, referee Bill Handley blew the final whistle. Don Howe approached him suggesting the match had to be abandoned because the pitch was now totally unplayable. In truth, he recognised that his flu-affected players were out on their feet. Frank McLintock had cramp in both legs, Peter Simpson had already been replaced and Bob McNab was in a state of distress. The pitch was a bog, but as the saying goes, 'it's the same for both sides'. Today the game would not have taken place.

The first half of extra time was almost up when I enjoyed making a special save. Perhaps, after all, it was going to be our day. From the corner that ensued, Don Rogers poked the ball through the mud and Bob McNab just failed to prevent it crossing the line. Swindon were rampant and, in the second fifteen minutes, ran us ragged. As the realisation of defeat entered my mind, Don Rogers broke free and it was one versus one. 'Oh well,' I thought, 'this situation is my party piece. There's no way you'll score.' I waited for him to lose control of the ball for a fraction of a second. Most players did. Don didn't. Instead, he dropped his shoulder and I bought the dummy. Skipping round me with a grace that made a mockery of the conditions, he made the final score Arsenal 1 Swindon Town 3. One of the game's greatest upsets was complete and I was part of it.

'The Shame of Arsenal' was the headline in the *Daily Express* piece written by the infamous Desmond Hackett. His pre-match promise to eat his bowler hat if Swindon won left him humiliated and resentful towards all of us in the famous red shirt. I believe that the success that followed in the next few years was born out of the stubborn belief instilled in the beaten Arsenal team that they would make their many critics eat not only their hats, but their words.

Reflecting now on the match programme from that memorable day and the newspaper cuttings that accompanied it, I still feel a sickness in the pit of my stomach that is almost as painful as it was more than three decades ago. Among the memories of the post-match wake, I recall skipper Frank McLintock, who had just become a four-time loser in a Wembley final, toss his runners-up trophy into the thick mud with the words, 'Another bloody tankard.'

At the subdued banquet at Claridges, I approached my great predecessor in the Arsenal goal, Jack Kelsey, and told him how wretched I felt. The Welshman's reply was straight and to the point.

'I played for Arsenal ten times as long as you have,' he said, 'and I'd have given anything to go to Wembley with an Arsenal team. You've done it in your first full season. Now have a drink.'

I did just that, and another and another, drowning my sorrows until late in the night. Then I fell down the stairs at the Playboy Club, was helped back to our London hotel and spent the night being sick. The 1968–69 season had promised so much only to betray me.

As a new boy, although a somewhat aged one, I was still thrilled with my progress. Conceding just twenty-seven goals had helped turn me from being a possible answer to Arsenal's goalkeeping problems to being a respected First Division player.

Nine games into the 1969–70 season I collected another injury. Fifteen minutes from the end of a 1–0 victory at Turf Moor, home of Burnley, I risked all with a headlong dive at the feet of Steve Kindon. As always, when serious injury occurred, I knew how bad it was. My right arm was numb, a lump two inches above the wrist clearly indicated a broken bone. A mixture of shock and stupidity got me through the final minutes as we protected our lead.

The bus journey to Manchester and train to London were not pleasant. Immediately, I was taken to a private clinic and arrived home at midnight with my arm in plaster and the break confirmed. Press interest and attention from everyone lasts for a few days only. There follows the long lonely road back to fitness. I filled it in the gym and, on this occasion, by producing and presenting a documentary on the 'Art of Goalkeeping' for the BBC. Their faith in me was flattering and ignited a small flame of interest in the possibility of regular work in the world of television some day. As I dived once again into unwelcome obscurity, Bertie Mee bought goalkeeper Geoff Barnett from Everton. He had no choice. There was no regular reserve to me that season and eighteen-year-old England youth keeper Malcolm Webster lacked experience, especially for our European campaign, which had just got under way ten days before I broke my arm.

Geoff was hugely likeable and, considering my relatively recent occupation of the senior goalkeeping position, presented a real threat. Serious injury can play tricks with the mind. Time seems to stand still, confidence disappears and worries about recovery, or lack of it, make life difficult. During my time on the treatment table, Geoff made thirteen appearances and in one played a starring role.

European competition was a totally new experience for all of us but the Fairs Cup, which later became the Uefa Cup, always included teams on the up, those that had shown promise and just missed out on their national championship. Having negotiated Glentoran in the first round, Arsenal drew Sporting Lisbon in round two. Playing away in Europe, the aim was to win if possible but, if not, to score an away goal, which would provide an advantage for the return on home soil. A goalless draw would be satisfactory but dangerous because 1–1 in the return game would put the visitors through.

Arsenal did indeed earn a goalless draw in Portugal thanks

to a great penalty save by Geoff Barnett. Immediately, the star of the night was catapulted into national press headlines and that dreaded scourge of journalism called speculation. The headline 'Will Bob Wilson get his place back now?' added to my frustration at the fickleness of the press corps, but a story is a story regardless of its effect on another party.

My documentary for the BBC attracted attention and kept my mind away from too many nagging doubts. Restoring my fitness brought me into contact with boxing legend and national treasure Henry Cooper, arguably Britain's best loved sportsman. In 1969 Henry was at the peak of his powers, with a world title fight against Cassius Clay very much in the offing. After an operation for a damaged cartilage, it was decided he should re-build his fitness at the football club he loved, which was Arsenal. We became instant friends and while Henry loved his involvement with the Arsenal players and marble halls, I became hooked on his stories of the boxing fraternity and the shadowy world that surrounded it. I learned how he disguised his famous left upper cut and, as his knee recovered, was on the receiving end of many a powerful right-foot drive. Even now, the first Christmas card to arrive in the Wilson household is invariably the one signed by Henry and his beautiful wife Albina. Fit again, Henry beat American Jimmy Ellis and produced two unforgettable fights against Cassius Clay, one at Wembley arena, one at his beloved Highbury. No one will ever forget the hook that dumped Clay on his pants at Wembley or the courage that Henry displayed as a serious cut ended his challenge to be heavyweight champion of the world.

I learned a lesson or two from Henry: 1, look out for number one, 2 have belief in your own ability, 3 practise the art of humility. When I returned from injury, I was ready to take on the world myself.

Thankfully, my arm healed simply and quickly over the next three months. I returned in mid December against the player who had inflicted the damage in the first place, Steve Kindon. Even more ironic was the fact that my first save found me diving at his feet. This time the feeling was not of pain but of satisfaction that the ball was safely in my arms. I was back and four other similar saves in our 3–2 win over Burnley restored my confidence.

Our league form was strangely erratic, and a third-round defeat in the FA Cup after a replay at Blackpool suggested that the progress made in the previous season had created false hope. Our route to glory lay in Europe and as Sporting Lisbon, Rouen and Dinamo Bacau were beaten, we suddenly found ourselves in a semi-final against one of the most promising teams on the continent. The young players of Ajax of Amsterdam had been losing European Cup finalists the previous season and included in their ranks twenty-three-year-old Johan Cruyff and Ruud Krol, who was just twenty-one.

We were approaching a pivotal time in the fortunes of Arsenal FC. The last time the club won a trophy was in 1953, and here we were in 1970. Seventeen barren years was much too long for a club that professed to be as famous and innovative as Arsenal.

Players had openly expressed their loathing of the bust of Herbert Chapman that faced them every time they made their way to the Highbury dressing rooms. Even Billy Wright, when he was manager, indicated a wish that it be removed to a less imposing position – but not Bertie Mee. Tactical genius he wasn't, but brilliant man-manager and organiser he was. He used Arsenal's history to inspire and, once established in his managerial role, he was never scared to make decisions.

For example, Bobby Gould was put up for sale in midseason, a decision which upset me simply because we got on so well together. Peter Marinello's signing from Hibernian created massive interest because he was dubbed the 'new George Best'. Frank McLintock was asked to change his role as cavalier wing-half to central defender alongside Peter Simpson. Of all the decisions made by Bertie, it was Frank's switch to the middle of defence that was the most inspired. At first, Frank's impetuous nature caused him to roam out of position, but with the skilful coaching of Don Howe and the defensive brilliance of Bob McNab, Frank quickly became more disciplined and even better placed to skipper the side.

More than 40,000 packed Highbury on 8 April 1970, attracted by Johan Cruyff's appearance as much as hope of success for their own team. Only occasionally do all the players in one side play to their maximum potential; for Arsenal, this was one of those nights. Ajax extended but never overran us while we made the most of every scoring opportunity and every tackle. Young Charlie George had his North Bank fan club ecstatic with a twenty-five yard drive past Ajax keeper Gerrit Bals. The thousands of visiting klaxon horns and sirens were silenced when Jon Sammels seized on a rebound off Bals to make it 2–0. Four minutes later, John Radford was tripped in the box and the precociously talented Charlie George elected to take his first-ever penalty for Arsenal, which Bals touched but couldn't keep out. The 3–0 scoreline was a surprise. Despite a flurry of action in our goalmouth during the second half, it was a great advantage to take to Holland.

The tulips of Amsterdam never had a chance to blossom seven days later. Our defence, marshalled expertly by Frank McLintock, restricted Ajax to a Muhren goal. The celebrations that followed the final whistle went on throughout the night. The headline 'Arsenal Poised for First Major Honour since 1953' greeted our return to England.

The final was a two-leg affair against Anderlecht, the best club in Belgium. The Parc Astrid Stadium in Brussels staged part one and Highbury was to feature six days later for the conclusion of the 1970 European Fairs Cup.

The biggest obstacle to glory was the desperation born of two successive years of failure in the League Cup final and the huge expectations always placed upon anyone wearing the famous cannon on their shirt. We needed to get rid of our 'loser' image. Few of us, I suspect, expected the tide to turn on the shores of Europe, but expecting the unexpected is something every footballer learns to do in his career, and it often happens in the most dramatic manner.

The first leg was played on Wednesday, 22 April. I was surprised that the Anderlecht ground was comparatively small for a leading European club, and the gates were closed on a capacity crowd of 37,000. The Belgians were a typically excitable foreign crowd, letting off fireworks and, with screeching whistles, creating a genuinely unfriendly atmosphere. Our travelling supporters responded with north London witticisms and chants.

Anderlecht, with eight international players, presented a terrific attacking force led by Jan Mulder, a brilliant Dutchman. Injury was later to rob him of a permanent pairing alongside Johan Cruyff in the Holland side, but he was almost as good a player as the legendary Ajax striker. Behind Mulder was Belgium's own golden boy, Paul Van Himst, who would later manage the club to European success.

Just as we seemed to be weathering the expected early flurry, Anderlecht struck with speed. Before we knew it, Mulder had scored twice and Devrindt once. At 3–0, a third defeat in a major final in as many seasons loomed large. We were lucky not to have conceded more by the time Charlie George was taken off and replaced by eighteen-year-old Ray Kennedy. With barely five minutes remaining, George Armstrong produced one of his special crosses and Kennedy squeezed his header past Trappeniers.

A 3–1 deficit was a very different proposition from 3–0. The away goal meant that a 2–0 victory at Highbury would be enough. It was a scrap of hope, better than nothing. Our dressing room post-match was as silent as a morgue at first but it became a place of passion and expectation before we left. That was entirely due to Frank's impulsive nature. Initially, he was the worst affected Arsenal player in the aftermath of defeat. Morose and muttering every swear word in his vocabulary, he stripped off his kit and trudged wearily and despondently into the showers. Somewhere under the warmth of the water that cascaded on to his body he became a man transfixed. His brain, dulled at the moment of defeat, suddenly became sharp and alive. The captain who emerged bore no resemblance to the one who had departed the dressing room, except that the swear words doubled in intensity and volume. Mel Gibson's performance in 'Braveheart' never bettered a McLintock rant.

'We'll fucking murder the bastards at Highbury. They're a load of shit. Van Himst's a fucking carthorse. Mulder will bottle it, it'll be a piece of piss,' was the gist of it. Frank's enthusiasm was infectious and that Anderlecht away dressing room became full of steam, belief and plenty of bullshit. If we could have played the return immediately, Anderlecht would never have stood a chance.

Few outside our close seventeen-man squad believed we could overturn the deficit. 'Arsenal Battered', 'Arsenal in Fierce Grip of Belgians' were the headlines that greeted us the day after the first leg, and *The Times* report summed up the general feeling among critics and public alike about our chances:

> Home advantage at Highbury next Tuesday will be small comfort to Arsenal after a demoralising defeat in the Parc Astrid tonight. The Belgian team have venom in their attack and strength in every department.

On the surface the omens weren't promising, but underneath there was a resolve in a group of young men to live up to the glories of yesteryear that had been continually rammed down their throats from the time they became Arsenal players.

Patrick Marnham of the *Daily Telegraph* was granted, by Bertie Mee, unusual access to our preparations on the day of the second leg. He wrote:

The expected takings from the two legs of the final are £100,000. The Arsenal team is insured for one and a half million pounds. Since tonight is a European game, the referee and linesmen will be from East Germany and will have to be paid in cash immediately after the match. This will cost £342 and despite urgent appeals from the Germans, it will not be given in Swiss francs. The manager of Arsenal, Bertie Mee, has been in since early morning. Part of the special problem he faces working at a club like Arsenal is that it is supposedly a name from the past, dominated by a family board and suffocated by its achievements in the thirties, of which the ornate stadium is a fearsome symbol.

Bertie Mee sees his main task as man-management, making the right noises to his board and the press, delegating daily coaching to Don Howe and all the time building a team that can win. He must have an extensive knowledge of finance and contracts. All his professional players start at a basic rate of £1,000 a year at 18 and can work up to a top rate of £10,000 by the time they are 25. When he retires, a top player with a club like Arsenal may receive a pension of £50 a week for life. At 3.00 p.m. Bertie Mee drives out in his Rover V8 to the South Herts Golf Club in Totteridge to meet Don Howe, physio George Wright and the players for the pre-match meal. It consists of cereal, crème caramel, poached eggs and tea. This is a high carbohydrate, high glucose diet. It is quickly digested, unlike the old system of high protein steaks, which often failed to have any effect until the game was over.

As a general principle, George Wright believes in making training rather uncomfortable. A player who is lingering over an injury may find that visits to the doctor can only be arranged at the most inconvenient times. The pre-match meal is an exception. Personal fads about food are tolerated, almost encouraged. George cossets those who are feeling the least bit precious with quantities of indistinguishable pills from large brown jars. For an hour or so they can digest these, playing snooker or putting on the green. At 5.30 p.m. there is the final briefing. Mee starts by announcing the team. Those who are not playing will have been told previously already. They sit with blank faces, quite failing to hide their disappointment.

During his talk, Mee sticks to general points. 'You know what this game means to you, your careers and this club.' Then Howe talks over the game as he wants them to play it. 'First 15 I want you forward, either you or the ball. Their best two forwards can be bullied. Well bully them. Hit them hard and do it quick. And when you've done it pick 'em up. Let the crowd see it was an accident. I don't want any messing with the offside trap. I want cover at the back. Don't let Mulder start running at you. He can take four on and go straight past the lot of you. I've got a lot of respect for him.'

Howe talks quickly, using gestures, pacing out attacks, living the moves he is describing. The team watch him intently. It is part of the weekly confidence trick that coach and players work on each other. They are going to win because they are the better team. It does not matter who they are playing, if it is a home game they are the better team. That is why they are going to win. Simple. Immediately after the talk there is a rush for the big Fords and Vauxhalls in the car park.

Outside the stadium the streets are filling up. The police recognise the players' cars and wave them through. It is going to be the game when the club defeats seventeen years of failure; for once, just for once, the papers are united in encouragement. All over North London the paper vans are decked out with red and white balloons. 'COME ON GUNNERS – SHOOT TO KILL' say the billboards. As they arrive, the players can sense the tension among their supporters. It is a still evening and Constable Alex Morgan, under direction of Major W. Williams, MBE, ARCM of the Metropolitan Police Band, can be heard at the bus stop a quarter of a mile away. He has just finished 'Mary's Boy Child'. Soon he'll have a crack at 'I'll Walk With God'.

For many of the boys and young men who have lived around Highbury during the last 50 years, the stadium has been the focus of their lives. It is the most important and the most impressive building for miles, a palace of delights, where Everyman can become rich and famous and brave. It is their battleground. When they go to football, they go to war. The chants have already begun. At the moment, an hour before kick-off, they are happy enough, but there is a cruel strain in them.

By 6.30 p.m. the players have changed into their training gear and are kicking around the indoor college training facility, going over dead ball situations. Don Howe makes various suggestions and then asks Frank McLintock for his opinion. McLintock and George Graham will argue about the details for several minutes. Then back through the crowds of autograph hunters. There is the usual pack of 14 year old girls for Peter Marinello and the older girls waiting in the corridor with gift-wrapped packets of after-shave for whoever will take them. For the next 45 minutes until the bell goes in the dressing room, the players will be changing.

On a big night like this, there are almost as many ticket spivs outside as buyers. Discreetly placed under a canopy, one can make out the considerable figure of 'Uncle' Stan Flashman, the king of the touts. Like as not the players would have had a call from him. 'Hello boys, it's Uncle Stan. Best of luck tonight. Got any spare tickets?'

In the dressing room you can hear very little of the din outside. Howe is still talking to anyone who will listen. There is the stink of camphor oil being meticulously rubbed in. Each player steps gingerly, preparing their legs like blades, to be stretched and oiled and bound. Once they have their boots on nobody stands still, the noise is deafening. With 15 minutes to go Charlie George is being sick, Bob Wilson is standing in the showers hurling a ball at the wall, which is a foot away, and

Peter Simpson has put on his cigarette and is saying, 'Relax, just treat it like a Cup final.'

The dressing-room table is covered with telegrams – from Wally Barnes, who was carried off during the club's last FA Cup final in 1952, a 2–0 defeat by Newcastle; from a 'nutty fan'; from Barclays Bank; from former colleague Jimmy Robertson at Ipswich.

Ken Aston the Fairs Cup Committee representative comes in from the Anderlecht dressing room to say that their studs are 2 inches long. 'Fucking 'ell,' says Radford, 'go over the top with those and they'll cut the leg in half.' His gloom invariably deepens before a match. He goes out to the pitch like a man facing the firing squad. Charlie George, famous for being the only man who could find a short cut across the cross-country course, is taping on his shin guards. 'Anybody puts a kick through that, I'll buy him a drink after.' The noise of running, jumping studs on the marble floor has reached crescendo. The brandy flask is going round faster and faster. Nothing unusual in that. Apparently, at Manchester City in the old days, they used to get through a bottle before every game.

Everyone is dressed now, except Frank McLintock who has neither his shorts nor his boots on and is still fussing about his laces. George Wright is checking his bag for pain-relieving spray, lint dressing, brandy, smelling salts, Deep Heat rub, eye wash, adrenaline chloride, Vaseline, an inflatable polythene splint, anti-tetanus shots, a field dressing, a camel hair eye brush and steel pin to adjust ball pressure. Plus the traditional sponge. Everything to keep an injured man on the field until the game ends. The bell goes. Bob McNab runs a last comb through his hair, Peter Storey applies the last clot of Vaseline to his eyebrows and the lads are lining up ready to run out.

The team was: Wilson, Storey, McNab, Kelly, McLintock, Simpson, Armstrong, Sammels, Radford, George, Graham.

Just ninety minutes separated these eleven men from a piece of footballing immortality. The alternative to victory was the obscurity that envelops whoever finishes second. We started as nervous as kittens despite a crowd support that, in all my time at Highbury, I had never heard before. The excitement and the tension affected everyone. Jack Kelsey had to leave his seat and sat in the marble halls throughout the game as the oohs and ahs increased. After twenty-five minutes they were replaced by a roar as Eddie Kelly's shot snapped into the roof of the net. When the goal went in, all the rhythm came racing back into our team play. George Armstrong was inspired; it was his greatest game. He beat man after man, time after time, and his wing play made a mockery of his non-selection for Alf Ramsey's World Cup squad, who were gathering to defend England's title in Mexico.

We needed another goal at least to win the Cup as half-time arrived. As usual, Bertie Mee had the first word and, to my amazement, began with me. 'Concentrate, Bob, one or two early moments.' Final or not, I went mad. 'Concentrate, fucking concentrate! What do you think I'm fucking doing!' The manager pressed on in a louder voice and then Don took over. Animated, in his shirt sleeves and braces, he was positivity personified. 'One will be enough, two will do nicely. The Cup will be yours.' Frank McLintock and Jon Sammels had long bloody gashes on their legs, which were caked in mud.

The bell went again. Anderlecht started the better in the second half and when Nordahl's shot rebounded off the outside of the post, I was glad to divert Mulder's follow-up for a corner. It was a critical save. With nineteen minutes to go, Bob McNab ventured forward, found some space and crossed to the head of John Radford. The face of the Yorkshireman, so often sombre, had never borne such a smile as his header beat Trappeniers. Thanks to Ray Kennedy's away goal, Arsenal now led, and two minutes later, when Jon Sammels raced on to Charlie George's pass to make it 3–0, a great club, its players and followers breathed a collective sigh of relief and pleasure.

As the final whistle sounded, delirious supporters surged on to the Highbury turf. The police and stewards did their best to allow a presentation area to be set up in front of the East Stand. The Anderlecht players were wonderfully sporting, their faces etched with exactly the same misery that we had experienced one year before against Swindon. The excitable antics of any winning team in a major final borders on the ridiculous – embarrassing to review later, but gloriously memorable at the moment of triumph. Sir Stanley Rous, then FIFA's President, presented the Fairs Cup to Frank McLintock, the third Scottish captain in succession to lift the trophy following Billy Bremner of Leeds and Bobby Moncur of Newcastle.

What followed was delirium. In Highbury's long history no game had thrilled the fans quite as much as that night in April 1970. The fans refused to leave the pitch and players quickly became engulfed. Frank was carried shoulder high until it became clear that, for safety reasons, we should retreat to the dressing room. Most did. I didn't. It had been too long a road to turn off now before reaching the end. Having swapped my jersey with Jean Trappeniers, I ran, walked, bounced my way round the whole of the Highbury pitch. All the way slaps of congratulations turned my naked upper body to a deeper red than the Arsenal shirts. Elderly supporters brought up on the 1930s sides and Tom Whittaker's team in the early fifties were in tears. So was Frank McLintock, his personal jinx of losing in finals broken at the fifth time of asking.

The 'Shame of London' at Wembley thirteen months earlier had become 'The Pride of London'. Bertie Mee had made history for the club by putting together a team who gave Arsenal Football Club their first-ever European trophy. Typically, he was thinking ahead in his press conference. 'We badly wanted to win the Fairs Cup but the players realise this is only an interim step', he said. 'The First Division is the toughest competition in the world and no club, whatever they achieve outside it, can call themselves great until it has been won.'

The twelve ties that led to the Fairs Cup triumph brought an extra £125,000 to Arsenal, enough to strengthen the squad and make a push for even greater success. Between them, Bertie Mee and Don Howe resisted the temptation to spend. Instead, they decided that the seventeen first-team squad players already in place knew how to win and, more importantly, had a respect, belief and love for each other that no money could buy. What they had achieved together was unforgettable. What lay ahead was unbelievable.

9
A perfect jigsaw – winning the double

'Teamwork divides the task and doubles the success.'

Anon

In the summer of 1970, following Arsenal's European triumph, the ninth World Cup finals took place. Mexico was the host country, England the defending champions, Brazil the ultimate winners. They lifted the Jules Rimet trophy for the third time and were allowed to keep it. The style in which the South Americans won it was as near to perfection as it's possible to get. If the opposition scored three, Brazil would knock in four. Their winning team is etched in my memory:

Felix, Carlos Alberto (Capt), Brito, Piazza, Everaldo, Clodoaldo, Gerson, Jairzinho, Tostao, Pele, Rivelino.

Not all great players in the true sense of greatness, they formed a perfect jigsaw, combining rough edges with smooth key pieces and supporting parts.

I watched Brazil's triumphs in a television studio, as a new member of the BBC sports team covering the tournament. Only one team came close to matching the samba boys and that was England, arguably a better team than the one that had lifted the trophy on home soil four years earlier.

Being made to talk about different teams and piecing together videotaped items on their respective merits and styles, challenged me in an analytical way. What makes a great team has always intrigued me. The word 'great' in a sporting context means 'excellent', 'fantastic', 'of exceptional talents or achievements'. On the world stage, Brazil of 1970 incorporated not just one, but all those interpretations. They remain my all-time favourite international team.

The timing of Brazil's triumph coincided with the most memorable season of my own footballing career. In 1970–71 I was part of the side that emulated an achievement that, up until then, had been accomplished on three occasions only, two of them in the previous century, the third in 1961. All four teams were accepted as 'great' but television coverage meant that the public could see the last two for themselves and make up their own minds. Arguments persist to this day about the prowess of Arsenal's double-winning side of 1970–71. Was it truly great? Does a team have to play with beauty to mark its greatness? To the seventeen players and supporting staff who made a bit of history more than three decades ago, the debate matters not one iota. All that matters is that we did it together.

The first club to accomplish the Double were 'Proud' Preston North End, 'The Invincibles'. In 1889, they won the twelve-strong Football League competition without losing one game, and the FA Cup without conceding one goal. Eight years later, Aston Villa emulated Preston's achievements in a sixteen-team League.

Sixty-four years elapsed before Bill Nicholson's Spurs became the first team in the twentieth century to achieve greatness. There was never any argument that the team that Danny Blanchflower led to glory was anything but great. Based as I was at Loughborough in 1961, I admired them from afar, watched them when possible. I still rate that side among the most stylish of British club teams. They had wrapped up the league title by mid-April, beat Leicester with some comfort to win the FA Cup final and were head and shoulders above all rivals.

Ten years later, our double at Arsenal went to the last league game of the season, away to Tottenham of all people, and into extra time in the FA Cup final. No club had ever been asked to win the league championship on a Monday night and the FA Cup the next Saturday. No previous winner played fifty-four competitive games in the season they made history, fifty-one of them in search of the coveted double.

The fact that only four clubs completed the feat over an eighty-two-year period signified the difficulty of the task. Another fifteen years went by before Liverpool made it five doubles by five different clubs. Between that achievement in 1986 and 2002, just sixteen years, winning the double has become much more likely, but not easier. Manchester United have won it three times – in 1994, 1996 and 1999 – and Arsenal twice, in 1998 and 2002. Football has changed dramatically. The rich have got richer. Competing with Arsenal, Manchester United and Liverpool no longer takes place on a level playing field. Money and how much you have or can generate has led to a situation where the battle for the league title is now between those three giants and two or three others whose housekeeping is excellent or who are prepared to gamble with finances.

What happens off the field, and to a lesser degree on it, bears merely a passing resemblance to what I experienced with my sixteen team-mates in 1971. Having been Arsenal's goalkeeping coach since 1976 enables me to make comparisons. I have been part of all three of the club's historic campaigns, a wonderful privilege, and I consider all three teams deserve the accolade 'great'. But the differences between the boys of '71 and the Gunners of 2002 are stark in almost every respect. Witnessing the transition at first hand has been fascinating.

Bertie Mee's squad was seventeen strong and totally British, nine Englishmen, five Scots, two Irish and a Welshman. Eleven were already, or later became, full international players. Arsene Wenger's squad numbered twenty-five and eleven were British. Of the others, six were French and two Dutch, and there was a Brazilian, Nigerian, Swede, Ukranian and a Latvian and one from Cameroon. All twenty-five were current full internationals.

Ten of our seventeen had been apprentices at Arsenal. In 2002, five had come through the youth-team ranks.

The biggest difference between the two managers, Bertie Mee and Arsene Wenger, was that the Frenchman was manager and coach, whereas Bertie left all tactical training matters to Don Howe. Where Wenger and Mee have earned their greatness in management, Don remains coach supreme. In 2002, as Arsene's men brought two trophies back to the training ground, Don could be found, or better still heard, on the furthest field from the main building, encouraging, teaching and rollicking Arsenal's latest recruits to the Academy. A triple heart by-pass operation has neither slowed him down or lessened his enthusiasm. His CV is amazing, having been coach to Arsenal, Leeds, Galatasaray in Turkey and, of course, England with Bobby Robson, whose 1990 team came within a penalty shoot-out with Germany of making the World Cup final.

When little Wimbledon created the biggest upset in FA Cup final history by beating Liverpool in 1988, their manager was my good friend Bobby Gould, their coach Don Howe. As a person, he loves to have a laugh and tell a joke, good or bad. As a coach, he can make a player feel ten feet tall when he plays well but, if he errs, Don will confront him passionately, toe to toe, face to face.

Within our flexible 4–4–2 formation, it was Don who decided to discard Dave Sexton's man for man marking, preferring a zonal system that suited us so much better. His coaching expertise plus Bob McNab's ability to enforce the zones taken up by the defenders, produced a formidable barrier that was penetrated twenty-nine times only in the League, five of those in one game at Stoke.

In front of me, the defensive pieces comprised Pat Rice, Frank McLintock, Peter Simpson and Bob McNab. Capable of filling in seamlessly were John Roberts and Sammy Nelson. Peter Storey had been a right-back before his conversion to right-side midfield, and he provided extra cover defensively.

The make-up of our midfield was equally adaptable and contained a terrific mix. Peter Storey was a defensive assassin, all the time, and a marauding attacker occasionally. George Graham was perceptive, creative and could slow a game down. The balance on the left side of midfield was terrific with George Armstrong the link between McNab and Graham. The fact that George never played for England will remain a permanent stain on the hands of those who selected the national side.

The other three midfielders were Eddie Kelly, Jon Sammels and Peter Marinello. A fiery little Scot, Eddie Kelly could patrol the entire midfield area, and he charged up and down the field tirelessly. Similarly, Jon Sammels was a vital if irregularly selected midfield cog. He could run for ever and was stylish and perceptive. Peter Marinello fitted in on even fewer occasions than Jon, but no one doubted his ability to beat defenders and get in crosses. Charlie George also featured in an advanced midfield role but his part in the overall construction of the jigsaw was, in my opinion, as important as skipper Frank McLintock's. The midfield produced thirty goals between them in the league campaign but the real firepower came from attack and two men who were as closely joined off the pitch as they were on it.

The partnership of John Radford and Ray Kennedy was a mighty weapon in our armoury. John provided 15 league goals, Ray 19, a total of 34 priceless strikes. Both were brilliant with their backs to goal and as target men. Where Ray Kennedy had the strength of an ox in holding off opponents, John's spins and mobility wreaked havoc in defences. The '71 side scored 71 First Division goals.

Within this perfectly constructed jigsaw there was one special rogue piece, a free spirit who could frustrate and inspire in equal measure. I knew of Charlie George's talent long before our special season. As a schoolboy in 1963 he trained alongside Pat Rice and me twice a week in the indoor gym. He was cocky, funny and blessed with a touch of footballing genius. When I taught part-time at Holloway School, he was just as cheeky and a bit of a problem to all the teaching staff with whom he came into contact. No one, but no one, doubted his ability or that he would make his mark as a professional footballer. He was made for Arsenal, loved the club and still does. In training we would sometimes challenge him to show his skills. In one test, we kicked a ball as high as we could into the sky and asked Charlie to control it on the way down. With a cushioned knee, outside of the foot, chest or even backside, he would invariably kill the missile instantly, give a cheeky look in our direction and with an 'OK!' stroll off. Charlie was the most glamorous piece in our puzzle, eyecatchingly similar to Manchester United's George Best. He cared passionately about his local team and before games was often physically sick.

Seventeen individuals with such differing backgrounds bonded into an immovable force. We were able to appreciate each others' weaknesses as much as our strengths.

My understudy Geoff Barnett, then twenty-five, was known as Marty because he looked similar to comedian Marty Feldman. He was great company, got on with everyone and proved his ability on many occasions.

Pat Rice was twenty-one years old in the double season. No member of the squad worked harder to improve his talent than Ricey; 527 first-team appearances and skipper of the Liam Brady inspired side of the late seventies illustrates just what determination Pat had. More important to me, he baled me out on numerous occasions by kicking off the line!

So too did twenty-seven-year-old Bob McNab. All his defensive team-mates appreciated 'Nabbers' for the way he provided an extra pair of eyes for them when danger occurred. Four England caps was a meagre return for his brilliance in the art of defending. He could certainly talk for England and hardly a week goes by even now without Bob calling from Los Angeles to keep up with events and news of his colleagues.

Within these pages there are many stories and superlatives about our oldest member, thirty-one-year-old Frank McLintock. Suffice to say, he was the best captain I ever experienced first hand. Our head to head confrontations never got as far as fisticuffs but plenty of spittle and verbal abuse flew around. It never dulled our friendship.

Alongside Frank was Peter Simpson, twenty-five, the best uncapped central defender in England at the time. 'Stan' did make Alf Ramsey's preliminary squad for the 1970 World Cup but the presence of Bobby Moore and Norman Hunter meant he was left at home. He was the most laid-back member of the squad and many a time he'd be found sneaking a last fag in the loos as the bell sounded for action.

Completing the defensive set-up was John Roberts. What a revelation the big Welshman was when Peter Simpson was injured early in the double season. His nickname, 'Garth', was a reflection of his muscles, especially the quads he'd built on his thighs to help overcome a career-threatening cruciate knee injury.

Sammy Nelson, who was twenty-two, made just four league appearances in 1970–71 but he was our joker. He could have been a professional comedian let alone such a good fullback. Whether dropping his shorts in fun in front of the North Bank, or appearing outside a hotel in the middle of the night after a fire alarm, clad only in his underpants and clutching his wallet,

Sammy was certain to amuse. Our journey to glory would have been infinitely less entertaining without the Irishman.

Twenty-five-year-old Peter Storey was our very own version of Nobby Stiles, Ron Harris, Norman Hunter and the other midfielders of the time who took no prisoners. Off the field, he was shy and polite; on it, he was anything but, and could scare his own team-mates to death.

Eddie Kelly was only nineteen when the double season began. His Glaswegian upbringing and toughness masked an impish sense of humour. The contribution he made in his twenty-three league appearances is too often overlooked.

'Stroller' was the affectionate nickname given to twenty-six-year-old George Graham. He was a footballer of style and poise, and that's describing him off the field as well as on it. Immaculately groomed, his strengths were his elegant ball skills and wonderful ability to head a ball.

Jon Sammels loved Arsenal FC. He was twenty-six when our big season began. An ankle injury sidelined him for the first three months. Sammy was a great runner with the ball, subtle in his use of it and yet missed out on the ultimate glory. My room-mate the night before the FA Cup final, I recognised his disappointment.

A popular TV programme of the time had a character called 'Catweazle'. Our version was Peter Marinello. The twenty-year-old, bought from Hibernian and dubbed 'the new George Best', he was weighed down by the expectations, and only briefly given the chance to shine. His talent was never in doubt.

'Geordie' Armstrong was a gem, a fighter, a brilliant winger, the most generous of men. He would fight anyone who tried to move him out of the pole position at the bar where he would be waiting to buy the drinks. No one underestimated George's contribution. He was twenty-six years old in 1970–71.

Also from the north east, Ray Kennedy was the baby of the squad at nineteen. His power and strength on the ground and in the air were formidable. He didn't win his seven England caps until he was a Liverpool midfielder. Recognition should have come earlier because his partnership with John Radford was England's best strike force at the time. Ray was a big, complex lad and suffered from phobias, including panic in lifts and tunnels; we would help him through those particular nightmare journeys.

As for 'Raddy', our twenty-four-year-old striker was as down to earth as you'd expect anyone born in Hemsworth, Yorkshire to be. We admired, and were wary of, his dry sense of humour, and I was often the butt of his mickey taking. You'd expect him to show his elder more respect wouldn't you? It was never needed. I thought he was the best centre-forward in England and he thought I was the best keeper around at the time. John was also a trendsetter, one of the first players to have a tattoo. It read 'Death before dishonour'.

These were the sixteen players who shared with me a remarkable rollercoaster ride. There was little we didn't know about each other. In a huge hot steaming bath after every game we laughed, cried or argued, but we never deserted each other. Those communal pools offered just one more difference in the thirty-one years that separated Bertie's team and Arsene's. In the interests of hygiene and preventing modern-day diseases, individual showers have replaced the plunge baths. Sad, because in 1971 the hours spent in them definitely played a part in creating a special spirit among a group of ambitious young men.

Sixteen of Bertie's boys played in the big season but only because injury demanded change. Arsene 'rested' all twenty-five of his men on a regular basis. Any one of our squad would have hated to be rested. Injury and poor form were the only reasons not to play for any one of us. The best team played every time. Modern players accept today's rotational methods; a massive change in mentality would have been needed for us to accept them.

In 1971, the training facilities were located a field or two away from where they are today. We rented the University College Hospital of London playing fields. In the main, the pitches were better than most but nowhere near the 'billiard tables' that make up the Arsenal first-team and Academy facilities of the modern era. Two of the first-team surfaces have undersoil heating.

Of course, the differences in the quality of matchday pitches, used for over forty-two games, was marked as well. Apart from the early season when the grass was fresh and lush, sides in the sixties and seventies were asked to play throughout the winter months on many pitches that resembled bogs and, at the end of the season, barren wastes. Modern-day pitches are much better, and if problems occur, they are simply relaid once or twice in a season.

As a result of the better surfaces and the more scientific approach to training, the modern game is considerably quicker and anyone who thinks differently is misguided.

After training we showered under seven or eight sprays none of which produced much more than a dribble of water, and soaked in six tin baths, which, if you were the last in the queue, would have a surface of scum and six-inch base layer of mud. State of the art showers, Jacuzzi, steam room, swimming pool complete with movable floor and gymnasium welcome today's stars.

We always thought we were fed well but in 2002 the club's chef, Rob Fagg, provided a varied daily menu approved by expert dietitians. Every calorie and carbohydrate was measured. The food was five star.

Bertie Mee had no option but to train on the University fields. When Arsene Wenger arrived, he was horrified that a club with such a great name rented a facility that had no office for the manager or staff. He made it a priority that Arsenal move into the twenty-first century. I wouldn't be surprised if he made the building of a new training ground a condition of his staying in the job. Purchasing Nicolas Anelka for about half a million pounds and selling him to Real Madrid for £23 million soon solved the problem. Immaculately managed by Sean O'Connor it has served as a blueprint for many other leading clubs.

Arsene and Bertie shared some things in common but in other areas were very different. Bert was light years ahead of his time on the medical and dietary front, but our squad never benefited from the scientific approach and expertise that Arsene brought to the club. In first-team matters, Bertie was assisted by Don Howe, his coach, George Wright, his physio, Steve Burtenshaw, the reserve-team coach, Tony Donnelly in charge of kit, chief scout Gordon Clarke and a club doctor, a total of six.

Alongside Arsene Wenger, twenty men were charged with supplying expertise in their respective roles. Pat Rice was assistant manager, Bora Primorac assistant coach, Eddie Niedzwiecki reserve-team coach, I was goalkeeping coach, Gary Lewin and Colin Lewin first-team physios, Tony Colbert fitness coach, Joel Harris and Craig Gant masseurs, Steve Rowley chief scout, Damien Comolli French-based scout, Paul Johnson travel manager. John Crane and Leonard Sash were the club doctors, Vic Akers and his son Paul, kit managers. Dr Yan Rougier was a specialist in diet and all matters relating to health and the body, Phillipe Boixel an osteopath and Tiburce Darrou's expertise was in rehabilitation from serious injury. Finally, there was Dave Elliott, a motivational speaker. In addition, a company called Pro-Zone was employed to analyse every kick, run, header, goal, free kick and throw-in that a game of football encompasses. Arsene's way was to extract, where possible, every fractional advantage that might help the winning process.

Where the physio that was Mee and the academic that is Wenger differed most was in the daily routine. Bertie's military and medical background demanded punctuality, precision in organisation, and dress 'becoming of anyone who represents

Arsenal'. I know he would have difficulty with Arsene's more fluid arrangements and in particular the dress code. Bertie had always been impressed with the way the top Italian clubs travelled in club suits emblazoned with the team badge. He saw it as a vital part of discipline, togetherness, pride. In 2002, tracksuits still bore the club badge but were much more sensible and comfortable for the mode of travel.

Private planes have become the norm for any trip outside London, except for Dennis Bergkamp, while a sophisticated team coach complete with DVD and satellite TV provides the transport for the closer areas of the Midlands. In 1971, it was train travel to the north west and north east and a coach for all other areas.

When Geordie Armstrong bought a Jaguar it looked extremely extravagant among the second-hand Fords and Vauxhalls, and was greatly admired. The car park at Arsenal's training centre just after the millennium was full of every prestigious make of car. Jeremy Clarkson would have been in his element. Most modern-day players have a choice of more than one. It indicates a lifestyle and salary that has changed just as dramatically as the speed of the game on the field and the structure off it.

However much those of us in the side led by Frank McLintock may raise our eyes at 2002 wage packets, the fact is we earned well for the day and age in which we lived. Just as pertinent, we loved playing in what was a golden age for quality and competition and would have done so for nothing. I was heartened to hear Thierry Henry say he loved football so much that he would play for nothing.

A basic weekly salary in our day varied between £50 and just over £100; bonuses were £4 for a win and £2 for a draw. Then there was a sliding scale of bonuses for the different rounds of the various competitions in which we played. Winning the FA Cup final was worth £700 to each of us. A loyalty bonus gave an extra 12½ per cent for each year the player represented the club and basically meant that if you'd been an Arsenal player for ten years, you doubled all the bonus money won in that season. Winning the double in 1971 gave the long-serving players a total of about £17,500 with bonuses, representing about £200,000 in modern-day terms. The house I bought a year after winning the double cost £26,500. Its value in 2003 stands close to a million.

Our earnings came nowhere near those of recent years. With bonuses, it's not uncommon for the salaries of Arsenal's top modern-day players to soar well beyond a million pounds per annum. Televised football in the early seventies meant that footballers became role models, heroes and commercial commodities, but on nothing like the scale of today.

If the FA had had video panels to assess bad tackles and bad behaviour back in 1971, most of the twenty-one teams who made up the First Division would have had half a dozen players suspended weekly. Referees would give as good as they got when players verbally protested. Trying it on and cheating did occur in those days, but on nothing like the scale of today. Shirt-tugging was virtually non-existent, but a right hook was common. In one respect, the two sets of players would speak with a single voice and that's the need for a panel of full-time professional referees and video replays to settle any controversy within ten to twenty seconds.

Signing autographs has changed little in the two eras, except we could still be found in the public domain, not closeted behind closed doors. Today's public are celebrity obsessed and make it difficult for well-known people to enjoy everyday activities with their families. Arsene's squad are asked to conduct signing sessions for charities and good causes once or twice a week within the training ground environment. Every Thursday or Friday between 100 and 200 items, including balls, banners, photos and shirts, are laid out for all the squad to sign. Football memorabilia has become a valuable commodity to collectors and therefore a good source of income for charity auctions and raffles. The modern-day players know how privileged they are and are always willing to help, in so many ways, people less fortunate than themselves.

Relations with the media have changed massively over the years. Reporters travelled with us openly and post-match we often had a drink together and a good laugh. Many became personal friends and we were able to trust the majority. In 2002, footballers had little or no trust of reporters, television presenters or interviewers. Players are always waiting for a loaded question and wary of the headlines that careless answers might provoke. If a player refuses to talk, his silence is interpreted in whatever way the paper and its editor decides is best for them. It's a Catch 22 situation. The game of football needs publicity and the tabloids sell successfully when there's a dramatic headline. There will always be a simple solution for players if they feel hard done by in dealings with the press and that is to keep on winning. It's the only way to humble if not silence a poison pen.

Proving the critics wrong in 1971 was probably a more difficult task than in 2002. Our season took on four very distinct phases, the Wenger team just two. We were written off so many times that it eventually strengthened our resolve. Most of us would freely admit we won it the hard way and without the style and panache of recent years.

Our start to the season wasn't brilliant. Of the first six games, between 15 August and 1 September, we won two, drew three and lost one; 7 points were gained from 12 – 5 points dropped.

The next eighteen games between 5 September and 9 January were special. Fourteen games were won, three drawn and only one lost; 31 points from 36 – 5 points dropped. However, the fact that the eighteenth game was at Stoke where we lost 5–0 pulled us up with a severe jolt.

Over the next five games, between 16 January and 27 February, we lost our rhythm, confidence and nearly our chance of glory. Only two games were won, the other three lost; 4 points from 10 – 6 valuable points discarded.

'Arsenal right out of it now', 'Derby's 2–0 victory puts tin hat on Arsenal's hopes of catching Leeds', 'Impossible task of overhauling the Leeds team already being hailed as League Champions North of the Trent' – such were the predictions following our defeat at Derby on 27 February, which left Arsenal 7 points adrift of Don Revie's lads. The last thirteen matches have gone a long way to settling any argument about Arsenal being a great team in 1971. Eleven matches ended in victory, just one was a draw and the sole defeat was at Elland Road, Leeds, three games from the end of the league season; 23 points from a possible 26 – a meagre 3 points dropped.

Sandwiched somewhere between the forty-two matches in the First Division were twenty-one Cup ties in the FA Cup, League Cup and Fairs Cup.

We lost our European crown controversially in Cologne, but before that we experienced a tie that could have wrecked our season; instead, it fired us up, in more ways than one. I have always loved Rome for its history and beauty. I even wrote a thesis on the gladiatorial games but I never thought I'd be caught up in a brawl that would have done justice to the mighty Colosseum. Our first opponents were Lazio. In the Eternal City's Olympic Stadium we took a 2–0 lead, but inspired by Welsh-born striker Giorgio Chinaglia, Lazio scored two goals and we had to settle for a draw. The whole game was ugly and ill tempered, spitting, hacking and verbal abuse allowed to prevail by the famous East German referee Rudi Glockner.

After the game, a restaurant near the centre of Rome hosted a reception for both teams. The Italians were late in arriving, by which time the Arsenal team were well into their pasta. They sat far removed from us and, although nothing was said or done to cause friction, there was a hostile atmosphere generated by on-field events.

Late at night, perhaps early in the morning, I was near the front door of the restaurant when I heard heated exchanges between some Italians and Ray Kennedy, unmistakable because of his Geordie accent. Within seconds Ray was attacked and a fight had started. It developed like a forest fire. My two most vivid memories are of John Roberts bear-hugging some of our lads and dragging them away from flailing fists and wild kicks. It's not easy to pull apart a passionate Italian and a couple of lads from the Gorbals; that was Eddie Kelly and Frank McLintock. Above the fight, shuttered windows were thrown open and locals in nightclothes watched in amazement. Only the arrival of the local police on two motorbikes subdued the fighting, which had got out of control.

Bertie Mee could be seen pulling players away and ordering them to the waiting coach. It was over as quickly as it had begun and, after being questioned by the police on our team coach, we left the scene and arrived back at our hotel at three in the morning. The paparrazzi in Rome and the scribes of Fleet Street enjoyed a couple of days of exaggerated headlines and the return game the following week was a damp squib as Arsenal won comfortably, 2–0.

The immediate after-effect of the trip to Europe and the scraps on and off field did, I think, have a bearing on our 5–0 drubbing at Stoke on the Saturday between the two games against Lazio.

So there was nothing smooth about the road to glory in '71. Our run-in bore some comparison to 2002 when Arsene Wenger's team eventually won the title by 7 points from Liverpool. The only three games they lost came in their opening seventeen games, when they won eight and drew six. Of the twenty-one matches remaining eighteen were won, three drawn, there were no defeats and 57 points were taken from the 63 available.

It's always difficult to compare teams who played when it was two points for a win with those who earn three points for a victory. We would have accumulated 94 points from our forty-two games, 7 points more than Wenger's team who played four less matches.

As we all know, there are 'statistics, statistics and damn lies'. The one feature that truly binds Bertie Mee and Arsene Wenger's teams together is the fight – the battles fought and lost, fought and won and simply fought. Charlton's defeat of Arsenal at Highbury in November 2001 was almost as sensational as the defeat we sustained at Stoke in September 1971. We travelled to the Victoria Ground on the morning of the match. Travelling such a distance would be unheard of these days. Tony Waddington's team played exceptionally well, we were poor. The result was that 5–0 humiliation in front of the 'Match of the Day' cameras. Imagine Bertie Mee's reaction when I appeared on 'Grandstand' the following Saturday with a filmed analysis of all five goals. He'd been very reasonable in allowing me freedom to do regular work for the BBC, but didn't anticipate my stupidity at trying to explain my own and the team's shortcomings. He was happy enough for me to describe winning moments, but not defeats, let alone annihilation. The press had already pointed out such dangers early in the season. My World Cup stint had received good response but the dangers involved in self-analysis or team analysis were obvious to all but me! No such mistakes were ever made again.

Manchester United featured strongly in both sets of glory years. In 1971 an early season win at Highbury over a team that had won the 1968 European Cup gave a massive psychological boost to all of us. Bobby Charlton, George Best and Nobby Stiles were playing, as were Denis Law and our old team-mate Ian Ure. United left north London after losing 4–0, and the game included a save from me at the feet of George Best, which will remain my favourite for ever, simply because it was George that I dispossessed. Eight times out of ten I reckon he'd have scored but this time he failed and later in a biography written by Michael Parkinson, George said:

> I still wake up at night even now reliving some of the awful things that happened to me on the field. Once we played Arsenal and I get the ball, thread through their defence and I've only got Bob Wilson to beat. He comes rushing out, dives at my feet and takes the ball from me. Now I still get the raving needle when I relive that moment. I always reckoned that when I got through with only the keeper to beat, you could put a million quid on me scoring and you'd be right a hundred times out of a hundred. I still can't fathom out what went wrong that game and it still worries me.

Years later George still found it difficult to credit me with one of the saves of my life. Over a sequence of photos showing the moment, he wrote, 'Kind regards, Bob. Sooner or later you get a lucky one – George.'

A 3–1 win over United in the return at Old Trafford was just as sweet, but neither game compared to the experience of Wenger's men in 2002. Having finished as runners-up to United in the three previous seasons, they were asked to clinch the title by winning at the theatre of dreams in the penultimate league game of the season. To respond with a win was one thing, to do it in a style that even United fans had to applaud, was sensational. Megs and I watched from home as Sylvan Wiltord's goal completed the first half of the double, and we were at the training ground with champagne at the ready when the team arrived back elated at 1.30 a.m.

That game was massive and I could appreciate the feelings of all the squad. In 1971 we had a similar dramatic conclusion to our league campaign, possibly a more difficult task than

Arsene's Army. It was Monday, 3 May 1971. The game pitched us against Tottenham Hotspur, the only previous winners of the double in the twentieth century. To take the First Division title we travelled to White Hart Lane with a clear mandate – win by any score and we would be champions; draw 0–0 and we would pip Leeds on goal difference, by the margin of 0.013 of a goal to be precise. A scoring draw would mean Billy Bremner and his team would be champions.

The gates were locked more than an hour before kick-off with 51,192 spectators inside; about 10,000 were left outside on the street. Referee Kevin Howley had to abandon his car a mile from the stadium and fight his way on foot through the crowds. Our journey from Southgate, north London, usually took twenty minutes; this time it was an hour and a quarter. The game against our fierce rivals was as expected – fierce. No quarter was asked for or given. Spurs desperately wanted to prevent Arsenal from achieving the double.

For eighty-eight minutes it was a goalless draw, which would have been enough. Then Charlie George passed the ball across the face of goal, John Radford's effort was kept out brilliantly by Pat Jennings, only for George Armstrong to retrieve it before it went for a throw-in and cross to the head of Ray Kennedy. The ball flashed by Pat, hit the underside of the bar and found the net. All the goal did was to provoke Spurs into a last-ditch assault in which a goalmouth scramble led to desperate measures – a loose ball, frantic tackles, deafening noise and a cut head for me from Alan Mullery's boot.

The sound of the final whistle produced the greatest rush of emotion of my entire playing career. Arsenal fans invaded the pitch, I looked for team-mates to hug and found myself doing a jig with referee Kevin Howley. We were champions of England and our forty-two league games had been watched by 1,662,528 spectators. Attendances at Highbury had averaged 43,771 and almost topped a million in total.

The Spurs players and fans were magnanimous in defeat. Our dressing room was a scene of delirium and we couldn't believe our eyes. Bertie Mee without a tie on! A telegram of congratulations arrived from Leeds manager Don Revie – 'Leeds have not lost the title. Arsenal have won it. You are true champions.' A further message reached the dressing room from Bill Shankly whose Liverpool team we were to face at Wembley five days later – 'Well done, you might even give us a bit of a game on Saturday.' Shanks was already using his special psychology skills on us.

As I went to the medical room to have two stitches in my cut scalp, I passed two enthusiastic Portuguese observers, Simoes and Eusebio of Benfica, giving interviews. In the *Evening Standard* next day Eusebio's quote gave me great pleasure – 'Wilson number one this place' it read.

As with the lads of 2002, the boys of '71 drank lots of champagne in the wake of victory. For us, though, it wasn't at the training ground or in a London nightclub, but a pub, the White Hart in Southgate. It wasn't my scene and I slipped away to family and friends waiting for me back in Enfield. Sleep could wait. The journey had been a long one – blue goalkeeping jersey, garage doors, amateur days, the stiffs, Wembley distress and now, in the space of twelve months to add to a European prize, I was one of the champions of England. I couldn't explain how or why it had happened for me, but the whole experience was immense and it wasn't quite over.

We had four days to sleep, get rid of excess alchohol and train on a pitch especially prepared as a Wembley lookalike. I'm glad our championship night preceded the Cup final. For the boys of 2002 it was the other way round – final versus Chelsea on 4 May, victory over Manchester United at Old Trafford on 8 May. For us, it was championship glory, glory night at White Hart Lane on 3 May with the Cup final date 8 May.

Our journey to Wembley had been awkward. Non-league

Yeovil provided a banana skin but we didn't slip up. The Pompey chimes rang out twice before we beat Portsmouth. Manchester City were removed on a mud heap at Maine Road. Leicester went the same way after another replay and Stoke City were 2–0 up and cruising in the semi-final but failed to win.

The half-time of that epic game against Stoke at Hillsborough illustrated the brilliance of Don Howe as a coach and Frank McLintock as a captain. A freak Denis Smith goal following a corner and a terrible back-pass from Charlie George that presented John Ritchie with a chance he took, left us trailing 2–0 after forty-five minutes. In the dressing room, heads were down, any thoughts of a double as far removed as is imaginable. Up stepped Howe and McLintock, leaders, wild men, urging, cajoling, bullying. They found and demanded inspiration from a team on its knees. Within three minutes of the restart, Peter Storey smashed a first-time volley past Gordon Banks. Stoke then missed two glorious chances with only me to beat before a challenge on Banks produced a last-minute corner for Arsenal. McLintock's header was goalbound when John Mahoney dived full length to stop it crossing the line. The penalty, which would keep our hopes alive, was too much to bear. As Peter Storey ran up to take the kick, I was kneeling, head on the ground, unable to watch. It evidently wasn't the greatest of penalties but the roar from the Arsenal fans gave a clear message to me. We had a replay.

Twenty minutes later I went into the Stoke dressing room to ask Gordon Banks for an autograph for my son John. He obliged, we shook hands and, as I passed their manager, Tony Waddington, he muttered, 'You bastard. If you hadn't dived at John Mahoney's feet we'd have been 3–1 up and in the final.' The dejection he showed, together with the quietness of the Stoke dressing room, was relayed by me to Bertie, Don and the lads. Stoke were stunned and unlikely to recover in four days' time for the replay at Villa Park. So it proved. We won 2–0 without drama.

Our preparation between the championship night at White Hart Lane and the Wembley final was planned and executed with military style – day off; light training day; small game day; gentle last tactical session on the Friday.

The only outside distraction that we were allowed during the build-up to Wembley was to undertake the obligatory interviews that brought a little extra income to the Cup final pool, monies made up of sponsorship, commercials, personal appearances and a 'hit' record. As soon as Stoke were beaten in the semi-final replay at Villa Park, the hunt was on for a tune and words that would take the musical world by storm. When we heard that Jimmy Hill had written new words to 'Rule Britannia' we fell around laughing. When we read the lyrics our mirth continued at a pace. How could something of such pomp and splendour be reduced to the following?

> Good old Arsenal, we're proud to say that name,
> While we sing this song we'll win the game.

The verse was repeated three more times deleting Arsenal and inserting 'Bertie' for verse two, 'Frankie' for verse three and 'Charlie' for verse four.

In fear and trepidation we arrived *en bloc* one Sunday at a studio near Marble Arch. As we waited, giggling and self-conscious, we heard for the first time the re-worked version of the tune. It bore little resemblance to the original but was beaty and catchy. Our confidence increased as we launched straight into a first rehearsal of Jimmy's Pulitzer Prize words. It took all of three rehearsals before producer Tony Palmer and arranger Brian Rogers decided to risk a first take. We were reassured by the three professional session singers placed right in the middle of our front row. 'Just go for it lads,' they encouraged.

The music began, the vocals were cued and to me it sounded great. Producer and arranger thought differently. Thirty seconds into take one a tapping over the internal PA system brought us to a faltering halt. The voice from the technical booth was complimentary but worried.

'Sounds great boys, but sorry to say there's a voice that's a bit flat.'

As laughter broke out, two of the session singers turned my way and said, 'Sorry, Bob, it's you.'

I was promptly removed to the back row and asked either to sing softly or, preferably, to mime. The lads loved it but I warned them that it now had no chance of becoming a hit. Wrong again. By Cup final week we were in the top twenty and booked for an appearance on a recorded 'Top of the Pops'. Only seven of us showed up, so Pan's People, the racy dancing troupe, were placed between us all. A backing group offstage, helped produce a far from perfect final product. Unbelievably, we all received gold discs in later years and mine hangs proudly in the most suitable place, the downstairs loo.

From our last training session at London Colney on Friday morning, we went straight to Wembley for the traditional look at the pitch the day before the game. When we arrived at the twin towers, it was pouring with rain. We made our way quickly up the famous tunnel and to our surprise found our opponents' manager standing challengingly by the cinder area behind the goal. There was no sign of any Liverpool players, just the great Shanks, in the rain, no umbrella. We all respected him so much, and acknowledged him, of course. We knew he was there to intimidate if he could. As I studied the soft and increasingly spongy goalmouth, I saw him watching me. I was getting a little worried about how slippery the surface was and how my long studs would cope with such a soft surface. I always had the longest metal studs allowable so that my 6ft 1in became 6ft 2ins but I was concerned they would dig into the Wembley turf. Bertie Mee ordered us to leave and, after letting most of the team go ahead, I left the field with Frank McLintock and George Graham. As we passed Bill Shankly and nodded, he returned our greeting. 'Good luck, Frank. All the best, George. Have a good game, Bob.' Hardly had I thanked Liverpool's great manager when he added a rider to me. 'Hey Bob, nightmare pitch for goalkeepers, eh?' Frank told me to keep walking and that's what I did but the words remained in my head, 'Nightmare pitch, eh?'

Most modern clubs, including Arsenal, have a sports psychologist or motivational speaker at hand. In 1971 we relied on our manager, our coach and ourselves. Liverpool didn't need a psychologist. They had Bill Shankly.

Playing in an FA Cup final at Wembley used to be one of the highlights of any footballer's life. The country would come to a standstill as twenty-four players took a short ride up Wembley Way to the twin towers, which seemed to represent all the successes and failures that had taken place since the great stadium was opened in 1923. The eyes of the world seemed to turn to England on FA Cup final day. Every footballer in every land would have loved to have had the same experience.

After inspecting the pitch, spotting families, tolerating TV interviews and battling the dressing-room nerves, came the knock on the door, signalling the arrival of royalty. It was time to go. We had planned, quite deliberately, to delay leaving the dressing room. A broken stud or a snapped lace meant Bill Shankly's young side were kept waiting in the tunnel. It can be an unnerving experience. Walking behind Bertie Mee and Frank McLintock, I was amused to see Bill Shankly agitated. He knew we had stolen a march over him and added to the nervousness of his players. We were champions, out to become only the fourth team in history to achieve the double. As we emerged into daylight, the first challenge to overcome was the cacophony of noise that tumbled down from the terraces as the long walk to the royal box began. It's the moment that inspires some players and paralyses others with fear. Moving off the cinder surround produced a momentary panic for me. My studs did indeed sink deeply into the turf. A little running on the spot eased my worries as we lined up for the national anthem and the presentation to the Duke of Kent.

As the two teams broke ranks and headed towards their respective fans, I could hear the Arsenal supporters bellowing what had become a familiar comforting greeting for me – 'Bob Wilson, Bob Wilson'. Just as familiar to them was the raised arm response from me. It was a gloriously sunny day and the heat, I knew, would be a problem for the outfield players. We had to exchange ends and the 110 yards gave me a chance to stretch my legs and rid them of more tension. Liverpool's young keeper Ray Clemence looked a shade edgy, like me, as we shook hands. The Liverpool fans, famed for their support of keepers, applauded me all the way to the goal. There was a last check of my red cap, which I knew I'd need, and my green cotton gloves, which I knew I wouldn't; then a final careful adjustment of my sleeves, which I always wore rolled up to just below the elbow.

Referee Norman Burtenshaw set the game in motion. During the ninety minutes, we had the vast majority of chances; they were either missed or Clemence saved well. Twice we hit the woodwork. My best moment came on half-time as Alec Lindsay sent a free kick thundering low to my left-hand corner. I saw it clearly and, at full stretch, kept it out. The follow-up block at the feet of Chris Lawler was effective and, as the ensuing corner was taken, the half-time whistle was blown. The second half was nearly all Arsenal, but still we couldn't score. My main work came in duels for high crosses with John Toshack.

The final had moved into extra time when substitute Peter Thompson pushed a ball into the path of Steve Heighway. The former university man cut inside Pat Rice and looked as if he was shaping to pull the ball back for a cross, as he had done all afternoon. Expecting another battle for the ball with Toshack, I edged away from my near post. Without warning, Heighway suddenly went for the narrow angle. In the fraction of a second it took for the ball to clip the bottom of the post and find the net, I knew I was badly at fault. Heighway danced away in delight submerged beneath his Liverpool colleagues. The looks on the faces of Peter Simpson and, in particular, Frank McLintock as they stared straight at me were full of accusation. At that moment Frank, who had been named Footballer of the Year, was facing a fifth losing Wembley final.

For just a few unhappy moments lots of negative thoughts went through my head. One of them briefly recalled that this was the same post where Bert Trautmann had erred against Bobby Mitchell in Manchester City's 1955 FA Cup final defeat. The worst thought was the realisation that if we lost, I would have cost Arsenal the double. My most consistent season, one in which I was to be named Arsenal's Player of the Season by the fans, would be ruined. There was even time for the image of Dan Lewis to flash across my mind. Lewis was Arsenal's keeper in their first-ever appearance in an FA Cup final, the 1927 game against Cardiff City, when he inexplicably allowed a soft shot to go through his arms and legs. The error was partly blamed on Lewis's shiny new jersey and, as a result, all subsequent Arsenal Cup final keepers wore sweaters that had been used or washed.

I put the bad thoughts behind me and just as well. Seconds later, I was forced into an instinctive reflex save from Brian Hall. Instead of going two goals down, we equalised within the next minute or two with a crazy, soft-looking goal. I thought George Graham scored it, but it was eventually credited to Eddie Kelly, who had come on as substitute for Peter Storey. Our never say die spirit had pulled us back from the brink of defeat yet again and when Charlie George, long hair flowing behind him, belted an unstoppable and deflected shot past Ray

Clemence, we were in the lead and within eight minutes of history.

As Charlie lay flat out on his back waiting to be buried by the team, my mind switched into a coldly calculating mood. There must be no mistakes. The photographers behind me, and BBC's Barry Davies, counted the minutes down. After one Liverpool attack, Davies rushed to retrieve the ball for me but as he threw it towards me, I volleyed it straight back, much to his surprise. The whistling from the Arsenal fans had reached a crescendo when Liverpool won a corner. Only seconds remained. It had to be their last chance. As I jumped around in my usual agitated manner, high on my toes, full-back Bob McNab slapped me hard on the back side and yelled, 'Be first, Willo!' The ball flew towards a blur of bodies. It stuck in my hands. The roar of relief from the Arsenal fans turned back into high-pitched whistles. I dribbled the ball to the left of the goal and then back to the middle. As I volleyed it upfield the final whistle sounded.

We had won the FA Cup. The glittering gold medal, which so many sought and so few found, was to be mine. The famous double belonged to Arsenal. Our names would go into the record books for ever. Players mingled and I searched for Ray Clemence. He had tears in his eyes and looked as dejected as I had been two years earlier.

'Don't worry, Ray,' I said. 'You've got years ahead of you. You'll be back. This could be my last chance.'

They were meant to be words of comfort but they were to prove prophetic in every way. Ray was to play at Wembley again on numerous occasions for Liverpool, England and Spurs. I was to be robbed by injury of a last appearance one year later.

For the moment, though, each and every member of the Arsenal squad and staff sought each other out. We had responded to the call from Bertie Mee ten weeks previously when he sat us all down in the Highbury dressing room and asked us to 'put family second for a short time and dedicate yourselves to creating history for yourselves and Arsenal Football Club'. Bertie embraced me and understood better than anyone what the achievement meant to the college boy he had persuaded to sign for Billy Wright.

Frank McLintock was out of control and eager to rush to collect the familiar old trophy. Instinctively, I held him back and told him to slow down, enjoy the moment, take it all in. It was a totally different set of steps from those we climbed when we lost to Swindon. These slabs of concrete seemed to have a spring in them where the others were magnetic in their pull. As we turned left towards the Duchess of Kent, I searched desperately for Megs. She had learned to live with a man driven by ambition and enthusiasm, and been understanding of the joy and despair, the highs and lows that are part and parcel of the professional footballer's life. She was excited and proud. My moment was her moment.

Much too quickly the Duchess had given me my precious medal and the base of the FA Cup. Without appreciating it at the time, we had become Arsenal legends. On the way down, my brother Hugh grabbed me and I hoped he understood the part he too had played in bringing me this far.

Our banquet was memorable, our appearances on 'Cup Final Match of the Day' with David Coleman embarrassing, our multi-coloured shirts and ties the height of fashion. For many of us, the night ended in Danny La Rue's nightclub where he and his staff entertained us as if we were royalty. Next day a quarter of a million Arsenal supporters lined the streets of Islington as we paraded the league championship trophy and the FA Cup aboard our open-topped bus. It was truly unforgettable. I never thought I'd do it again but, in fact, I made the same journey, celebrating a double, twice more in 1998 and 2002.

On the steps of Islington Town Hall, our skipper fell asleep, exhausted after nine months of effort and leadership. Waiting for mayoral speeches, I studied the Cup final programme for the very first time. Priced 10p, its main content were the two teams.

Arsenal 1. R. Wilson, 2. P. Rice, 3. R. McNab, 4. P. Storey, 5. F. McLintock (Cpt), 6. P. Simpson, 7. G. Armstrong, 8. G. Graham, 9. J. Radford, 10. R. Kennedy, 11. C. George. Substitute J. Sammels [on the day Eddie Kelly was sub]. Manager Mr B. Mee. Trainer Mr G. Wright

Liverpool 1. R. Clemence, 2. C. Lawler, 3. A. Lindsay, 4. T. Smith (Cpt), 5. L. Lloyd, 6. E. Hughes, 7. I. Callaghan, 8. P. Thompson, 9. S. Heighway, 10. J. Toshack, 11. B. Hall. Substitute A. Evans. Manager Mr W. Shankly. Trainer Mr R. Paisley

On the page headed 'Who's Who for Arsenal' it read:

> Bob Wilson. A late arrival on the First Division scene, he has fast become soccer's best uncapped goalkeeper in just three seasons of regular first team football. Fast off his line and a fearless diver at opponents' feet. Joined Arsenal as amateur from Wolves in 1963. Professional March 1964. Became TV personality as BBC's 1970 World Cup analyst. Ex schoolmaster. Born Chesterfield. 6ft 0½ ins. 13st 11lbs.

Pretty accurate, apart from half an inch short on height and four pounds too heavy on weight. Also in the programme, the BBC's Sam Leitch wrote:

> We're delighted that in the same season as he's played his part in taking Arsenal to Wembley today, goalkeeper Bob Wilson has become a popular and regular face on BBC screens with his action analyses, and it says a lot in his favour that one of the first to spotlight the menace of Liverpool's Steve Heighway was television commentator Bob Wilson.

Reading Sam's words I laughed out loud. You'd have thought I'd have known what Steve Heighway was likely to do!

The season, which had begun for me by admiring the greatness and colourful play of Brazil, had ended with my being an ever-present member of a club side whose style of play was described in one quarter as 'a horrible grey'. Had the Arsenal team of 1998 or 2002 been in our place, the accolades would have been entirely different. You could genuinely make comparisons between Arsene Wenger's entertainers and the Brazilians coached by Mario Zagalo thirty-two years previously.

The strength of Bertie Mee's team lay in the respect every member had for each other. Every player was a vital part of the jigsaw and each would have given all for the guy next to him on the pitch. Almost thirty years later, we were standing round the graveside at George Armstrong's funeral, all but Ray Kennedy, Parkinson's disease having made it impossible for him to attend. Bob McNab had even flown in from Los Angeles, California. As we stood stunned by the loss, the Arsenal captain at the time, Tony Adams, remarked on our amazing camaraderie three decades on from our moment of glory. He pondered whether the same gathering would occur with the team he captained in similar circumstances. Of course it wouldn't, and couldn't. The geography of the modern game makes it at best very unlikely.

Arsenal's double-winning side of '71 were like family and will remain so. The term 'great footballing team' may have eluded them. 'Great team' they most certainly were.

10
Dreams fulfilled

'Success is getting what you want. Happiness is
liking what you get.'

H. Jackson Brown

I was helping my children John, Anna and Robert to build a boat
in the sand in Ibiza. The sea was warm and welcoming. The sun
beat down relentlessly. From the time the double was clinched,
Megs and I had been entertained and feted. My diary became the
property of one of Fleet Street's favourite men, Reg Hayter. His
famous sports agency had taken me under its wing and the diary
was full of commitments and deadlines. Two books were on
the way to publication, there was a weekly newspaper column
for the *Sun* to fill, work with two of my favourite charities to
be undertaken and many bookings to open fetes, garages, new
shops and any number of similar events to be fitted in. My link
with BBC TV Sport had been strengthened and two adverts for
showing on ITV were to be shot on my return from holiday.

For the moment, though, deciding on two funnels or three for
the kids' boat was the priority. A Scottish accent interrupted my
designing skills. 'Och Bob, da ya ken the news? Ya wun 'o us now.'
Fellow Brits on holiday had been kind and left us alone despite the
recent publicity and fame I had acquired, but this news was too
important to ignore, and no, I didn't know about it.

The international footballing board had seen fit to change
the rules concerning a player's eligibility. A Welshman, the

172

late Trevor Morris, had debated long and hard about the real nationality of those children born outside the borders of their parents' origins, whether it was for the lack of hospitals or the necessity to work abroad. The old rule stated that footballers could play only for the country in which they were born. In the summer of 1971, a new rule gave players permission to choose either the country in which they were born or the country of either parent's birth. My mind raced at the realisation that the dream that my dad always had of my playing for his beloved Scotland was a possibility, as long as I continued to play well.

When we arrived home, more good news was tempered by a newspaper rumour that Don Howe was about to be lured away from Arsenal to join his former club West Bromwich Albion. Don's appointment as manager at the Hawthorns was quickly confirmed and totally overshadowed the letter informing me that the Arsenal fans had chosen me as their Player of the Year for the 1970–71 season. I maintain that all seventeen of Bertie Mee's squad should have shared the award, but to be chosen individually was very humbling, a high point of my career.

The pre-season photographs for 1971–72 were enhanced by four gleaming trophies – the league championship trophy, the FA Cup, the Manager of the Year trophy and the Footballer of the Year award, which went to Frank McLintock, together with the MBE.

The new season promised much for Arsenal and delivered nothing in terms of silverware. After winning the opening two games against Chelsea and Huddersfield, we went down 3–1 to Manchester United. That game was played at Anfield, the result of an FA punishment United had incurred following crowd problems at Old Trafford. It remains memorable for me because of a new episode in my personal duel with George Best. He had famously 'nicked' the ball out of Gordon Banks' hands in Northern Ireland's home international match against England, although the goal was disallowed. At Anfield, George did exactly the same to me. Where he came from and how he did it I'll never know. It was like a sleight of hand, except it was achieved with his feet and performed at amazing speed. Only a desperate dive to stop the ball crossing the goalline avoided embarrassment.

There was no avoiding a red face when it came to my first television commercial. I had turned up at a studio to film an advert for Tuf shoes. The producer had asked me how I intended to deliver my lines about the product. In my gentlest and warmest tones I delivered what I thought was the perfect sell. It wasn't how the client saw it. 'What's the name of the shoes, Bob? TUF, TOUGH, TUF!' He shouted so loud he almost scared me to death. If that's what he wanted, that's what he'd get. It was neither subtle nor subliminal and a totally different shoot from the one where I sat by a lake with young footballers extolling the virtues of Shredded Wheat. That ad would have done Hollywood proud, such was the soft focus on the perfectly arranged footballer and his young admirers. The irony was that no one remembered my Shredded Wheat commercial, but no one forgot Tuf shoes.

The changes behind the scenes at Highbury created an unsettled squad and it was reflected in results. Don Howe had taken physio George Wright and youth-team coach Brian Whiteside with him. Don's replacement was reserve-team coach Steve Burtenshaw whom we all knew so well. It was a sensible and well-deserved promotion for Steve and he was joined by the effervescent Fred Street, who became our new physio.

Our league form was dreadfully erratic. By the end of November, any chance of retaining our champions tag had gone, eight games out of seventeen lost, the other nine won. We were out of the League Cup as well, at the fourth-round stage, but were progressing well in the club's first attempt to win the European Cup. The early rounds had all been negotiated with some comfort and the quarter-final wasn't due until March. It promised something special, another double header against

Johan Cruyff and Ajax. For the moment, I was unaware that I would meet the great Dutchman and other Ajax stars before March.

I was visiting John Groom's Home for the Disabled in Edgware on 5 October, my mum's birthday. The charity's offices were close to Highbury and my association with their impressive work had gained momentum as a result of the Arsenal team's success. A phone call temporarily interrupted my afternoon. It was Megs, in happy mood. She had just taken a call informing her that the new Scotland manager, Tommy Docherty, had included me in his first squad to play Portugal the following Wednesday. Also included was Alex Cropley, who had been born in Aldershot but lived most of his early life in Scotland, and there was a first call up for my Arsenal team-mate George Graham.

The papers had a field day. 'The Doc picks MacWilson' was a kind headline, 'Docherty calls up Englishman Bob' less enjoyable. I liked Tommy Docherty. I think he was perfect for international management. The Doc's enthusiasm was infectious making his international players feel ten feet tall. 'To hell with the man's accent, he's as good as Gordon Banks,' was how he described my selection. It probably wasn't too accurate an assessment but it was flattering and boosted my confidence.

No words could express my parents' delight at my selection, but there were plenty of words on the subject from the Glasgow press camp, questioning my national status. It so enraged my mum's brother John that he wrote forcibly to the *Scotsman* newspaper. My uncle John was extremely well known in Scotland, having been Lord Provost of Perth for nine years. He bore the same name as my great uncle, who had opened Hampden Park, and had been the recipient of a knighthood. Any letter from Sir John Ure Primrose to Scotland's leading broadsheet was bound to cause a stir. The basis of his argument was that the family tree showed not a trace of any English until his sister Catherine's children were born in

England. He felt therefore that I had a great right to claim my Scottish heritage.

International selection for one-off matches takes players out of club routines for two or three days at a time, when concentration is on an entirely different type of football, in unfamiliar surroundings and often with unfamiliar faces. It was important for me that George Graham was there when we joined up with the rest of the Scottish squad at Glasgow airport, if only as my interpreter. Despite a great reception from the other players, I felt dreadfully conspicuous simply because of my English accent. I tried like mad to insert a few 'ayes' and 'ochs' but it was difficult. The other keeper in the squad was Bobby Clark of Aberdeen, who seemed genuinely delighted that we could work together.

After Tommy Docherty announced that I would be playing, an invasion of the Wilson clan descended on Hampden Park. Hugh watched from the terraces while Mum and Megs lauded it in the South West stand, row F, seats 116 and 117, priced £1. Arriving at Hampden was as special as I'd anticipated and, on entering the old ground, one of the Scottish FA officials called out, 'Welcome home, son.' The Scotland eleven was:

Wilson (Arsenal), Sandy Jardine (Rangers), David Hay (Celtic), Billy Bremner (Leeds Utd, Capt), Eddie Colquohoun (Sheffield United), Pat Stanton (Hibernian), Jimmy Johnstone (Celtic), Alex Cropley (Hibernian), John O'Hare (Derby Co.), George Graham (Arsenal), Archie Gemmell (Derby Co.).

The 2–1 win against Portugal was deserved, and although Arsenal would not release me for the next international, a friendly against Belgium, I was back for the game in Amsterdam against Holland on the first day of December. I anticipated a lot of work during my second international and was not disappointed. Cruyff and Co. were brilliant, but with a bit of luck and Scottish passion, it remained 1–1 going into the last minute.

The Dutch were awarded a corner and the delivery to the near post was perfect for tempting me to collect. Barry Hulshoff's head beat my despairing hands and Holland won 2–1.

I was bitterly disappointed having played so well, and I've never been allowed to forget it by a certain Kenneth Dalglish. The great Kenny made his full international debut in the game and whenever we meet up, he reminds me that I 'threw the jerseys' in the closing seconds. I, in turn, love being able to tell everyone that I was in goal when the great Kenny Dalglish made his first full appearance for Scotland and that between us we won 104 caps. Kenny won 102 and I won two. It would have been more, but 1971–72 was a season when upsets and injuries made me start to think about my future.

Between my second appearance for Scotland and the weekend prior to our European Cup quarter-final against Ajax, we were unbeaten in eleven league games and four FA Cup ties. Our fine form had a lot to do with Bertie Mee paying a football league record of £220,000 the week before Christmas for Everton's Alan Ball. Bally had, of course, made his name as a member of the England 1966 World Cup winning squad. He was a fantastic player and an argumentative team-mate, and he hated the fact that I'd been chosen for Scotland. I soon got used to his high-pitched voice pouring scorn on my nationality. 'You, a Jock? You're no more a bleeding Jock than I am.' It was the first of many discussions that Alan and I were to have together, mostly on return coach trips from games or late at night on tours. I might not always have agreed with the little redhead, but I never failed to enjoy his company or his rhetoric.

The highlights of the early rounds in defence of the FA Cup were knocking out Swindon on their own ground, for obvious reasons, and a three-match saga with Derby County and Brian Clough. This was the season he was to gain immortality at the Baseball Ground by leading Derby to the championship. He was brash, brilliant and, in his own words, a 'big 'ed'. He bullied not only his own players when required, but the opposition when he could. A good example came in the first replay of our fifth-round tie. Having drawn 2–2 at Derby, the second meeting attracted 63,000 to Highbury. The score was 0–0 after ninety minutes and the two teams stayed around the centre circle prior to extra time. When the referee signalled the managers to leave, Cloughie walked straight into the Arsenal group who were receiving a final word from Bertie and quite deliberately collided with me and knocked me flying. He was trying to rattle me, and succeeded. I chased him and was about to punch him in return when Bob McNab stopped me. The outcome of our tie with Derby was settled at the third attempt, at Filbert Street, Leicester, when Ray Kennedy scored the only goal of the game. Cloughie was not best pleased. He didn't like the Arsenals and Manchester Uniteds of this world. Brian Clough was brilliant at making small clubs great rather than great clubs greater.

Cup games were coming thick and fast at the time, none more important than the European Cup quarter-final against Ajax. The Dutch champions were outstanding in every way and every department, from coach Rinus Michels to the brilliant Cruyff. We shocked them, though, in Amsterdam, matched them throughout ninety minutes and were unlucky to lose 2–1 as a result of a late and disputed penalty.

All we needed was a 1–0 victory at Highbury in the return. The scoreline was 1–0 but it was in Ajax's favour. Peter Marinello, replacing the suspended John Radford, had a great chance in the very first minute, but his shot was blocked. Within fifteen minutes, I called for a long cross, but the shout was lost in the roar of the crowd. George Graham didn't hear and inadvertently headed the ball into the path of Arie Haan. Ajax had gained revenge for our Fairs Cup semi-final win two seasons earlier, and our only consolation came in the fact that they went on to win the European Cup that season and the two that followed.

All that was left to aim for was as high a league position as possible and to retain the FA Cup. After disposing of Leyton Orient in the sixth round, we once again drew Stoke City in the semi-final. Surely it couldn't be as dramatic as the previous year at Hillsborough. In the event, it most certainly was but only on a personal front.

In the first few minutes, a difficult cross-cum-shot from Jimmy Greenhoff produced a desperate save at the expense of my colliding with the far post. George Armstrong had put us ahead in the first half and Stoke rarely looked like scoring. With about twenty minutes to go they were awarded a free kick, which was curled tantalisingly into the box. From the moment it was struck, it was a ball I had to take. There was a swirling wind at Villa Park and as I timed my jump alongside Stoke's John Ritchie, I realised I needed to help the ball on and away from danger rather than catch it. At the height of my jump and twisting to make contact I managed to clear the ball, but by the time I hit the floor I realised I had badly injured my knee. Fred Street the physio was always optimistic and encouraged me to stand and wait until I could get some strength back in the leg. Here we were, twenty minutes from another FA Cup final appearance and my mobility was down to zero.

A decision was taken by Bertie Mee, Fred and myself to give it a go. It was a poor decision. Every time I was asked to gather the ball in the next five minutes my leg gave way underneath me. On about the third occasion Peter Storey ran up to me and screamed abuse, assuming I had lost my nerve and was looking for a way out. For the fourth time I tried to play on but a minute later the decision proved foolhardy. A low cross, which normally would have been mine, concerned Peter Simpson enough for him to attempt to clear, but he succeeded in turning it past me into the net for Stoke's equaliser.

At last, Bertie Mee realised I had become more of a hindrance than a help. John Radford, who in training had always fancied his chances as a keeper, took over my jersey and performed heroically for ten minutes. By then I had been stretchered off, examined by a sports injury specialist and diagnosed with ligament damage and a ruptured cartilage. Back in London, Nigel Harris, an orthopaedic surgeon, examined my injury and surgery was booked for the next morning.

The game had ended in a draw and in the replay at Everton, John Radford scored Arsenal's winner after penalties from Greenhoff and Charlie George. I listened to the match and watched the TV highlights from my bed in the Harley Street Clinic. My recovery was expected to take a minimum of three months, very different from the short period of time it now takes after microsopic surgery, which has revolutionised the treatment of such injuries. My season was over. Any possibility of playing in successive FA Cup finals was gone, too. Geoff Barnett would be in goal. The squad put me in charge of running the players' pool. I hated it. Sums for interviews with the daily newspapers were around £100 to £150, an Esso Petroleum photo shoot brought in a princely £1,000 but the greatest amounts came from the boot and shirt companies. For wearing their equipment in an FA Cup final, the pool received £2,000. The BBC's payment for television facilities was £1,000, bringing the total amount to £10,000 to be shared between seventeen players.

The final itself against Leeds United commemorated the centenary year of the competition and the occasion was marked by the presence of Her Majesty the Queen and the Duke of Edinburgh. I had been asked to give my views on the game for BBC TV and alongside me on the gantry was Leeds' Terry Cooper, who missed the final because of a broken leg. We looked a rare pair, perched on stools, each with a leg in plaster and our crutches within handy reach. We cheered each other up until the moment the two teams emerged from the tunnel. In unison, and thankfully not on air, we both reacted in the same way. The expletive was identical. We simply felt we'd been robbed of our rightful place in the line-ups. It didn't help that the game was dreadful and settled by Allan Clarke's diving header. Geoff Barnett and I together would have struggled to keep it out.

I began the long, slow road to recovering fitness after the injury on 15 April. My return to the first team came on 25 November. Complications with the knee meant what seemed like an interminable seven months out of action. When the knee kept breaking down in training or in specially arranged games, there were serious doubts about my future. None of the treatment was pleasant and only the optimism of Fred Street kept me afloat.

Finishing fifth in the League in 1971–72 meant we just missed out on a Uefa Cup place. The new season began well enough without me, just three defeats in the first sixteen games. A couple more games were lost before I made my return against Derby at the Baseball Ground. It was the twentieth league game of the season and attracted much publicity, as much for my return as for the meeting between the two previous season's champions. The 5–0 scoreline in favour of Brian Clough's team centred on one person only – the returning Arsenal goalkeeper. The worst trait of the British press is to knock off the pedestal those they helped put in such a position. They predicted that my future in the game was in the balance and that the serious injury would hasten the end of my career. Eventually, it could be said to have done just that, but not immediately as was suggested.

The weekend after the Derby débâcle, in which, incidentally, I felt myself culpable for only one of the goals, we beat Leeds 2–1. I was more delighted at that result for my son John than myself. The press reaction after the Derby game led to him receiving a rough ride at school. Children can be unwittingly cruel and on the Monday he arrived home in tears and seemingly heartbroken. Many of his class-mates had been saying, 'Your dad's finished.' I tried to explain how unpredictable football was and how we could still chase Liverpool for the title. I said the words more out of hope than in belief.

After beating Leeds, we lost just once in the next fifteen games. In the end, we had to settle for second place in the championship, three points behind Liverpool, but right up to the season's end we were chasing a second double.

In the FA Cup we reached the semi-final and were expected to beat Sunderland, even though they were heading for promotion to the First Division. The game took place at Hillsborough and I couldn't wait for Arsenal to secure a place in a third successive final and so make up for my disappointment a year earlier.

Three things conspired in our defeat. The way Sunderland played was the main factor, with the support of the Wearsiders' fans hugely significant as well. But for once, Bertie Mee's attempts to treat players like men backfired. Frank McLintock was injured and his replacement, Jeff Blockley, was not fully fit. He should never have played but when asked by the manager if he was OK, he nodded in the affirmative. Bertie should have taken matters into his own hands. The 2–1 defeat was a bitter blow and remained so even when Sunderland surprised everyone again by winning the final against Leeds, thanks to an Ian Porterfield goal and a wonder save from Jim Montgomery.

Returning to training for the 1973–74 season, I became more aware of the difficulties I was finding with my damaged knee. My left leg had always been the natural take-off leg when I went for crosses and drove upwards off the ground. I was finding it difficult to adapt to right-foot take-off. I was also aware that I had not overcome the muscle wastage that followed the initial operation, now over a year ago, and that I couldn't fully straighten my left leg. I discussed my concerns with Fred Street, the club's specialist doctors and Bertie Mee. Their reassurances helped to a degree, but not significantly. I had nagging doubts about how long I could play at the top level. Circumstances again conspired to hasten my departure.

During the opening three months of a season, players get a good idea of whether they'll be in the running for the championship race. Seven defeats in Arsenal's opening fourteen games provided too quick an answer. There was dressing-room discontent and Bertie Mee knew it. He asked to see four of his senior players, Bob McNab, Alan Ball, George Armstrong and me. There was no Frank McLintock. He had been allowed to leave for Queens Park Rangers at the end of the previous season. Too often managers and coaches worry about a player's age and let that cloud the value that experience can give to a side. In Frank's case, he also had outstanding leadership qualities. He was to play on at Rangers for three seasons and narrowly missed another championship medal in 1976.

Bertie asked the four of us for a frank assessment of the current feelings in the dressing room. The manager was told that feelings were running high against Steve Burtenshaw as our coach. The fault really lay in the fact that we were simply in transition. Frank had gone, Jon Sammels had gone, so too had Peter Marinello, John Roberts and George Graham. The only truly promising replacement came from within our own ranks; the talent of Liam Brady was just beginning to emerge. The manager's decision was to replace Steve Burtenshaw with Bobby Campbell, who had been making a name for himself in coaching circles.

What Bobby did immediately on his arrival is still talked about by the players he faced. On his very first morning, Bobby sat the squad down in a dressing room at the London Colney training ground and, with barely an introduction, he began to tear in to the group. I was the first to be told success had made me soft and that I wasn't producing what I had shown previously. Seven months out with injury never came into his assessment. Pat Rice came next, Peter Simpson and Peter Storey followed. There was amazement and growing anger among the players. Turning to Bob McNab, Bobby Campbell was stopped in his tracks. Nabbers had had enough.

'You can stop right there,' he told the new coach. 'The majority of these lads have worked together and fought for each other for the last six seasons. We've been to three Wembley finals, one European final, won the championship and been runners-up in the League again last season. We've finished first or second in a major competition for the last six seasons and you're telling us we've gone soft. Fuck off.' With that, Bob McNab stormed out of the dressing room.

The mood in the camp was despondent and darkened within the next few days. Newspapers reported rumours of McNab's possible transfer to Wolves and the pursuit by Arsenal of three of Bobby Campbell's old players at Queens Park Rangers. They included goalkeeper Phil Parkes.

On the day of the rumours I waited until training was finished before cornering Bobby Campbell and Bertie Mee. I knew my knee was good enough to play on in the top division but I didn't want to play for any other club. I was determined I'd have a say in my own destiny. My mind was working overtime when I got home, and Megs bore the brunt, as usual, of my concern. What was going on at the club, and the manner it was being carried out, was not the Arsenal way. We sat and debated the possibilities, which by now included a half promise from BBC TV Sport that 'when you are ready to call it a day playing, let us know because we'd like you on board'. I was now giving serious thought not so much to whether I could carry on playing but whether I even wanted to, and for whom. A further consideration was the testimonial game that was due to me after being an Arsenal player for almost twelve years. The trouble was I was in a queue behind George Armstrong, Peter Storey, Peter Simpson and John Radford. Any firm decision was put on hold for the time being, but meanwhile I started to set up meetings with my agent Reg Hayter and the BBC.

Megs made it quite clear that whatever decision I finally took, she would support it. The form of the team did nothing to help the dilemma I faced. We were capable of playing the brilliant, the ordinary and the dreadful. Results over the season read: played 42, won 14, drawn 14, lost 14. We finished fifth, 20 points behind champions Leeds.

Midway through the season there was an FA Cup tie that helped make up my mind. We were drawn against Aston Villa in the fourth round. The tie took place at Highbury and we were being outplayed, losing 1–0. The opposing centre-forward, Sammy Morgan, had stopped me taking a quick free kick on two or three occasions. The red mist descended partly as a reaction to his gamesmanship, but mainly because our Arsenal team looked as if they were preparing to go down to defeat meekly. Under the full gaze of the ITV cameras, I was caught angrily gesticulating at Sammy to move backwards to the obligatory ten yards to allow the free kick to be taken. He refused. Referee Clive Thomas quickly booked him. Five minutes later a pass into our eighteen-yard area left the ball tantalisingly placed between Sammy Morgan and me. I dived head first, he kicked, I won the ball, his feet connected with my head.

It was the last thing I recall until I heard Fred Street asking me to tell him how many fingers he was holding up in front of me. I was quite unaware of my surroundings or the fact that Clive Thomas had sent Sammy Morgan off for dangerous play. Against ten men and with an extra determination in our step, the Arsenal team equalised to earn a replay at Villa Park.

Press interest centred on the sending-off incident. The Villa manager Vic Crowe openly accused me of deliberately 'taking a dive' and getting Sammy Morgan dismissed. The version of the event put forward by the press sickened me. They had no compunction about savaging my reputation, which had been so well nurtured by them.

We lost the replay at Villa Park and Sammy Morgan scored

one of the goals. I was pilloried throughout the game and accepted the crowd abuse with as much good grace as I could muster, but I was badly affected by the experience. Only once before in my career had the opposition been so hostile towards me. That was in October 1971 when a collision with Hugh Fisher left the Southampton player with a badly broken leg. It had seemed so innocuous but as I picked myself up from the floor and went towards Hughie, he screamed, 'You bastard! You've bust my leg!' I couldn't believe it but his instinctive reaction fired a few of his team and a section of the crowd. I was totally exonerated for the accident and generous apologies were forthcoming. Two seasons previously at Burnley, it had been me with the broken bone.

I discussed the impact that the Sammy Morgan saga had upon me with Bertie Mee and he was shocked that I was now considering retirement from the game. He tempted me with talk of my testimonial and a new contract. I told him I'd think about it.

A week or two later I met Sam Leitch at a restaurant in Notting Hill. Sam was Head of Sport but also presented 'Football Preview' at the start of the BBC's flagship programme, 'Grandstand'. He told me he was going to vacate the presenter's chair and concentrate on his senior role as Head of Sport. The big Scottish journalist invited me to take his place. It was an amazing offer. The only professional footballer to be involved in television sport up to that moment was Jimmy Hill, who was the analyst on ITV's 'Big Match' alongside presenter Brian Moore.

The Wilson household had much to consider. Family and selected friends were taken into our confidence. The Arsenal squad and management were unaware that my playing career might be drawing to a close. A big drop in salary was one of the biggest hurdles to be faced. My Arsenal contract by now guaranteed maximum loyalty and incentive bonuses. The BBC's offer to present 'Football Preview' couldn't extend beyond £4,500 per annum.

It didn't totally deter me, especially when a chance meeting with Eric Morley led to the offer to a job with Mecca, the company that had dancehalls and clubs right around the country. Eric loved football and clearly liked me. He told me how I could be a help to Mecca, the beauty contests – including Miss World – and possibly his television programme 'Come Dancing'. At the latter suggestion I begged to differ. I felt that if I accepted the BBC's job offer, it would be wrong for the presenter of 'Football Preview' to be a co-presenter of 'Come Dancing'. Quite simply, the two were not compatible. My quickstep was strictly confined to a goalmouth. He reluctantly agreed but the offer of around £6,000 pa was still there. I thanked him profusely and told him I'd be in touch.

Events were now moving quickly. The combined salaries of Mecca and the BBC would not come near to matching Arsenal's bonus-related contract but my fitness, and thus playing career, was beginning to be a concern and here was a chance to secure the future for my family.

The promise of what lay ahead clearly outweighed the present and immediate prospects. My international career had come and gone with Tommy Docherty's defection to Manchester United. His successor, Willie Ormond, was said to be biased against selection of English-based and English-born players and never came to see me play. My dream of making the Scotland squad for the 1974 World Cup finals was gone.

The first person to be told about my decision to retire, outside my family, was Bertie Mee. I was unprepared for the obstacles and temptations he quickly put in front of me. The biggest was my testimonial, due to any player who shows club loyalty beyond ten years. 'Leave and you forgo your testimonial' was put to me very forcibly. He understood my concern to create a future for my family. He knew I would never play for any other club but he also knew the testimonial would benefit Megs and the children immensely.

'I need one more year, Bob,' he said, 'just one more year from you.'

I respected Bertie Mee and he, in turn, respected me. I told him that Megs and I would have one more discussion but I warned him my mind was almost certainly made up already.

The *Sun* newspaper, for whom I had written a weekly column for two or three years, broke the news on Friday, 19 April 1974. 'Bob Wilson Quits Arsenal' was the headline. I didn't like it. Sub-editors write headlines and they often bear no resemblance to the story beneath the block type. 'Quit' was a powerful word, but I never quit on anything in my life. 'Retires' was too soft and gentle a word for tabloid use, then and now.

One more terrible event had helped my decision and made me appreciate even more the fragility of life and the need to enjoy it without regrets. On Sunday, 3 March 1974 a phone call from Robbie Brightwell informed us that our mutual Loughborough College friend John Cooper had been on board the Turkish Airlines DC 10 that had crashed just after noon that day. It was the world's worst air disaster with 345 people perishing in a wooded area just outside Paris.

'Coop', as John was endearingly known, was one of our best friends. His heroics in gaining two silver medals at the Tokyo Olympics in 1964 would never be forgotten. A few months before his death we had celebrated his wedding to Jo, the event especially arranged for a Sunday so Megs and I could both attend. I had supported him throughout the brilliance of his athletics career, and he had similarly stood shoulder to shoulder with me throughout my moments of joy and turmoil as a goalkeeper for Arsenal.

His death was devastating for Jo, his family and friends. The manner of it was cruel, not just because of its ferocity, but because he had originally been booked on a different flight. Having represented his company, adidas, at the France v. England rugby international, he'd arrived at Orly airport to be offered a single seat on the ill-fated Turkish Airlines flight to London. Somebody had missed the flight. Coop took the vacant place.

The final weeks at Highbury were emotional, littered with feelings of self-doubt. My decision to go was public and Arsenal were already looking for a replacement in the guise of former Manchester United keeper Jimmy Rimmer, who was on loan to Swansea. Jimmy joined up with the squad prior to our game at Anfield, three weeks from the end of the season.

I had always enjoyed my appearances at Liverpool, win or lose. Bill Shankly's presence helped the occasions. In the team hotel before the game, just prior to his team-talk, Bertie Mee took me aside and asked me if I'd be prepared not to play. He knew how much I loved Anfield and that I was one of only two ever-presents, with Ray Kennedy, in the team that season. I wanted to say no, but realised the dilemma Bertie faced. Reluctantly, I stepped down and agreed to help Jimmy Rimmer through the ordeal of his trial game. He was a fine goalkeeper and his performance in our 1–0 victory showed it. Bertie asked me what I'd thought and while paying the newcomer many compliments, I expressed my surprise and concern at the generous slug of whisky or brandy the keeper took before playing so well.

All that was left for me were two games, at Coventry and at Highbury against Queens Park Rangers. The few days leading up to my last game were full of reflection. In the eleven seasons since arriving at the marble halls, I had worn the Arsenal shirt 532 times in total, of which 309 were in major first-team competitions. From the time I made the breakthrough, a seven-year spell, Arsenal had finished winners or runners-up in a major competition in all but one season. It was an amazing reward for a lad from Chesterfield who had natural agility, was quick, had a good pair or hands, but who had to work like mad at the other key areas required of a top-class keeper. The diamond in my game was the ability to dive at feet. It looked courageous but wasn't; it was a God-given asset. Being so spectacular, it caught the eye and lifted me above the pack. It brought many serious injuries in its wake – more than twenty stitches to head, face and body, a punctured lung, broken arm, dislocated elbow, chipped shoulder bone, broken ankle, two dislocated fingers, a lacerated left ear, six broken ribs and a torn cartilage and ligaments. The long-term effect of many of those injuries hasn't lessened the pleasure of the achievements gained.

Preparations for my farewell appearance at Highbury were unusual. I would normally lock myself away from public gaze, but this time I was happy to go along with the media scrum of interviews and photographs. Had we been in with a chance of winning a trophy, I wouldn't have smiled or talked so freely. Only when I arrived at my beloved Highbury did the enormity of my decision to retire from playing really begin to hit me.

I was shocked by the number of good-luck messages and needed little warm-up after the back-slapping and handshakes that followed my every move. Once I was in the sanctuary of the familiar home dressing room, though, I went back into automatic pilot. Only one aspect of my pre-match preparation had changed from the time I made my breakthrough into the top flight. Originally, I had taken Bert Trautmann's autobiography with me to every game. It was called *Steppes to Wembley*, a play on words relating to the great German keeper. Without it, I thought I would feel naked and vulnerable, but when it went missing one day and I still went out and played well, it was the end of my superstition about good-luck charms.

I was not alone in changing and preparing in a methodical and well-practised way. What is good preparation and what is superstition is too close to call. Jacket went first followed by tie, shirt, trousers, shoes and finally pants. Naked, there were never any inhibitions in a dressing room. Putting on playing kit also followed a ritual – jock strap, socks, shorts, boots, undershirt and, much later, goalkeeping jersey. Checking my thin cotton gloves and cap was left to the end. My warm-up was similarly exact and executed with military precision. It was conducted in the bath area, a series of stretch routines and running on the spot exercises with the sound of metal studs resounding off the marble floors. Next came my handling work, hurling the ball at the walls and catching the rebound, just as I had done as a kid off the garage doors in Ashgate Road, Chesterfield.

On the way back into the main dressing room, I would stop at a wash basin and splash cold water over my face, clearing my eyes. I would then put on my jersey and move close to the tiled wall a yard or two from where I changed. The final act of preparing my mind involved charging that wall with right and left shoulder as hard as I could. The aim was to shake my system and make sure I wouldn't be 'caught cold' by any shoulder charge from the opposition, as I had in my initial first-team games. All that was left was to do the rounds and shake hands, pat backs or simply wish good luck to the team. As a senior player, I enjoyed adding my voice to the skipper's, manager's and coach's words of encouragement.

By now my nerves were at breaking point. It had never been any different but I knew that the moment I hit daylight the worries would instantly dissipate. Bertie reminded me that I was to be presented with a silver cannon by the club's chairman Denis Hill-Wood and that the QPR players would be lining the way. Even now, all I wanted from the evening was to play really well. It was not the moment to doubt my decision to go or to let my vulnerable emotional streak run amok.

The sound of the bell increased the heartbeat. It was followed by the familiar shouts, 'Come on, let's go, get into them, let's play!' It had been almost twelve years to the day since Billy Wright had led me down the same corridor to the tunnel. Much had happened in that time, most of it totally unexpected. On the way down the tunnel we passed the halfway house players' room where wives and friends of the team would meet up before and after matches. It was here, early in my time at Highbury, that Frank McLintock had remarked on the nice company I kept after he'd seen me chatting animatedly to a small guy with a lived-in face.

'Do you know who that is?' Frank had asked.

'No, but he's a really nice guy isn't he?' was my reply.

'Oh yeah, that's Frankie Fraser,' said Frank.

'Who's Frankie Fraser? What does he do?' I asked.

'He shoots people,' Frank said with a laugh.

'What do you mean, he shoots people?' was my naïve response.

'Bang, bang, you're dead,' was our captain's telling final words on my meeting with one of the infamous Kray twins' hitmen, who was an Arsenal fan.

Now I was taking in every sight and sound, passing the club chairman *en route* as he waited to join us on the pitch. I knew the silver cannon was reserved for special presentations and only when I saw it in his hand did the significance of this moment hit me fair and square between the eyes.

The noise as we emerged from the tunnel was, as ever, inspirational, the moment when our amazing fans provided the support that was the backbone of our latest quest for victory in the name of Arsenal Football Club. Strangely for me, there were no tears of emotion. I was told other members of my family and friends were less stoic, especially my eldest son John, who was inconsolable that his dad would, after this evening, no longer be wearing the No. 1 jersey.

For most footballers, playing a last game is the end of a dream. It was different for me because the dream had been fulfilled and there was a possibility of an exciting 'after life'. In part, my decision had been made for me by a dodgy left knee and an unshakeable loyalty to the club I played for. I could have carried on somewhere but I knew my injuries and style of play had already reduced my effectiveness. I was already on a slippery downward slope.

The correctness of my decision to leave at the top was emphasised as Rangers England keeper, Phil Parkes, shook my hand. Had he been captured by Bertie Mee and Bobby Campbell at the start of the season, this moment of farewell may not even have happened. Leaving the game of football presents a desperate challenge for the majority of professionals but for me it simply signalled a journey to fresh fields.

I was just thirty-three years old, the date was 30 April 1974, as I ran out for the last time as a first-team player in this the final match of the season, against Queens Park Rangers. When 42,000 people turned up at Highbury for a game that meant nothing as far as the championship was concerned, I knew that the fans had appreciated my efforts.

In the match programme on that poignant evening, Bertie Mee paid me a very great compliment when he wrote:

Bob Wilson has all the hallmarks that place him above his fellow keepers. First of all, he has a very high standard of consistency. Of course he makes mistakes sometimes, but I can say, in all honesty – and I mean every word of it – that during our double year, I do not remember Bob making one mistake. This must have been worth 14 points to us over the season. He is a player with great courage and his enthusiasm for the game has never wavered. For a manager, he is the ideal team man. He certainly takes his place in the Hall of Fame with the great Arsenal goalkeepers of the past, and will be very difficult to replace.

Back in the dressing room after my last game – a 1–1 draw in which Alan Ball broke his leg – I read that tribute, thanked Bertie and the rest of the lads for their kindness and support and picked up the telegrams off my bench. Staring out at me on the top of the pile were the words, 'Good luck, play well, keep 'em out, have a good game.' Those were the words John, Anna and Robert had said to their dad, loyally, as they kissed me goodbye before every game. They had served me well.

ne time – the Arsenal goalkeeper, with trademark rolled up sleeves.

Training session before the Scotland–Portugal international.

The beginning of the end, a torn cartilage and ligaments in the 1972 FA Cup semi-final versus Stoke City.

ughborough's gymnastic training comes in ful at Chelsea.

Superstars on the beach in the Algarve, Portugal. Robert and John meet Johan Cruyff and Eusebio in 1973.

ways packing a punch – Henry Cooper proves his cartilage problem is over as we both over from surgery in 1972.

Charity cricket match – Arsenal versus Spurs 1972. *Left to right, standing*: Jeff Blockley, Charlie George, me and Alan Ball. *Sitting*: Geoff Barnett, Bob McNab and Peter Storey.

Chairman Denis Hill-Wood presents me with a silver cannon before my last game for Arsenal, against Queens Park Rangers in April 1974. It was later stolen.

Home in Hertfordshire after retiring as a player, ready for the next phase of my life.

Fiddling with early logging equipment for 'Match of the Day'. It was much quicker when videos arrived on the scene.

Presenting 'Grandstand' was one of the great challenges in the television world – five and a half hours of live sport and no autocue. Frank Bough was professional to his fingertips.

'Young man, you said we wouldn't be champions!' – Brian Clough proves his point to the 'Football Focus' presenter.

Accosting a likely looking interviewee the run on Tower Bridge as part of the BBC's coverage of the London Marath

...vays a pleasure to interview Arsenal players, here it's captain Pat Rice prior to the 1979 ...Cup final victory over Manchester United.

...holiday with Megs, John, Robert and Anna.

John and Robert with Anna on her wedding day, 26 September 1992.

11
The Beeb

'The nice thing about egotists is that they
don't talk about other people'

Lucille S. Harper

No job, however glamorous, could adequately replace the one
I was leaving. My dream had always been to be a footballer. I
had fulfilled the dream. It was the best job in the world. Success
was an unexpected bonus. Never had I anticipated that my face
would be known throughout the British Isles in and around
those circles of the population who were interested in sport.

Even more of a surprise was what happened next. It didn't
happen overnight, but over the next twenty-eight years many
more people came to recognise my features, if not the name
behind them, such is the power of television, a medium that
people love or hate, but can rarely ignore. For twenty of those
years I worked for an organisation respected throughout the
broadcasting world, but not without its faults. The Beeb, as
the BBC is affectionately known, retains a certain allure and
mystique that is beyond the capability of its rivals. It is no
longer able to claim that it is the best organisation in its field,
but it likes to think it can.

For the vast majority of years that I remained in its employ, I
was challenged, satisfied and proud of my association. In return,
I gained a lot of respect, some affection but ultimately was taken
for granted and had to leave. There never was, or is, any feeling

of ill will between us. The BBC will remain my spiritual home when it comes to talking about the third of my career moves. Schoolteacher to footballer to TV sports presenter would be an accepted route in today's media. In 1974, the progression was viewed with scepticism and a shade of envy in some journalistic quarters.

As a public service, the values at the BBC three decades ago were different from now. Their standards were high and there was an air of Oxbridge about the corporation in both the way it was run and those who produced, edited and presented the programmes. In short, it regarded itself as the flagbearer for broadcasting. Criticism of anyone who displayed a broad colloquial accent was common but the advent of the Beatles era changed all that. Michael Parkinson was one of the early presenters to break the mould of those with cultured accents. It says a great deal for Parky that his strong Yorkshire voice still rules the airwaves in the new millennium.

On my arrival, I received no special training whatsoever for the role I was about to undertake, just a morning visit to understand how autocue, the method of prompting the scripted words, worked. I had, of course, been inside TV studios on many occasions, as part of a World Cup panel or guest on football programmes. Indeed, my second appearance ever, in 1969 in the BBC's 'Sportsnight' studios, could have been my last.

Invited to comment on a wonderful display of goalkeeping by the Romanian keeper who had faced England, I got carried away with the word 'tremendous', so much so that when I got home, full of myself and my appearance on the programme, I was surprised that Megs' congratulations were tempered by a cautionary word.

'You'll have to be a little more careful in the use of certain words,' she told me.

'What on earth do you mean?' was the edgy response.

'Well, for instance, when describing the keeper's saves or Bobby Charlton's strikes you said "tremendous" rather a lot.'

I disputed the fact and said I couldn't have said it more than a couple of times.

'Actually, you said it thirteen times,' Megs replied.

I was convinced only when I watched, highly embarrassed, the video recording she had made of my appearance.

Early in my television career I was excited by the possibility of using recordings to analyse players and teams, and by the potential of logging match action. Initially, I had been provided with a Heath Robinson contraption that spooled 16mm film. Bulky spools, about 16ins in circumference, were transported from the BBC to our home almost daily. In a time-consuming process I would wind the film with one hand and watch the match action through a central viewer approximately 6ins square. I would set the counter below the viewer to zero and log the timing of every piece of action that I considered appropriate. Eventually, the BBC changed from using film to video and the onerous task was transformed by the installation of a video recorder at home. For twenty years I was responsible for producing logs of every goal, save, close-up or worthwhile moment caught by the cameras.

Apart from Sam Leitch, the men at the Beeb who encouraged my employment were seasoned professionals Paul Fox, Bryan Cowgill and the editor of 'Grandstand' Alan Hart. The first thing they did was to find me an editor, a great film-maker Bob Abrahams, and the second was to sit down together to find a new name for Sam's old programme. We settled on 'Football Focus' and for the entire time I was a BBC man, it was the one programme associated with me alone. I never missed a show in those twenty years and travelled the length and breadth of the country collecting stories and interviews.

My earliest days in the new job produced as big a culture shock as is imaginable. Only my enthusiasm and optimism kept me going as I struggled to learn the basics of presentation. Up until that moment I had felt comfortable in a TV studio because I simply had to sit, watch match action, listen to questions and answer them. From the moment I arrived in the summer of 1974, I was expected to write the scripts for 'Football Focus', and instantly cope with the technicalities of talk-back and autocue while 'driving' the programme from the presenter's seat. Some of the early lessons learned will haunt, and amuse me for ever.

On the Friday before my first programme, I went to the 'Grandstand' office in Shepherds Bush to discuss the following day's running order with Bob Abrahams. To my surprise, Bob told me he was going off to put together a film item and that he'd pop back regularly to see how I was getting on with the script. The only advice I received was to keep my links down to fifteen seconds, twenty seconds maximum. There were usually twelve or thirteen links, dependent on whether there was a studio guest or not, to fit into a twenty-minute programme, as it was then. It doesn't take many words to fill that time, the task becoming more difficult when trying to incorporate names of players and the fixture being previewed together with a touch of humour or interest.

My first effort took me more than four hours to get together. Alan Hart, 'Grandstand's' main editor asked to see the script and, as I sat in front of him, he read my words quietly and then, like a schoolmaster, proceeded to put his pen through the majority of my efforts. With great patience he proceeded to explain, for the first and only time, some of the peculiarities required of television scripts. At that time, 'Grandstand' depended hugely on still photos or photo slides. There was very little use of moving pictures outside the prepared film items. Consequently, Alan explained that when referring to any player in the script, the name must precede everything else so that the viewer had time to recognise to whom and what you were referring. In my initial script there were names at the end of sentences, not at the start, and the use of the personal pronoun 'I' was apparent on far too numerous occasions.

Cruel though it seemed at the time, I decided Alan Hart's way of teaching me was effective. The finished version of my first 'Focus' script was eventually accepted at seven o'clock on that Friday night, some nine hours after I began to write.

Nerves were biting at me the following day as I sat in the 'Grandstand' studio, awaiting rehearsal. It was the first time I had worn an earpiece, a plastic moulding that fits inside the ear and through which the production gallery keeps in touch. The presenter would be counted down into items that were to be shown and, at the zero count, should have ended his link. Today, there is no countdown, only an instant run of videotape.

I was studying my script on autocue when the producer, Brian Venner, decided to start rehearsal. Lots of advice and best wishes were forthcoming since everyone present appreciated I was nervous. They knew what a risk the BBC were taking employing a professional footballer for the first time in such a role. The first words came out pretty well, but just as I was starting to relax, my concentration was broken by the producer's voice in my ear, shouting 'Run TK'. Startled by the command, I stopped speaking in mid sentence and, turning my head away from the camera towards some invisible person, said, 'Pardon?' Quickly, through my earpiece, I was told to keep looking at the camera and carry on talking.

Frank Bough was presenting the 'Grandstand' programme on my debut. With his help I survived my first programme, but when watching a re-run, I didn't have to be told that I looked like a block of wood. There was plenty of room for improvement. Frank Bough was one of the first great sports presenters I worked with in my twenty years at the BBC. He was a great professional and had an uncanny knack of making the presenting task look easy. Inadvertently, he embarrassed me once in the opening weeks of my new job.

After presenting 'Focus', it had been decided that I should go off to some big match in the afternoon and return by car in time to deliver a one-minute report to camera at the end of 'Grandstand'. Two things made me argue against attempting such a difficult task so early in my new career. One was the fact that you often had to leave the game twenty minutes before the end in order to reach the studio in time. The other was my lack of experience in delivering a one-minute report without the assistance of an autocue. Yet again, Alan Hart decided the sooner I tried it the better. The first game I was to report on involved Arsenal; they thought that would make it easier.

Leading up to the day, I asked for guidance from experienced commentators Barry Davies, John Motson and David Coleman. The best advice came from David. 'Make sure your opening line includes no big or difficult words. If you make a mess of the first sentence, you'll struggle. So remember, easy, small words.' Two minutes into the game at Highbury, Alan Ball scored. Fifteen minutes later, he scored again, playing brilliantly. Remembering David Coleman's advice, I wrote down an opening line without any big words, which I could easily memorise for my one-minute report. It read, 'I have just got back from Highbury where Alan Ball has been the star of the day.' As the game progressed and Frank Stapleton scored a third Arsenal goal, I was continually repeating to myself the opening line, 'I have just got back from Highbury where Alan Ball has been the star of the day.' I must have repeated it to myself fifty times or more by the time I had been driven back to Lime Grove and taken the lift to the 'Grandstand' studio on the fourth floor.

As I entered, Frank Bough was just leading to a match report from Barry Davies at Goodison Park. I had less than a minute to get into my seat beside Frank, who was studying the afternoon's results and scorers and taking no notice of my own mutterings,

'I have just got back from Highbury where Alan Ball has been the star of the day.' I don't think I have ever felt as nervous, even walking out at Wembley and Hampden as I did at that moment. All I needed to do was to follow David Coleman's advice. Deliver the first line without a stutter and everything would flow. Suddenly I heard Frank beside me say, 'Sounds like a great game at Goodison. Now it's time to hear about Arsenal against Manchester United and here, just back from Highbury, where I gather Alan Ball's been the star of the day Bob?' Unwittingly, Frank had delivered my opening line. As my mouth dropped open and improvisation deserted me, I heard myself utter the words, 'Yes, indeed Frank, I have just got back from Highbury where Alan Ball has been the star of the day.'

I marvel now that after those early amateurish experiences, I eventually came to present not just 'Focus' but the complete 'Grandstand' programme on more than 200 occasions – five and a half hours of live sport and no autocue. It was one of the supreme challenges in the television world. The best of those privileged to fill the role were David Coleman, Frank Bough, Steve Rider and Des Lynam. Each was different in their approach but all had star quality. Frank was like a favourite uncle and I was fascinated by his pre-programme warm-up when he concentrated simply on perfecting his opening greeting of 'Hello' or 'Good afternoon'.

David Coleman's advantage was that he had been a fine amateur athlete. He understood the emotions and reactions of sportsmen and women. None of the others ever mastered the results sequence towards the end of 'Grandstand' like David did. Steve Rider's presentation was flawless and I don't ever recall him losing his way or mixing up his words. As for Des Lynam, he was a consummate actor and had a unique delivery that embraced whimsy and fun.

There have been other excellent BBC presenters of course,

including Harry Carpenter. There was a spell when boxing received a lot of coverage and Harry was perfect for the midweek 'Sportsnight' programme. His boxing commentaries added great authority.

I unashamedly watched and learned from each and every one of the presenters I respected. I also learned from my own mistakes, although occasionally slip-ups are inevitable on live television. Another early *faux pas* would have resulted in a red face if I'd actually realised what I'd said at the time. In the middle of 'Focus', my hotline phone went off. Bob Abrahams told me some news had come through from Old Trafford about their striker Joe Jordan and that he'd now definitely be playing, when everyone expected him to miss the game through injury. With thirty seconds available and no time to put the information on autocue, I found myself thinking of two different ways of giving the news. I ran out of time and was caught in two minds. I meant to say, 'We've just heard Joe Jordan has just passed a late fitness test.' Instead, as I heard the producer say, 'Cut to Bob,' I came out with, 'Before we move on, we've just heard that Joe Jordan has just pissed a late fatness test.' Unaware, I ploughed on with the script but couldn't understand the laughter I was hearing from the gallery through my earpiece.

Frankly, I'm surprised the BBC showed so much patience with me during those early days. The thing that saved me was my inside knowledge of the game of football. It was the only advantage I had going for me over the other presenters, who all had a background as professional journalists.

Within a very short period of time I began to understand the content of sports programmes. Televised sport should be, first and foremost, entertaining. If along the route it can educate and provoke thought among the viewers, that is a bonus. Television as a whole is a very subjective medium. You either like certain programmes and their presenters or you don't. I believe that I survived the first year or two at the BBC because the public already knew and liked me as a footballer. The press were less supportive, maybe because I had appeared to gate-crash the system. Arguments will always persist about whether a professional journalist is better suited to presenting sport on TV than individuals who have become national heroes. It is just one area of resentment that exists in an industry full of egos. I like to think there is now a place for people from both fields. As far as sportsmen and women go, I'm sure there are very few viewers who don't appreciate the presenting skills and knowledgeable insights of Peter Alliss, Sue Barker, Roger Black, Clare Balding and, of course, Gary Lineker.

I owe a great debt to Des Lynam for his understanding of the true worth of sportsmen in the key role of presentation. During one of the BBC's Olympic Games stints, when Des presented the prime-time coverage and I presented the day-time schedule, I made reference to his script with a degree of awe and envy. His words appeared so superior and adroit to mine. He listened to me and remarked, 'I've only got the words. You've got the inside knowledge. How do you think the viewers would take to me talking about pitch conditions or technicalities?' The advice was a great help to me and I carried on doing what I knew best and Des always concentrated on his unique strengths.

Only once, to my knowledge, during my time at the Beeb did I come close to getting the sack. It was at the same time as Des helped my confidence. Arriving in the editorial office at five in the morning, the place was buzzing with the overnight success in Los Angeles of Daley Thompson in the Olympic decathlon. My editor for the daytime programme was Brian Barwick, who was also, by then, editor of 'Football Focus'. He was a scouser, idolised Liverpool Football Club, had a great eye for what was good on screen and was extremely ambitious. The beginning of our morning programme was going to be on Daley's gold medal. Brian asked if I'd watched the medal ceremony. I told him I had and was surprised at Daley's apparent rudeness during the playing of the national anthem. He appeared to be whistling at one point and talking to people behind him throughout. Instead of just accepting that Daley Thompson was a laid-back character, Brian and I decided to insert a line about his disregard for the anthem. Although we both agreed the words, the buck stops with the presenter. Over the pictures of Daley Thompson on the rostrum, I delivered the following; 'Brilliant, brilliant Daley Thompson. I just wish he'd shown a little more respect for the national anthem.'

By the time we came off the air, Brian and I had been summoned to the office of the Controller of BBCTV, Bill Cotton. Brian told me we were in trouble and that the script line had led to an unprecedented reaction in phone calls to the switchboard. My role as presenter was supposed to reflect the voice of the BBC and I had rather stuck my neck out by giving a contentious opinion.

For some reason the meeting with Bill Cotton was delayed and I went home fearing for my job. Megs, as ever, thought the comment made was justifiable. She also fended off the numerous phone calls from the press, looking for a quote from me as they started to pursue a good story. As the evening news bulletin began, we were very deflated but by the end of it we knew my remark had been overshadowed. The main story on the news surrounded a press conference given by Daley following his decathlon victory, when he wore a vest emblazoned with words that suggested that Carl Lewis was gay. It was an unwise jibe at the great American athlete and was received badly by the host nation.

Brian Barwick and I never did get to see Mr Cotton, but received an admonishment and warning not to step over the line again. Interestingly, and as a direct result of the press follow-up to my rash comment, I received almost a thousand letters about the incident. They took me a whole month to reply to personally and were split almost equally between letters of condemnation at my words and letters of support. With time and experience behind me, I think it was perhaps stupid to question a national hero at the moment of his greatest triumph.

Being controversial is appealing to most television editors. They search endlessly for guests who, if not controversial, deliver opinions with conviction and passion. Just before and just after I arrived at Television Centre, the BBC's favourite analyst was Brian Clough. He was brash, brilliant and too opinionated for his own good, but his success at Derby had more or less given him *carte blanche* to say whatever he liked. We all laughed and listened to Cloughie, even when he was totally wrong.

One example of his over the top opinions was the view he expressed about Poland's goalkeeper, Jan Tomaszewski, after England had been knocked out of the World Cup. Totally ignoring the brilliance of Tomaszewski in keeping out numerous shots, albeit in an unorthodox way, Brian insisted in calling him 'a clown'. The media in general loved the description and the sarcasm in its delivery. Jan Tomaszewski went on to become the only keeper in a World Cup finals tournament to save two penalties and, playing brilliantly throughout, finished in a team that took third place. It is a good example of the thin line that exists between good journalism and sensationalism.

Both BBC and ITV executives courted Cloughie for years, such was his magnetic appeal, but I felt sorry for him. Both organisations always put him under too much pressure. In every single appearance he was expected to come out with a dramatic Tomaszewski-type statement.

Who is good and bad is a matter of opinion. In my three decades in the industry, I have seen and listened to a wide diversification of punditry, which is the term given to analysis. The role of analyst has become an increasingly dangerous one because of the number of cameras covering controversial incidents. The pitfalls come with the tendency to condemn players instantly and without recourse. Only the footballer involved in debateable moments knows whether any dubious contact has been made and to what extent. There is huge responsibility on pundits because their view can quickly inflame and colour the truth. Over the years, those best placed to talk about all the areas of the game, management, coaching and playing, have been Jimmy Hill, Brian Clough, Terry Venables and, during major tournaments, Bobby Robson. The vast majority of the current experts have never managed, or coached at, a football club.

Jimmy Hill's contribution to television has been almost as great as his contribution to the game. One of the best Professional Football Association union leaders, he became a successful football manager at Coventry and was Head of Sport at London Weekend Television, as well as ITV's top analyst, before moving to BBC Sport. I don't understand why Jimmy Hill has never received a knighthood for services to football. Very few recipients have been more deserving than he is. He is one of the greatest characters I have met and worked alongside. For about ten years, Jimmy presented 'Match of the Day' while I sat alongside him, bringing the day's football news. The programme, with its catchy title tune, was a national institution; at least it was when it used to go on air at ten o'clock every Saturday night. Once the executives at the BBC started, in their infinite wisdom, to move the starting time to 10.15, 10.30, 10.45 on an irregular basis, the programme's ratings, often surpassing ten million viewers prior to the change of time, plummeted dramatically. 'If it ain't broke, don't fix it' was a saying completely ignored by the BBC.

Working with Jimmy was a lively experience. His enthusiasm for the game of football never wavered; his views were nearly always sound. Occasionally, he would go over the top. Laughter was never far away when we were preparing or presenting 'Match of the Day'. From the outset of my television career, I had been told to check the autocue prior to starting time.

The girls who tried to decipher my long-hand scrawl could not be blamed if the occasional letters in a word I'd written were misread. So I always checked scripts scrupulously. Sometimes Jimmy was just too busy and consequently we were treated to a few unusual moments.

One night, the autocue girl misread the 'a' in the word 'same' for an 'o'. Jimmy didn't check his script and consequently came out with 'That's all for tonight. "Match of the Day" some time next week. Goodnight.' Even funnier was when the letter 'l' was missing in his final link telling the nation that the clocks needed to be put back. There was no time for him to retrieve his error by the time the 'Match of the Day' end titles began. 'Oh, and don't forget to put your cocks back. Goodnight.'

Those of us who were in the studio one Saturday night when all the fire alarms sounded were treated to a JH classic. The noise was deafening but we were still on air. Various make-up girls, camera crew and floor assistants were advised to leave the studio. Calm as you like, Jimmy turned to me and said, 'Bob, what shall we do?' Somewhat flustered I said, 'Jim, I think we should get the hell out of here.' Quick as a flash came the reply, 'No, no, we can't do that. The nation needs us!'

Where Jimmy Hill's achievements in football thoroughly merited an ego, the television industry is inundated with individuals, in front of camera and behind, who too quickly believe in their own power when they find a modicum of success. It is a highly competitive arena but, unlike football where good performances demand inclusion in the first team, television accomplishment is much more subjective. A presenter's skills aren't always the main criteria when it comes to a deserved promotion. Decisions are in the hands of executives, heads of department, editors and even artist's agents. Sometimes huge pressures are put on television executives by powerful agencies who have several artists on their books, one of them an established star. Agencies will always have more bargaining power than individual artists representing themselves.

I have learned that survival is the main goal in the television world. Whether you like it or not, or whether it suits your personality or not, you must develop a tough skin. Success can be hugely rewarding; disappointments, for all but a few, are more common. During twenty years at the BBC I resigned or prepared to leave the Corporation on three occasions. The harder I worked, the more I felt I was being taken for granted. Had the rewards been lucrative, I might have been less irate, but they weren't.

To supplement my early salary I accepted the offer from Eric Morley to work for Mecca. We had an agreement that I would work for them when BBC commitments and programming schedules allowed. I was given an executive's office on Oxford Street, but quickly realised that sitting in it or touring the various dancehalls around the country was not for me – and I never did get the hang of the quickstep. The money kept me there for a year or more – that and Eric's insistence that I would grow into the job.

Part of my remit involved working on the beauty contests that culminated in the Morleys jewel in the crown, Miss World. In the time I was on board, a beautiful Welsh girl called Helen Morgan won her way through regional events and became Miss UK. Helen eventually won the Miss World title and my involvement with the contest ensured her presence at the 'Grandstand' studios the following day. Her appearance was well received by all involved, but we were shocked later that day to learn that she had been stripped of the title only a day after she had been crowned. It emerged that she had a baby, something that she had hidden from the Morleys and in contravention of the Miss World rules.

It was while I was in Blackpool helping with the Miss UK contest that I received a phone call from Megs in a rather distraught state. She had returned from a visit to her parents to find that our home had been robbed of every item of value that we owned, from coats to electrical goods to the children's pocket money. Practical items can always be replaced but many of my footballing awards were unique. The silver cannon presented to me by the Arsenal when I retired had only been in my possession for a few months. The Arsenal Player of the Year trophy was missing and so, too, was my precious FA Cup winners' medal.

In a second robbery a year later, the jewellery that Megs had been wearing during the first one was taken. No item has ever been recovered. The Football Association allowed me to buy a replacement Cup Final medal from the makers Fattorini. In the greater picture, the loss of such possessions is not of huge importance, but anyone who has had their home defiled by criminals is never likely to forget the experience.

It was not long after the Helen Morgan episode that I went to see Eric Morley to tell him that I was not suited to the job and that I couldn't accept a monthly pay cheque when it wasn't deserved. It was a relief to be concentrating my mind once more solely on football. Hard work and a willingness to learn and improve were assets instilled in me from an early age by my parents.

Throughout my BBC career, every week was planned like a military campaign. 'Focus' was always my main concern. The planning meetings on Tuesdays became the place to air ideas for items on football's main talking points. The editor would make the final decisions but the input of commentators John Motson, Barry Davies and Gerald Sindstadt and reporter Tony Gubba was hugely influential.

The afternoon following the planning meeting would be taken up with numerous phone calls to football clubs, their managers and even players. Fixing a time and place to film was rarely easy. On a Wednesday or Thursday, I would set off to drive to any part of England or Wales with a producer and just hope nothing would go wrong with the intended story. Some clubs were wonderfully co-operative and others were simply unhelpful. It did help that I had been a player. Doors were opened and areas filmed or discussed that might otherwise have been banned.

My many interviews for 'Focus' ranged between the memorable and the instantly forgettable, but one that lives on in my memory does so for an off-camera moment when I was instantly elevated to the status of greatest player ever.

Edson Arantes do Nascimento, better known as Pele, remains the favourite player of most football fans throughout the world. 'Football Focus' had been granted an interview with the Brazilian hero and I was pacing up and down outside his suite at the Savoy hotel, waiting for my film crew to arrive. Suddenly, a hotel cleaning lady came running towards me down the corridor, paper and pen in hand, poised for an autograph request.

'Excuse me, love, are you Pele?'

Just as I was about to say, 'No,' Pele opened his door and the embarrassed lady realised her 'slight' mistake.

Most clubs had also heard that I was back in the game, when time permitted, as a coach to goalkeepers at a variety of clubs, including Arsenal. My insistence that keepers needed specialised tuition fell on appreciative ears, but it was difficult to combine my BBC work with a coaching role. I was also a member of the Sports Council for three years, a body chaired by Sir Roger Bannister.

I thought that maintaining contact with the game was hugely valuable to my work at the BBC. I even played, in emergencies for a variety of clubs, helping a Danish First Division side, Naestved, avoid relegation over eight games, standing by for Bobby Gould's Bristol Rovers when a flu epidemic hit his team prior to an FA Cup tie against Leicester City and similarly playing four games for Arsenal's reserves leading up to the 1978 FA Cup final versus Ipswich Town.

There were also summer tours with an Old Internationals XI to Holland, South Africa and Brazil. It was great to experience playing behind Bobby and Jackie Charlton and Bobby Moore. One day in Rio, I saw at first hand the hold that football and its best players have around the world.

We had just landed in Brazil and reached our hotel on the Copacabana beach when Bobby Moore asked me if I wanted to get the flight out of my system and join him for a run. So it was that England's 1966 World Cup winning captain and I began a gentle jog along the edge of the sea. We had barely run two hundred yards when I was aware that a wave of humanity was moving in our direction. I knew they weren't running to speak to me. The men, women and young people who excitedly reached us had only two visions in their minds. One was of Bobby lifting the Jules Rimet trophy in 1966 in England; the other, and more pertinent, was the famous embrace and exchange of shirts between 'Mooro' and Pele after Brazil had beaten England 1–0 in the 1970 World Cup.

With my feet in the water, I watched as Bobby spent twenty minutes signing shirts, shorts and human flesh. He was brilliant with each and every one of them, a wonderful ambassador, a great, great man. At that moment, I was again aware of how the game of football embraces a world audience in a way no other sport does.

In the early period of 'Focus' we were in direct opposition to ITV's 'On the Ball' programme with Brian Moore. Whenever we met up, Brian and I would debate the merits or otherwise of our respective programmes. He would claim a larger midday audience and I would challenge his figures. We always liked each other; Brian had an uncanny way of putting me down and picking me up when our discussions became heated. Eventually, he concentrated solely on his great commentary skills and 'Saint and Greavsie' took over ITV's Saturday football spot, but later in the day than 'Focus'. Ian

St John and Jimmy Greaves had both been icons at Liverpool and Spurs respectively, and the Saint followed my steps from football pitch to presenter's chair.

Presenting 'Focus' became very comfortable for me and equally enjoyable. Supplying me with all the relevant facts was Albert Sewell, the finest of football statisticians who always guided me brilliantly. I knew I was beginning to improve when I started to be asked to present 'Sportsnight' and 'Match of the Day'. Both programmes were heavily scripted and rarely too demanding for a committed professional. Only 'Grandstand' seriously challenged all those who presented it. The ones who made the task look easy became legendary BBC presenters. A few others, including me, are proud to have been given the opportunity to try. If homework was not done on the day's events the programme would find you out. On the couple of hundred occasions I was in the hot seat, I always had two or three times more facts at hand than I'd ever normally need.

The Hillsborough disaster was not normal. An FA Cup semi-final between Liverpool and Nottingham Forest cost ninety-six people their lives after extra fans had been allowed to enter an area of the ground that was already filled to capacity. The tragic events were reported throughout the afternoon on 'Grandstand' and I happened to be its presenter.

It wasn't always easy to get the programme on the air, talk through the menu and the events to be covered and then hand over to 'Football Focus', which I was to deliver as usual. But semi-finals day always provided extra interest. The other main sports that day were horse racing and the world snooker championships which were taking place in Sheffield, too, at the Crucible theatre.

I had handed over to the snooker when the first indications of trouble at Hillsborough came through to us from the BBC production van at the ground. Very quickly we learned that a terrible disaster was unfolding at the end where the Liverpool fans were. John Shrewsbury, senior producer at the ground, kept updating us but no live pictures were permitted. By the time of the scheduled kick-off, everyone within the 'Grandstand' studio was aware that lifeless bodies had been taken close to the area where our TV vans and scanner were located.

The instructions delivered into my ear changed by the minute. A directive came from the Head of Sport, Jonathan Martin – 'Watch your tone, consider your words, no mention of fatalities.' For almost two hours the decision was upheld not to mention any loss of life even though we all knew that at least fifty people had been crushed to death. Many fans were still in or close to the ground and it was obvious that families, on hearing of the problems, would be turning on the television for further news. By then, fourteen years into my BBC career, I had learned how to stay calm in frantic situations and to use words with sensitivity.

In the last ten minutes of the scheduled programme, the police advised us that we should mention that there had been some fatalities. We were asked to provide a phone number for viewers worried about events at Hillsborough. The lines I had to deliver were difficult enough, and it was important to choose my words carefully. I could envisage the panic in hundreds of thousands of households in Liverpool. For two hours a desperately serious picture had been painted and now, for the first time, families would learn that people had died. Within five minutes of my reporting the loss of several lives, the BBC's main news programme, which followed 'Grandstand', announced a figure approaching fifty deaths.

It was the custom after 'Grandstand' came off the air to go to the bar and have a drink with the editorial and production team. We were all in a daze, lost for words, caring little for the traditional glass of wine. We had all been party to a terrible piece of history, one we would never forget. I drove home, sat down with Megs and cried.

Dramas of such scale are thankfully rare in the sporting world. Programmes usually provided wonderful action, supreme skills and lots of entertainment and fun. Unlike more than 90 per cent of television, sport output is transmitted live. There is only one chance to get it right and, for me, it produced an adrenaline rush very similar to those I experienced as a footballer.

Viewers love nothing more than spontaneous actions or reactions. Presenting 'Focus' from Aintree on Grand National day, I was to interview comedian Freddie Starr. I knew what to expect and Freddie didn't let me down with his antics, but it wasn't exactly easy to turn from him and deliver the next link to camera while his tongue licked the side of my face and deep into my ear!

The one guest whom I always had some difficulty in under-standing was Kenny Dalglish. If Kenny delivered his answers quickly, I would catch every third word or so. Then I wished I'd been born in Scotland rather than Chesterfield.

Arthur Cox, who was a coach at many clubs and a special ally of Kevin Keegan's, was the most nervous interviewee. He sat alongside me throughout a 'Focus' programme in which he was to appear towards the end. During the video-taped items, he kept saying he couldn't understand how we could do the job, looking so calm, getting so many instructions in our ears. After ten minutes, sweat poured off his brow, after fifteen his shirt was totally wet and when we told Arthur he'd be on in thirty seconds he let out a terrified groan. When his time arrived, he was terrific.

For the second ten years at the BBC, I became a regular replacement for Des Lynam, Steve Ryder or Jimmy Hill when they were taking a break. Occasionally, I even presented the Grand Prix programmes and for many years enjoyed an inter-esting role with the London Marathon. In the first year of Chris Brasher's great event, the interviewing on Tower Bridge was conducted by Des Lynam. He would walk alongside the fun runners and club runners and basically see how they were feeling after twelve miles on the road. For the following twelve years, I took over Des's role on Tower Bridge and, as the race progressed, down below the bridge at Traitor's Gate which was approximately twenty-two miles from the start, six miles from the finish.

With my coaching involvement at training grounds with various football clubs I still felt pretty fit, so I suggested that I could interview on the run. It was a fairly novel idea and was an instant success. The runners preferred not to break their rhythm while being interviewed and therefore were more relaxed generally. During the course of the marathon I would interview anything between seventy and a hundred competitors; some chats went out live, others were recorded and slotted in. On Tower Bridge I would pick out interviewees, run with them for a hundred yards up the slope to the bridge, put my arm in the air so cameras could pick me out in the mêlée, be given the order to talk, run two or three hundred yards while conducting the interview, wish the folk good luck for their remaining fourteen miles and sprint all the way back to my pick-up position ready for the next one. It was an identical procedure on the cobbles alongside the Tower and Traitor's Gate. My presence over the years received a mixed reaction from the competitors. The wheelchair bound Tanni Gray-Thompson wasn't too happy with my interruptions, whereas other runners looked out for me and our chats became an annual event.

There were many funny moments but perhaps the best was when I was set up by the producer who had spotted a group of six clearly running as a team. I was on live, had to sprint to catch them up and was into the first question when I realised they were all Japanese who didn't speak one word of English. In the space of three hundred yards, and in my best pigeon Japanese, I managed to prise out of them that they were 'OK!' and that they came from Tokyo. All the time I was party to great guffaws of laughter in my earpiece and the words, 'Great interview, Bob, keep going!'

We worked out that on an average marathon day I would run between six and ten miles while working. As I got older, it took its toll. After returning home one year, I was lying on the settee drinking a cup of tea and relaxing when the phone rang and as I reached for the receiver, both my legs went into cramp. The caller was Graham Taylor, then the England manager, who immediately went into an in-depth conversation about players. I didn't want to interrupt him so I clamped my hand over the mouthpiece and I mimed my agony to Megs. She rushed to my aid and pressed my feet backwards to stretch my cramped-up calves. Quite what Graham thought of my strange conversation and staccato delivery I'll never know.

The vast majority of programmes I was involved in at the BBC provided great fun and memories but I was always happiest with football, preferably as a main presenter with Des. Including the 1970 competition in Mexico when I was an Arsenal player, I helped the Beeb cover seven World Cups.

The BBC always recognised and appreciated the value I could provide on the goalkeeping front. They used my expertise at every opportunity. A good example came in the 1986 tournament in Mexico when Maradona's sleight of hand against England was not spotted by Tunisian referee Ali Ben Nasser or his linesmen. The instant Peter Shilton was beaten to the ball by 'the hand of God', as Maradona described it, I was out of my seat, yelling and shouting, 'That's a foul, it's handball!' The BBC staff around me, including Head of Sport Jonathan Martin, didn't agree. They thought the Argentinian had simply outjumped the England keeper. Protesting to the point of exasperation, I demanded that the goal should be replayed and freeze framed on the moment of Maradona's contact with the ball. The point was quickly proved and my credibility enhanced.

I was unhappy with my role in the 1982 World Cup held in

Spain. I was given the job of England reporter, following them to Bilbao, Madrid and any other venue. Reporting was not why I joined the BBC. My expertise lay in presenting; a reporter's role is very different, requiring special skills. The decision had been made, though, and for three weeks I lived in the shadow of the England squad.

Gaining access to Ron Greenwood's men was never simple, but I had strong contacts within the team and access to their phones. It was very useful to keep in daily touch, especially after closed training sessions. Just how useful was illustrated when I found out that Kevin Keegan, England's star man, was unlikely to play in the opening game. We were within minutes of delivering our report live and until that moment every other branch of the media, including our ITV rivals, had included Keegan in their probable England line-up. I went strongly on the information received, reporting 'Shock news from the England camp. Kevin Keegan will miss tomorrow's game.' Within seconds our small BBC reporting team was inundated with calls asking how accurate the news had been. Ron Greenwood was forced to admit that the story was true and that Kevin would not play. It was a huge scoop, made possible with a touch of luck and close contact with my footballing friends. A week or so later, it was ITV's turn to scoop a Keegan story; the England star was spotted by chance in a German airport by ITV staff, when he should have been in Spain. He was secretly visiting a German osteopath.

My biggest moment in a reporting role was followed very quickly by my worst and again it revolved around Kevin Keegan. On his return from his visit to Hamburg, where healing hands had failed to cure his injury properly, the great player agreed to give main interviews to the press and television. I spent several hours thinking about and preparing my questions to put to Kevin. When my producer Bob Abrahams failed to contact me to tell me about time and place, I approached him. To my utter amazement, Bob told me very sheepishly that I was not going to conduct the interview but to have a day off. It had been decided that Tony Gubba would take my place. Tony was a very good, at times extremely incisive, reporter. He didn't seem to care about the effect loaded questions would have on those he interviewed. In my view, he should have been given the England reporting role and not me; but he hadn't and it was my job. I had done the task effectively with the bonus of a big story. No one was going to ride roughshod over me and so I took the BBC sports department on and threatened to walk out if I wasn't reinstated on the Keegan story.

Apart from one or two notable exceptions such as David Coleman and Des Lynam, the BBC dictated to those they employed. My request to be put back on the interview was refused. Immediately, I asked for a flight to be arranged for my return to England; again I was refused. The only allies I could count on were Megs, my agent at the time Dennis Roach, and those in our small reporting team. I finished up spending a day in my Spanish hotel room organising my own flights and stewing to the point where my anger was boiling over. I arranged to fly home that evening and accepted that my time at the BBC was at an end. I didn't care. There was a principle at stake and for that I was prepared to give up my job.

A phone call from Dennis Roach delayed my departure. He had agreed to fly out immediately to try to resolve the situation. He was soon at the hotel arguing the case for me to stay. The other mediator was Bobby Charlton. Bobby was always a great choice by the BBC when covering major events. His world fame meant he opened doors everywhere we travelled. As soon as he was aware of the row, he cleverly shut the door on my departure. He understood my angst but he made me appreciate the magnitude of my decision to leave. 'Think of your family and not yourself,' was Bobby's message to me. It took one of England's greatest footballers to make me stay in the job. Tony Gubba conducted the interview with Kevin Keegan.

Within days, my anger and despair had been replaced by more elation. The reigning world champions, Argentina, had been knocked out by Brazil 3–1 in Barcelona, a game in which Diego Maradona had been sent off. The Falklands war had been over for just three weeks. No one could get near the Argentina team. I remembered that the former Tottenham Hotspur player and Argentine midfield player Ossie Ardiles had given me a phone number after I'd interviewed him for 'Football Focus'. I rang the number and to my surprise Ossie answered. He understood that, whatever the rights and wrongs of the Falklands conflict, an interview with him to be shown in England about Argentina's demise and his view on the war would be worthy. Ossie was a great gentleman. The problem was how to get me into the Argentine's hotel. No Brits were allowed in, but he was prepared to try if I was prepared to take the risk. I put the story to the BBC's editorial team. They knew I was still seething with anger over the Keegan interview and they agreed that I should go ahead.

Fortunately, the BBC had a private plane at their disposal throughout the tournament. Within an hour, a producer and I were on it heading for Barcelona. Time was running out when we arrived at the hotel. I called Ossie and he told me to stay outside. Security was incredibly tight. He came out, we shook hands and briefly discussed the Brazil defeat and Maradona's dismissal. Then he told me to follow him into the hotel but not to utter a word. Tension over the war was at its height. As the daylight began to fade, he found a quiet space at the back of the hotel and we proceeded with the interview. Ossie was emotional, revealing and frank about his distress regarding the fighting between his own country and his adoptive land. The interview would have huge appeal and impact back home. Thanking him profusely, we headed back to the tiny aircraft and took off for Madrid. Already the tape had been transmitted.

The producer and I drank champagne as a frightening thunderstorm bounced the light aircraft around the skies. When we landed, there was genuine relief at our safe return. Congratulations on our story were led by Bob Abrahams. Our disagreements were put on hold, but not forgotten.

The other occasion on which I came close to walking out on the BBC was very different from the fit of pique I had in Spain. Working alongside Lawrie McMenemy many times, we had discussed football management and coaching. He had asked me to go down to Southampton to assess and coach his goalkeepers. Lawrie knew that I was not completely satisfied with television work, or indeed the pay. He could understand my frustrations and anxieties about whether I had done the right thing by choosing television, or whether I would always regret not staying in football as a manager. I think he believed I was a better football coach than television presenter – a theory with which I would concur.

Out of the blue, he asked if I would consider joining him at Southampton. Megs and I went down to the Dell and we talked further with Lawrie and his wife Ann about my becoming assistant manager. I could see that working alongside Lawrie I would quickly learn how to manage a club. He had input into all areas and activities during his successful reign at Southampton. Just as I was beginning to think the time might be right to re-enter the professional game full time, Lawrie was offered the manager's job at Leeds United. Suddenly, a decision that had looked comparatively easy became confused. When Megs had a miscarriage around the same time, the priorities became much clearer. We decided, together, that the time was not right to go back into the precarious world of football coaching or management, if ever.

Quietly I got on with 'Focus' and anything the BBC threw

my way. I wrote to Lawrie McMenemy after he had turned down the job at Elland Road. He understood my decision but clearly believed it was just a matter of time before I left the BBC. In his letter he referred to the 'anxiety' Megs had shown on her face, adding, 'It was certainly good experience for when she has that worried look permanently.' I never did enter football management, although foolishly, not having any managerial experience, I allowed my name to be put forward for the Arsenal job just before George Graham became manager at Highbury.

The extra income that I was looking for came from within the BBC and in particular the news department. Shortly after 'Breakfast News' was launched in January 1983, I was approached by the programme editor Ron Neil with a view to taking over the main sports presenting from David Icke. David, a former goalkeeper at Coventry, was a very promising newcomer to television sport, but he did have a tendency to self-destruct. His pronouncements on the future of the world and his political leanings didn't endear him to the BBC and ultimately his career floundered.

Two or three months after the breakfast programme began, I took David Icke's seat and spent twelve years in the job. It meant getting up at 3.20 four mornings a week, but it was well paid and I was appreciated throughout my time on the early morning show. Initially, Frank Bough and Selina Scott were the main presenters. Frank I knew well from our 'Grandstand' days. Selina was a very special lady and did the job outstandingly well, bringing her own serenity to the screen. There were plenty of laughs as well and another female presenter, Kirsty Wark, produced one of the funniest lines when handing over to me. She was telling the viewers about a golf course in Japan where literally thousands of balls were lost daily, requiring a diver to retrieve them from the lake into which they had been hit. Turning to me to introduce the sports news, she said, 'Well, here's a man who never gets his balls wet – Bob.' When I responded, 'I beg your pardon?' Kirsty instantly realised what she had said and turned a lovely shade of red.

In twelve years, I sat alongside many different presenters and, although constantly fighting the fatigue factor, I managed to combine the role with coaching and my ongoing involvement with the sports department, who had come up with an improved contract and role for me. Four days a week I faced a demanding routine:

3.20 a.m. – alarm call
3.45 – leave home
4.30 – arrive BBC Television
4.45 – run through sports scripts and video-tape inserts
6.30 – first sport spot
7.25 – second sport spot
8.25 – third spot
8.40 – depart TV Centre for Arsenal training ground
9.15 – arrive London Colney
10.0 – start training session with Arsenal keepers
1.00 p.m. – depart training ground
2.00–6.00 – preparation work/interviews for 'Football Focus' 'Grandstand' etc.
6.30 – depart for evening football games at Arsenal or other London clubs
10.45 – bed
3.20 a.m. – alarm call

Another remarkable lady joined the 'Breakfast News' team later. Jill Dando had arrived from Plymouth without the promise of a contract but she was as natural a girl as you would ever find within the television industry. She was and remained unspoiled. We would meet up between four and five o'clock in the morning for a cup of tea when she would pour her heart out about her anxieties regarding the job, her looks, her romances and anything else that happened to have worried her. Like many others, including Bob Wheaton who became 'Breakfast News' editor, I thought she had a real chance of stardom. Jill was Bob's partner for a considerable period of time, but suffered criticism and jealousy because of her personal involvement with the editor. Bob was responsible for the huge change that Jill made in her appearance, influencing her diet, her hairstyles and her taste in clothes, bringing out greater confidence as her magnetic personality began to come across.

Of all the friendships I made during twenty years at the BBC, Jill's was the strongest. When, in February 1994, my daughter Anna was diagnosed with a rare form of cancer, Jill's natural compassion supported my increasing concern for my beautiful daughter's plight. Megs and I would meet up with Jill for a few precious hours to try to bring a form of normality into our lives.

She was thrilled that I received some recognition during the 1994 World Cup tournament. The finals were in America and I was co-presenting with Des Lynam. Some exciting games and controversial moments fell my way and allowed me a personal view on major talking points. A special half-hour documentary following a failed drug test on Diego Maradona received generous reviews from the press. It seems a rival television organisation were also impressed.

They didn't contact me immediately but when, in the summer, Megs and I returned from the tiny island of Montserrat in the West Indies, one waiting message put us on red alert – 'Please ring Trevor East as soon as possible.' It was from Dennis Roach who had been my most recent agent and who, when Megs undertook that role, remained my contractual adviser. Trevor East was Head of Sport for ITV. The independent company had received very poor publicity during the '94 World Cup finals after broadcasting from Dallas.

The day after our return from holiday, Trevor East came

to our home. His approach was brief and to the point. ITV wanted me to front their football coverage – all major world and European tournaments, plus the emerging Champions League, the modern version of the European Cup, the rights for which they had on a long-term exclusive basis. We listened, laid bare our immediate concerns, discussed salary and agreed to talk again within forty-eight hours. Two days later the talks continued when salary and length of contract were agreed, but I insisted I should meet the main editors and producers at ITV before any final decision was taken. Megs was working tirelessly. As my agent, she had insisted on a salary that reflected not just the importance of the job but the necessary enticement to leave an organisation where I had built a reputation over twenty years. ITV were offering a two-year contract. Megs demanded a four-year minimum stay. Agreement was quickly forthcoming. I slipped into ITV's Grays Inn Road and met their senior staff.

My opening gambit was simple – 'Do you really want me here?' It seemed to take at least two of the six people by surprise but the overall consensus was very much in my favour. As I departed, I knew in my heart that this was the chance I had worked so hard for at the BBC. Megs was less convinced. She had informed Jonathan Martin and Brian Barwick that ITV had made an approach. She also reminded them that my contract had been up for renewal towards the end of the recent football season, and despite many reminders they had continued to put off the meeting at which it would be discussed. Therefore I was conveniently out of contract.

We were totally surprised by the BBC's response. For three days following my meeting at ITV, Megs went to Television Centre and was promised more than we ever thought possible for me to stay. The BBC, whose pay has often been the centre of some derision, agreed to match the offer made by ITV. That in itself was both amazing and annoying. Four years more was not a problem and they clearly didn't want me to go. Megs was elated when she returned home and revealed the BBC's new deal. I was staggered by her successful negotiations but I needed one final question to be answered truthfully and in my favour if I was to stay at the BBC – 'Who will present the FA Cup final, the World Cup final, European Championship final and all major football including "Match of the Day"? Des Lynam or me?'

I knew the answer. Megs knew the answer but she asked anyway. With my agreement, Megs told the Beeb that I would stay if I was given 'Match of the Day'. She was despondent on her return. The best offer she could secure was a large proportion of 'Match of the Day' programmes. Des would still present World Cup, European Championship and FA Cup finals.

Megs was concerned that I was leaving an organisation that, despite the fights, I had been thrilled to work for. At the same time, she appreciated that at fifty-three years of age and with a four-year deal guaranteed, our future would be secure. Even then, she was clear-thinking enough to anticipate possible future problems and as a final condition to my joining ITV Sport she insisted my contract included the words 'ITV's principal football presenter'. Her instinct told her that commercial television was not to be trusted and that there had to be safeguards. The significance of her wisdom was to be revealed five years later.

When I told Jonathan Martin and Brian Barwick of my final decision to join ITV, they made direct individual appeals for me to stay. Jonathan warned me of the shortcomings I might expect and Brian talked of ITV's inconsistency in their standards of production and presentation. I told him it was up to me to change that situation if indeed his view was accurate. I shook hands with both of them and the rest of the BBC Sports department.

Both 'Grandstand' and 'Breakfast News' seemed to be genuinely upset that I was leaving. Humorous video-tape tributes appeared on both programmes. Steve Rider bade me a public farewell with the words, 'Good luck, Bob, but make sure you keep an eye on your near post,' a direct reference to the rivalry I could expect from the BBC when I sat in the ITV chair.

I was sorry to be going but equally excited at what lay ahead. It was the first and only time I had been seriously headhunted in my television career and I was going to enjoy the challenge presented by an organisation that was driven by adverts and audiences.

12
Coaching the goalies

'You get the best out of others when you give the best of yourself.'

Harvey Firestone

Most people who know of me think of the footballer or the television presenter; through both careers I enjoyed a high profile and an element of success. However, my first career was significant because teaching is in part coaching and coaching is in part teaching, and my most original, perhaps best, role is goalkeeping coach.

The inspiration for my specialisation in coaching goalkeepers came from Brazil. In 1966, the Brazilians were defending world champions. I was three years into my Arsenal career, a newly qualified FA full badge coach and fascinated by different coaching ideas. The South Americans were famous for their samba-style warm-ups, all rhythmical and loose limbed, and I was lucky enough to be able to see at first hand a typical training session; but it wasn't the warm-up that set me thinking, it was what followed.

Team coach Vincente Feola was in overall charge, but he was surrounded by assistants, all of whom were specialists in given areas. As the squad split after the warm-up, the defenders went away with a defensive coach, midfield and strikers with similar experts. It was the goalkeepers who interested me most, of course. The three men who played in the same position as me made their way to a goalmouth where their specialist coach awaited. The exercises they undertook were all designed with goalkeeping in mind – not just pressurised catching or shot-stopping drills, but activity that was clearly based on game situations.

Watching them sowed a seed of thought in my mind about how goalkeepers should be developed in Britain and how they might best flourish. At the time, coaching generally involved the whole team. Keepers were never catered for in the correct manner because few coaches or managers understood the complexities of the position. Keepers were usually stuck in a goal and lots of shots were directed at them; within minutes they would be exhausted.

Immediately following that Brazil experience, I concentrated on developing my own playing career but whenever I was asked to put on a coaching session, my priority was goalkeepers and their welfare.

I had barely left Highbury as a player before I was asked back as a part-time goalkeeping coach. Bertie Mee had resigned as manager and was succeeded by Terry Neill, a former team-mate of mine. Early in his seven-year reign, he pulled off a master-stroke by signing Pat Jennings from Arsenal's fiercest rivals, Spurs. How the management at White Hart Lane allowed the great Irish keeper to leave I will never comprehend. He was thirty-two when he arrived at Highbury, still in his prime and one of the world's best custodians. Terry phoned me and asked me whether my BBC job would permit me enough spare time to work with Pat. He felt my enthusiasm could help Pat prolong his playing days.

I had watched and admired Pat Jennings from the terraces as well as from the other end of the pitch, and I'd learned a lot from him. I asked Terry Neill whether I would be given a free hand to train the big man in my own way. Terry, who knew Pat well from their Northern Ireland international duties together, told me that he and his coach Don Howe wouldn't interfere.

Payment was never an issue as my job was with the BBC. Terry and I struck a deal whereby I would coach two or three days a week and Arsenal would pay expenses of £2,000 per season and provide four matchday tickets for my family. So began a relationship with the new generation of Arsenal goalkeepers.

Since I returned to Highbury as a coach, many keepers have passed through my hands, but only thirteen have worn the Arsenal No. 1 shirt. Six of them have gained winner's medals of one sort or another, and three of those have gained legendary status at the club. That trio, Pat Jennings, John Lukic and David Seaman, were similar in a few goalkeeping respects but very individual in their thinking and attitude to life.

Getting to understand what motivates the player is where the coaching of goalkeepers starts. Creating a realistic working environment is hugely important but not as vital as having the ability to read their minds and to act as their mentor.

Pat Jennings' style of goalkeeping was unique at the time. No one had developed the ability to save with feet in the natural way that Pat had. These days, saving with feet is commonplace, essential, and its origin lies with the man from Newry.

By the time I appeared for my first session with Pat, I had decided to suggest something to him that I would normally never contemplate. I told Pat that he alone must guide me on when he wanted to work hard and for how long. I based my thinking on the fact that I couldn't teach him anything new. His age was a minor factor. I insisted that if he wanted little or no work on any particular day, he must still help the other keepers with words of advice or service of footballs alongside me.

Pat's reaction was typical. He agreed to my terms and without fuss or drama he began to inspire all around him during sessions, either with a few words of wisdom, but mainly by his remarkable skill when he took to the goal himself. Only one other keeper has come close to playing in Pat Jennings' style and that's David Seaman; both had an extraordinary presence in their goalmouths, and both could make saves that turned games.

In between Pat's departure in 1985 and David's arrival in 1990, the main Arsenal goalkeeper was John Lukic. Like me, John was born in Chesterfield. Before joining Arsenal, he had played for Leeds United, where in his early career David Seaman had been a young professional but released a month before he turned nineteen. John arrived at Highbury with a view to becoming Pat Jennings' successor, an aim he achieved plus a lot more. An amazingly hard worker, John had a style that mixed intensity with intelligence and a marvellous understanding of the goalkeeping art. He was by no means a natural.

My relationship with all three keepers exceeded the boundaries of the training ground. Personal friendships developed and still exist. Such closeness is not essential. The only important factors in any player–coach relationship are respect and an exchange of knowledge.

Goalkeepers alone understand fully the extent of the role but equally vital is an acceptance that different custodians will have different styles. What works for one keeper doesn't necessarily work for another. I learned a lesson when I was a player in direct opposition to Pat. I had marvelled at how he could make goalkeeping look easy. While I dived headlong among oncoming forwards' feet and appeared so anxious, he was the epitome of calm. It took a well-known journalist to help me identify our respective strengths. Eric Todd wrote for the *Guardian*. Following a truly outstanding display by Pat for Spurs at Leeds he wrote:

> If Jennings had been available on that memorable day when the Romans met the Etruscans, Horatius surely would have had to be satisfied with a seat on the substitutes' bench.

I read the report and was in awe. It perfectly summed up the glorious manner in which Pat kept goal. One week later, I played in goal for Arsenal against Leeds and had a very decent game. The report of the game in the following Monday's *Guardian* was again written by Eric Todd. Here was a chance to see if my type of goalkeeping was beginning to bear comparison with the great Pat Jennings. I quickly scoured the print until I spotted my name. The report read:

> To play the way Wilson plays you need courage, speed of thought, determination and an IQ of 20.

I might have reacted with surprise but Eric Todd had perfectly reflected two hugely opposing styles. Pat's style worked for him, mine suited me. Both ways of keeping a football out of the net were effective. In eight years working with Pat Jennings, I never taught him anything. I didn't need to because he was so naturally gifted. Where I was of some use was to keep his enthusiasm high. Pat played until his fortieth birthday, bowing out with a brilliant display in the World Cup finals against Brazil, and I knew I had fulfilled the role Terry Neill had asked of me, to keep the big man motivated and interested.

Working with John Lukic was, to a degree, a different proposition. In two spells at Arsenal, John was always receptive to my advice and new exercises. He needed and wanted to work all the time. He was a perfect student. Winning the championship so dramatically at Liverpool in the final game of the 1989 season was the highlight of John's first period at Highbury. Two seasons later, back at Leeds, he became the first keeper ever to win a championship medal with different clubs. A huge disappointment for me is that all the coaching ideas we talked about and carried out together have not yet led to John being employed as a top goalkeeping coach. In that respect he is a natural.

When John left Arsenal for the first time, the fans were upset.

They liked him, trusted him. Unfortunately, he fell out with the manager, George Graham, who allowed him to return to Elland Road. It was at this time that George asked my opinion about Queens Park Rangers goalkeeper David Seaman. Rangers were one of many clubs at which I had coached on either a regular basis or intermittently. Luton, Watford, Southampton, even Spurs, had asked for my help but, other than Arsenal, I spent most time at Queens Park Rangers.

When we were first introduced, I thought David was a little wary of what I might ask of him. He gave me the impression of being very much his own man, single-minded, bloody minded and a proud Yorkshireman. Very quickly, I believed that the man from Rotherham had the potential to be the best of his generation. By the time George Graham needed my assessment, David Seaman was already in the England squad and a full international. I told George that buying the Rangers keeper wouldn't be a risk; he could be as good as, if not better than, Pat Jennings. The move appealed to David. Arsenal was a big club, always expected to be in with a chance of honours. It would enhance his England opportunities to play for them, and he liked the idea that the weekly sessions we undertook together would now increase threefold.

My coaching methods and belief in how keepers should train did not come out of any Football Association manual or handbook. The governing body of the national game did what they thought was best in laying down standard techniques and drills for goalkeeping, but the difference between theory and practice is massive. Even now, with the advent of full-time specialised coaches at most clubs, the FA have not decided whose methods are best. Only when a recognised standard system is forthcoming will the British Isles again consistently produce a group of keepers capable of ousting the clutch of foreigners from within our league clubs.

My thoughts on how keepers should be coached are centred

on a series of basic essentials and the need to replicate what happens in a game. I have held the same beliefs for almost thirty years, with an occasional addition or subtraction of an exercise. All the keepers I have worked with have been treated identically, regardless of their respective styles, strengths or weaknesses. The ultimate objective is to help the keeper to perform consistently, game in, game out. Any method of stopping a football from hitting the net is legitimate. The use of any part of the body must be encouraged. To achieve that aim, I concentrate on three basic areas: the hands, the feet and the head.

Good 'hands' are essential tools for goalkeepers, but when I stress the importance of hands to my charges, I tell them it embraces not just fingers, palms, wrists, but forearms and shoulders. In short, it requires complete upper body strength. The 'feet' are the means by which goalkeepers travel around their area to produce a balanced and set position, which enables them to make saves. The importance of the 'head' cannot be overestimated.

The speed of passing and movement of a football means that keepers are constantly having to adjust their position. Ideally, goalkeepers should be perfectly set to save and suitably balanced as a ball is struck towards them. Unfortunately, keeping goal is not a perfect science; therefore it's imperative that the head should be still at the moment a ball is hit, even if the rest of the body is on the move. So head, feet, hands, balance and a set position are the bare essentials of goalkeeping and when combined with game-related exercises to sharpen understanding and reactions, one or all of these basics comes into play.

All the keepers I've worked with have had these beliefs repeated to them on a weekly, sometimes daily, basis. My aim is to reproduce for them exactly what they are likely to face in any match. Every game situation is explained and reproduced. Correct decision-making holds the key to success. What I hope will happen is that the students will gradually develop an insight into what might follow at any given moment, so that although obviously they won't know precisely what is going to occur, they will know what the possibilities are. For example, if an opponent is moving square across the face of the eighteen-yard line with the ball and makes enough space for himself to shoot, there are only four possibilities – a misdirected shot that goes wide of the post or over the bar; a shot that is within the keeper's reach and therefore saveable; an unstoppable shot across the keeper into the far corner for a goal; or, an even worse scenario, the opponent pulls the ball back inside the near post guarded by the keeper. The last is the worst possibility because keepers are not expected, in theory, to be beaten in this manner. In practice, when the cut back occurs, making a save is difficult.

Try to picture Gordon Banks' great save from Pele in 1970 when the ball was crossed from the goalline. In that case it was a chip cross to the far post for a header. That's just one of six possible moves that could have been attempted given the position. A direct shot could have been tried, a low near-post cross, a deeper pulled back cross, a mid-goal cross or a cross to beyond the far or back post.

Recognising the possibilities as attacks build can give a goalkeeper a fractional advantage over his opponents. All match situations created in training are carried out without any rush. It must be similar to the real thing. Only occasionally do keepers have to make a double save. Rapid work is about fitness, not reality. The goalkeeping coach no longer has the responsibility of being fitness trainer to the Arsenal keepers. A full-time qualified expert carries out that duty, which leaves the coach more time to concentrate on the ultimate objective – instilling knowledge and honing the ability to make saves, ordinary or crucial, on a regular basis.

Jennings, Lukic and Seaman believed in my aims and objectives, as did most of the keepers I coached on a regular basis. The only difference between those three and the rest is in the success they achieved. Pat played in three successive FA Cup finals between 1978 and 1980, picking up a winner's medal in the dramatic 1979 success against Manchester United. A year later he was in goal for the Cup Winner's Cup final defeat on penalties by Valencia. Apart from that epic championship decider in 1989 at Liverpool, John Lukic played in winning and losing League Cup finals in 1987 and '88. No one, least of all David Seaman, could have anticipated his success after joining Arsenal. Between arriving in the 1990–91 season and 2002–03, David has been a winner in a major competition on nine occasions, and a runner up on another seven. Having become one of only three footballers ever to surpass 1,000 first-team appearances at his four clubs, and represented his country seventy-five times, he should be remembered as one of the greatest goalkeepers ever. He's known as 'the Goalie'.

Physically, David Seaman has inherent attributes. At 6ft 4½ ins and around 15st 3lbs, he is also a natural sportsman, excelling at cricket, tennis, golf and, most important to him, fishing. The patience required in fishing has often been of huge assistance to him when his goalkeeping has been called into question. It would fascinate me to see how Gordon Banks, Peter Shilton, Pat Jennings and other great keepers would have coped with the back-pass rule and the modern lightweight football. I can only hazard a guess but I think they would have experienced as much difficulty as do the modern men.

David Seaman's consistency is second to none. For the vast majority of his time at Arsenal, he conceded fewer goals per season, or second fewer, than any other keeper at the top level. On the training field he always demands perfection of himself. When a shot escapes him that should have been saved, he reacts with genuine anger at himself. If he pulls off a wonder stop, a loud deep chuckle will ensue. He loves his job, goalkeeping in general, and appreciates the lifestyle it affords him.

I tried to set him targets. For major games I usually left a keepsake and a message as a harbinger of luck. Before one of his three FA Cup winning finals I placed a pair of my old green cotton goalkeeping gloves on his bench in the Wembley dressing room. They were, more or less, the only ones available in my playing days and looked like a pair of gardening gloves. They were certainly not of today's high technical quality. In fact, they were pretty useless but we all wore them in wet conditions. In dry conditions we used bare hands. With those gloves I left a message: 'If I could play well in these, there can be no excuses for you today.' Sometimes the message would be a simple explicit note. Before his first FA Cup final in 1993 I wrote down the names of all the previous Arsenal Cup winning keepers: '1930 Preedy, 1936 A. Wilson, 1950 Swindin, 1971 R. Wilson, 1979 Jennings, 1993 Seaman?'

Before the 1998 FA Cup final, which led to Arsenal's double, I popped into the dressing room *en route* to my ITV presenter's seat, and left a favourite photo. It showed my daughter Anna at a very young age, standing in the Highbury goal, a tiny girl next to a giant goalpost. At the time of the final Anna was at a particularly difficult stage of her fight against cancer. She and David had formed a special bond. The words that time read: 'Do it for Debbie, do it for your family, do it for yourself and please try and do it for this beautiful girl. This is Anna at Highbury in 1971. Good luck, play well, keep 'em out.' In the post-match interviews, David made special reference to Anna, dedicating the win to her. We were touched, she was thrilled.

David Seaman is a genuinely nice, fun-loving man, who has had to accept that the art of goalkeeping produces moments of sheer exhilaration and moments of desperation, often in equal measure. Constructive criticism he would always accept; the destructive element would eventually take its toll. Euro '96 and the performances he gave as England reached the semi-finals, only to lose on penalties to Germany, made him a national hero. Presenting ITV's coverage of the tournament was made doubly difficult for me on the day David was playing. It was the pinnacle of his international career. He was almost flawless throughout, and against Scotland he produced two world-class saves. For the first, he travelled the full distance of his goalline from post to post before clawing out Gordon Durie's header. It was reminiscent of Banks' save from Pele. He followed it up minutes later, with Scotland the better side at the time, by keeping out Gary McAllister's fiercely struck penalty. The two saves turned the game, allowing Paul Gascoigne's goal to determine the match for England. Similar saves of great quality and another dramatic penalty stop against Spain from Nadal, which decided the shoot-out, thrilled the public and press. Despite the cruel exit against Germany, the English nation applauded the honour of an MBE bestowed on David Seaman.

Just as important to me as his coach was the international technical report that followed the tournament, listing David as the best in the world. I remember almost every great save David made in his international and Arsenal careers – I could fill a book with them – including the three penalty saves against Sampdoria that took Arsenal to the final of the Cup Winner's Cup, which they had won the previous season against Parma.

For keepers, strange goals, bizarre goals and downright bad goals remain on instant recall. One of the cruelties of the game at large, and goalkeeping in particular, is that at the top level, the media who help create heroes seem to revel in moments of despair when wonderful keepers occasionally fall off the tightrope they attempt to walk in every single game. A less resilient person than David would have had his belief and confidence destroyed. Despite David's great consistency season after season and despite the knowledgeable support given to him by most fellow professionals, a section of the press have systematically decided that age has lessened his ability. Age gradually reduces reflexes but increases knowledge and reading of the game.

The goals that David let in against Nayim in the last minute of the 1995 Cup Winner's Cup final and against Ronaldinho in England's 2–1 World Cup defeat against eventual winners Brazil in 2002 have been regurgitated after many of the goals he has conceded since. Both Nayim's and Ronaldinho's goals were in their own ways bizarre. On each occasion, David held up his hands and expressed his disappointment at being beaten in such a manner. As his coach, I could look more objectively and clinically at the possibility of keeper error. Against Nayim and Ronaldinho, David's starting position, a crucial factor in making saves, was perfect. Keepers have no alternative but to play the percentage game. When Nayim had the ball at his feet in Paris, David spotted the run by Real Zaragossa's Argentinian striker Juan Esnaider and rightly moved off his line to cut off the possibility of a through ball. The chances of Nayim striking for goal, let alone finding the target, from that distance would have produced incredible odds against. But it happened, he scored, Arsenal lost, David Seaman took the blame. In the dressing room afterwards, his tears and the desperation of feeling he'd let the Arsenal team and their fans down were overwhelming. The words from the coach that it was a fluke meant nothing to him at that moment. He was similarly inconsolable after the Ronaldinho goal.

Until that moment he had been one of England's star performers in World Cup 2002, the most solid and consistent of all the World Cup keepers, including Oliver Kahn and Brad Friedel. His position as Ronaldinho kicked the ball anticipated a free kick arriving somewhere between the England defenders and Brazilian strikers. Any top keeper would have adopted a similar position. Whether any other keeper would have retrieved the ground behind him once the ball was goalbound is hypothetical.

In the case of both goals, had David not been in those starting positions, he would have been highly vulnerable to a through ball or inswinging cross, either of which appeared more likely than any direct shot on goal. Fans, critics and press are all entitled to their opinion, but when criticism becomes deeply personal and offensive, as it did, those who proffer such views let down themselves and their profession.

David Seaman's ability to recover from setbacks has been remarkable. Working with him has been the most rewarding of experiences. Sharing in his moments of glory has been humbling; sharing his worst nightmares has increased my admiration for him as a person.

When the Goalie played in the 2003 FA Cup semi-final at Old Trafford, it was his first game in a month, following a hamstring injury. Sheffield United were the opponents and six minutes from time they created a great chance for an equaliser. Paul Peschisolido's header from six yards seemed to be almost over the line when David, throwing himself backwards, clawed the ball back into play. It was a save of supreme athleticism, great experience and huge upper body strength. The watching Peter Schmeichel, there as an analyst for the BBC, called it 'one of the best saves I've ever seen'. It was certainly ranked alongside Gordon Banks' 'impossible play' from Pele thirty-three years earlier.

There was something of a mutual admiration society between the great Danish keeper and Arsenal's custodian. David and I discussed many things together, particularly other goalkeepers, their styles, strengths and weaknesses. He was most admiring of Schmeichel, whose presence was similar to his own but whose technique differed greatly. He was also fascinated by Bruce Grobbelaar. We regularly laughed at the Liverpool keeper's rushes from his goal, but equally we acknowledged and appreciated Bruce's athleticism and extraordinary reflexes. Only one other top-flight keeper had quicker feet than Grobbelaar and that was Wimbledon's Hans Segers. Fractionally short for a top keeper, Hans made up for lack of inches with lightning footwork.

In late 1994, just after I'd moved to ITV, I was shocked to read of charges made against Bruce Grobbelaar and Hans Segers, two of the country's best-known goalkeepers. I knew Bruce only as a result of television interviews conducted with him during the course of my job. Prior to the 1986 FA Cup final when Liverpool added the old trophy to their championship triumph, he wrote in my copy of his autobiography, 'All the best Mr Double, Bruce Grobbelaar. 10.5.86'. Two hours later, he became the fifth keeper in the history of the game to help achieve the feat.

I knew Hans Segers better than Bruce. He had regularly attended my goalkeeping school, which I had set up in 1983 in an effort to provide specialist goalkeeping coaching for young aspirants. Hans never asked for a fee to come and talk to the young keepers who attended. Often he would join in and demonstrate his skills and speed of action.

The whole of the football world was shocked when Bruce and Hans, together with John Fashanu, were charged with attempting to fix a number of Premiership games so that a Far Eastern gambling syndicate could win vast sums of money by betting on the results. The trial received huge publicity. The *Sun* newspaper broke the story in the November after an incredible sting operation involving Bruce and a bitter former business partner of his named Chris Vincent.

Grobbelaar faced an additional charge in relation to accepting, allegedly, a sum of money from Vincent, which had been supplied by the *Sun*. The initial story ran for days. Some time later, I received a call from sports lawyer Mel Goldberg whom Hans Segers had called upon for help in answering the charges. In meetings with him and David Hewitt, who was building a defence for Bruce Grobbelaar, they asked if I would be prepared to be called as an expert witness in the trial of the two keepers. They explained that my experience and reputation as a goalkeeping coach could help clarify whether there had been any goals deliberately let in by either goalkeeper. It was explained that I would need to view and review five key matches involving the performance of Bruce Grobbelaar, and eighteen games in which Hans Segers had played. These were the games the prosecution were alleging they had fixed.

Over many hours and many days I began to study and collate every incident involving Hans and Bruce in the games that had been cited. There is often talk of the 'goalkeepers' union' and the unwritten bond that all those who've played in the position will defend and remain uncritical of one another. I hated the fact that two of our so-called 'union' were being accused of deliberately making errors to affect the scorelines of games. I didn't want to believe it but had I found any evidence at all that could prove that Hans Segers and Bruce Grobbelaar were corrupt, I would have identified it without compunction. I watched every game a minimum of three times. All really pertinent incidents I studied innumerable times. When Mel Goldberg and David Hewitt revisited me, I told them I was quite happy to go into a witness box on behalf of both goalkeepers. I was entirely confident that if there was anything untoward in the action of either man, it certainly wasn't in relation to their goalkeeping.

My reports on the two preceded me to the court at Winchester in Hampshire. My summaries included the following:

I have reviewed 18 matches involving Hans Segers the Wimbledon goalkeeper and overall this entailed 478 incidents. Out of these 478 incidents I would question and criticise Hans Segers position or choice of save on no more than a dozen occasions. I have looked constantly and diligently for incidents that were dubious or without explanation from a goalkeeping point of view. All keepers have to live with making poor decisions but there is nothing obviously or blatantly untoward in these 18 matches . . .

In each of the 5 games I have viewed, Bruce Grobbelaar performed well and in the Manchester United game, outstandingly. Overall I cannot criticise his performances at all and there is not the slightest hint in any game that he has behaved improperly or suspiciously. Any suggestion that he attempted to 'fix' the result of any of the games by seeking to ensure his side were defeated gains no support whatever from the video recording of these games. I would be happy to give evidence in court on Bruce Grobbelaar's behalf in accordance with the terms of my report.

Going into the witness box during the two trials in Winchester, which led ultimately to the acquittal of both goalkeepers, was a huge ordeal. At times during the questioning, I felt as if I was the one being accused. The manner of the two judges was very different. In the first trial, the judge was helpful to me as an expert witness; in the second trial, the judge had a considerably harder approach and was seemingly less sensitive to the pressures placed upon witnesses.

The strain on the face of the accused and their loved ones was obvious for all to see. I was happy when the verdict arrived at 'Not guilty'. In Mel Goldberg's account of the trial, *The Final Score*, he wrote:

I will never forget the day Bob Wilson was called as a witness at Winchester. He faced a fierce attack from the prosecuting counsel, but maintained his poise, authority and dignity to deliver evidence in such a thorough and professional way that the jury should have been left in no doubt that Hans was innocent. The prosecution referred to a 'goalkeepers club' but Bob reminded them that when a goalkeeper was 'out of line' such as the West German Harald Schumacher in a World Cup match some years ago against France when he rushed out to flatten a French player, then he would be the first to criticize him. He gave that impressive answer to a prosecution question, so he could not have known it was coming and it was not a rehearsed answer. What a man to have on your side. Very few people knew that Bob Wilson was concealing a very distressing family matter. His daughter was seriously ill. Yet still he insisted on turning up at the court and delivering his evidence in the calm, unflappable manner that has been a hallmark of his years in television.

I had hoped that the conclusion of the Winchester trials in January and August 1997 would be the end of the matter, but a libel action brought by Bruce Grobbelaar against the *Sun* newspaper eventually came to court in July 1999, nearly five years after the original article. In the thirteen-day case, held in Court 14 of the High Court in London, I was again in the witness box. This time, I faced the legendary QC George Carman whose celebrity status stemmed from his representing such people as footballer George Best, politician Jeremy Thorpe, 'Coronation Street's Peter Adamson and comedian Ken Dodd.

Carman seemed to be polite enough and respectful in his early questioning of me, but quickly turned in mood and manner as he set out to discredit Bruce Grobbelaar. He was intimidating to the point of making a witness confused but I thought he made two errors with me. The first was when he attempted to 'mock' goals Bruce had let in. He was seeking an explanation of how a great professional goalkeeper could make such slips. Perhaps a great QC doesn't make a slip of the tongue but in goalkeeping, time to prepare for any unusual eventuality is fractional. I cited the case of when Ray Clemence allowed a Kenny Dalglish mishit shot to go between his legs during a Scotland v. England international. More pertinent, I told him how I had left too much of a gap for Steve Heighway to score in the 1971 FA Cup final. 'Why shouldn't I have deliberately left that gap? How can you prove beyond reasonable doubt that what happened was not intentional?' I asked Mr Carman.

When he then produced a copy of the *Sun* newspaper that contained a purported quote from me about 'the possibility of keepers throwing games', I respectfully told him that the words were not mine, but had been taken out of context from an article I had written on the precarious nature of the goalkeeping role. George Carman more or less accused me of being economical with the truth. In reply I told him, with great respect, that the *Sun* newspaper was renowned for its lack of ascertaining the real facts.

Bruce Grobbelaar won that case and was awarded £85,000 damages. The *Sun* lodged an appeal and, amazingly, three high court judges, who were not present at any of the three previous trials and who never heard evidence first hand, overturned the verdict. Eventually, Bruce Grobbelaar was to reverse this judgement as well, but his damages were reduced to £1. It was a hollow victory, but still a victory.

I was happy to be free of the accusations that had brought discredit to the goalkeeping community. Being an expert witness was an unusual experience. Since I began my coaching role at Arsenal, I was more than content with simply being cross-examined by the club's succession of managers about the state of mind and fitness of their keepers. Terry Neill didn't have to worry overmuch. For most of his time as manager he had Pat Jennings in goal. The only serious challenger was George Wood, who was Pat's deputy but still amassed seventy appearances in the first team. Apart from being a Scottish international, George was an avid birdwatcher and a member of the Royal Ornithological Society. One morning I arrived at training to find George squinting and with very red eyes. I wasn't aware he wore contact lenses at the time. He explained that he'd been foolish the previous day by wearing new lenses for too long while watching birds in a wooded area. When I asked George how difficult it was to see clearly without them, he told me to start walking backwards. After two and a half steps, George was screwing up his eyes in an attempt to see where I was. He was our keeper and he couldn't see clearly beyond two or three yards. We laughed and I cancelled the training session.

My relationship with George Graham was always based on mutual respect. We knew each other extremely well. However, when he arrived in the spring of 1986 to take over from Don Howe, he surprised me by asking if I'd had any involvement in the search for the new Arsenal manager. He had obviously been told that I had put forward Graham Taylor's name, which was true. Graham had indicated to me, after an interview I had conducted with him for the BBC, that he would like the Arsenal board of directors to be aware that he was interested in the vacant job. He wasn't going to apply formally. I, in turn, informed vice chairman David Dein of the conversation with Graham, but George clearly believed that I had put forward Graham Taylor for the job.

In a way it was an indication of his form of management. He was a proud, clear thinking, independent man and demanded loyalty from everyone, especially old team-mates. What he achieved in his nine-year reign, without the resources afforded to Arsene Wenger, was truly remarkable. He won two championships, one FA Cup, two League Cups and the European Cup Winner's Cup and lost two finals in the League Cup and Europe.

After at first encouraging me to continue working for three days a week with his goalkeepers, he eventually asked me to coach on a daily basis. Beating Parma with a massively understrength side to lift the Cup Winner's Cup was fantastic to observe at close quarters. Winning at Anfield to pip the Liverpool team for the 1989 title was breathtaking. They were the supreme moments during George Graham's management.

The manner of his departure from Highbury following the infamous 'bungs scandal' came as a shock and was sad. Most people intimately connected to football thought that George took the rap for many other guilty parties.

When Bruce Rioch took over from George Graham in 1995, he was as supportive as the previous manager had been of the job I was doing with the Arsenal keepers, young and old. I liked his concern for players' families, loved his signing of Dennis Bergkamp, but will never know to what heights he could have taken Arsenal because he was sacked after a year in charge. Stewart Houston and Pat Rice became acting managers and my role remained the same. I looked after the development of all Arsenal's young keepers and sustained the senior men as best I could.

The arrival of Arsene Wenger in the summer of 1996 marked the start of a French revolution that re-established Arsenal's position as one of the most respected clubs in world football. My role as coach changed rapidly as Arsene began to unveil his blueprint for the future. He is not in the mould of most managers. Being an original thinker, he is studious, a perfectionist, multilingual but, on occasions for me as the goalkeeping coach, frustrating. The Arsenal teams that have evolved under him have possibly produced the most attractive style of football in the history of the club. He usually gets what he wants and intensely dislikes losing. David Dein is on record as saying, 'Arsene Wenger is a miracle worker and he revolutionised our club.' In turn, the board have backed him financially in a manner previously foreign to club policy. Arsene's ability to make good players great is just one attribute of this mightily talented man. Vieira, Pires, Wiltord, Henry and Ljungberg arrived as talented footballers full of potential; under his guidance they have exploited their talent to earn world status. Dennis Bergkamp was already one of the best footballers in the world.

Arsene's philosophy is based on youth, power, pace, skill

and technique, intelligence and supreme fitness. I admire the fact that he is prepared to admit he can sometimes be wrong. He was surprised and taught a lesson about the value, to any team, of experience and age when he came in daily touch with David Seaman, Lee Dixon, Tony Adams, Steve Bould and Nigel Winterburn, the famous back five. All would generally fall outside Arsene's parameters of youth, power and pace. Each one proved to him that youth can succeed consistently only if supported by experience. When he introduced special diets and new stretching routines for the ageing defenders, he added two or three years at least to each of their playing careers.

No previous Arsenal manager involved me so much in team affairs as Arsene. He included me on all pre-season training camps in Europe and would always ask me for a view not just on the Arsenal keepers, but all the current top number ones. The signing of Alex Manninger from Sturm Graz was done entirely on my recommendation. A three-day trial period was all I needed to be convinced of the young Austrian's potential. He was to play a massive part in securing Arsenal's second double in 1998, filling in brilliantly when David Seaman was injured, but that huge promise went no further. Alex and another protégé, Paul Barron in the late seventies, are my biggest disappointments. I feel personally responsible that these two didn't achieve more than they did.

My admiration for Arsene Wenger will never be affected by our disagreements about goalkeeping and goalkeepers. The differences of opinion have usually centred on the abilities of Arsenal's goalkeepers and the amount of time I have had to work with them. Fitness and footwork in the gymnasium are vital but for every keeper, basic handling and positional work are the most crucial factors in building the confidence required to meet the demands of the goalkeeping role.

There are those who believe Arsene is wary of all talent that is English, but he is happy to acknowledge the universal respect felt for the famous back five and for others including Sol Campbell, Ray Parlour and Ashley Cole, although with Ashley it was a close call. He may well have been allowed to join Crystal Palace on a full-time basis had the Brazilian full-back Silvinho not been injured. There is little doubt that Arsene believes foreign players hold an edge over the British in technique, but he's grown to appreciate the value of the spirit and competitiveness of home-grown players. Ultimately, his judgement is based on players' ability to cope with the very highest levels of the game.

I know just what a difficult decision it was for Arsene to allow David Seaman to move on from Highbury after the 2003 FA Cup final triumph against Southampton. He would have weighed up the pros and cons in minute detail.

The against argument would have included David's age, nearly forty, slower reactions than in his early days as a pro and especially the longer recovery time anticipated if injury struck. The argument for keeping him as number-one choice would have been his immense experience, the ability still to make match-winning saves and definitely his influence in the dressing room and on the training ground. It must have been a close call, even for Arsene, but his thinking would have centred on his long-held belief that youth, speed and supreme physical fitness are essential if the best of Europe are to be conquered.

As for David's decision to continue playing rather than to take over from me as Arsenal goalkeeping coach, making an occasional first-team appearance, I have no doubt it is correct. His talent and ability remain, as well as his enthusiasm and ambition. Football in this country needs home-grown stars of stature, character and greatness. Kevin Keegan knows that only too well and the Manchester City fans will surely have their love of the game furthered by watching David Seaman follow in the footsteps of not just the retiring Peter Schmeichel, but former

City favourites Joe Corrigan, Frank Swift and a man called Bert Trautmann.

The best young English keepers I've been able to help become professionals are Stuart Taylor and Graham Stack. I have high hopes that both will achieve great things. In the third of Arsenal's double successes, in 2001–02, Stuart made enough first-team appearances to earn a championship medal alongside David Seaman and Richard Wright. It was the first time in the history of the top division of English football that three goalkeepers were presented with a championship winning medal. Seaman and Wright were in the full England squad, Taylor in England's Under-21 international squad and Graham Stack made the Irish Under-21s.

Stuart Taylor's progress has been more erratic than I would have liked and it's one area in which Arsene and I have sometimes held a different view. Perhaps my own difficult journey to becoming Arsenal's number two keeper has helped me sympathise with Stuart when he's been frustrated by his manager's squad selection. In the modern game, it is necessary to have three top keepers, but I think it's still important for them to earn the right to be the number one, two or three choice. Stuart Taylor has done exactly that since 2001 but still Arsene rotated all three of his keepers, leaving the young Englishman angry enough to review his future at the club. Richard Wright, like Stuart, played a significant role in the 2002 double success, but Arsene allowed him to leave for Everton. It clearly enhanced Taylor's chances, a keeper at least the equal of the two other young England potentials, Paul Robinson and Chris Kirkland.

Rami Shaaban was signed from Djurngardens in Sweden as the new number three. Not long into the 2002–03 season, David Seaman sustained injury. To my surprise, and Stuart Taylor's dismay, the manager chose Rami ahead of one of England's more promising keepers. It was not hard for me to give Stuart advice on how to react; I had been there once under Billy

Wright. It would have been easy for him to ask for a transfer he didn't really want. The alternative was to prove Arsene Wenger wrong. When Rami Shaaban broke a leg in training, Stuart's chance came again. He performed brilliantly in the second half of a Champions League game against Ajax at Highbury, after David Seaman came off with a calf strain, and was voted Man of the Match by Manchester City fans after Arsenal's win at Maine Road. The following Saturday, at Highbury, David was back as number one. Gus Warmuz, just signed from Lens as a third choice for the injured Shaaban, was on the bench. Stuart Taylor was not selected at all. I was less than pleased at Arsene's decision and Stuart was even more unhappy.

It's much easier for Arsene to include outfield players in a matchday squad than keepers and it's possible he had told Gus that he would be involved with first-team matches in order to secure his services. Nevertheless, his selection of Gus Warmuz was a huge risk. Had David Seaman been injured or sent off during the game, the French standby would have been much less prepared for a vital championship game than Stuart Taylor.

It is only on these goalkeeping decisions that I often have a differing view from the manager. I have always tried to make it clear where I stand with my goalkeepers, but it's Arsene Wenger's job to make decisions; that's what he's paid to do. I hope that Stuart Taylor will accomplish great things with time.

Both he and Graham Stack were products of the goalkeeping school I set up in 1983, which gave me enormous pleasure until 1996. In that time, Megs and I hosted one-day and one-week courses for goalkeepers of all abilities, shapes and sizes and of any age, male or female. The visits of great top professionals including David Seaman, Pat Jennings, Joe Corrigan, Hans Segers, Eddie Niedzwiecki, Perry Suckling, Alex Chamberlain, Bob Boulder, Paul Heald, Nicky Hammond and Eric Steele helped inspire the students. Intensive practical work was interspersed with video teaching and question and answer sessions. The courses demanded complete dedication to the weird and wonderful art of goalkeeping.

After seven years of increasing success with three magnificent assistants in Mick Payne, Alex Welsh and Shaun Dudgeon plus a host of other regular coaches, we began to lay out a blueprint for goalkeeping coaching in England. We sent if off to the Football Association's coaching department led, at the time, by Charles Hughes. No similar school existed in the British Isles, no structure for the development of keepers existed within the FA. We were asking for approval and support. We obtained neither. It was a huge disappointment because we all felt we had got everything right.

Rarely in my life have I experienced the joy I got from watching the students at work. Up to 150 students, twelve sets of goalposts, a ball per keeper, devoted staff and lots of learning, fun and laughter, spread across an acre of playing field was my kind of heaven. If Stuart Taylor and Graham Stack achieve success, plus others signed by different clubs, it will provide a wonderful reward for all involved, not just Megs and me.

An end of course presentation gave Megs one of her most embarrassing moments. Parents and families arrived on the last day to watch the final session and collect their goal-keeping protégés. A large hall housed the final presentation of certificates and awards, organised by Megs. The parents made their way to find favourable seats in anticipation of the ceremony, and to keep them entertained until all the students were assembled, Megs would play them the video of the week's activities showing their sons and daughters performing various goalkeeping exercises.

On one occasion, over three hundred parents were seated as Megs put on the video and pressed 'play' so that the activities could be viewed on the two giant television screens at the front of the hall. She walked away confident that the parents would be glued to the pictures in anticipation of seeing their own son or daughter displaying their skills. It was only after a minute that she suddenly became aware of the grunts and groans coming over the loudspeakers and a few guffaws from the watching audience. To her horror she saw that the bluest of blue films was in full flow. No one had ever seen Megs move so fast as she rushed to retrieve the situation. As she reached for the stop button a watching parent shouted out, 'No wonder my lad always wants to attend your school.' It wasn't exactly the 'blueprint' for which I had held out such high hopes. Megs never did find out who switched the tapes.

Sadly, the goalkeeping school came to an end as our energies were needed more and more in helping Anna in her battle with cancer. She had helped her mum in the administration of the school and was a vital member of staff, but when her illness began to take over daily life, our priorities were firmly with our daughter.

There is no goalkeeper I have ever worked with who hasn't provided me with rewarding moments. One of those in whom I continue to have great pride is Gary Lewin. Arsenal and England fans know Gary as an outstanding physiotherapist. So do I, but before he ventured into that role with such success, he was an apprentice goalkeeper at Arsenal.

Gary was talented but not quite good enough to fulfil his dreams of playing for Arsenal. Recognising that fact is difficult for both coach and player. I'll never forget the tears Gary shed when he was told he wasn't going to be offered a professional playing contract. He only ever wanted to play for Arsenal and the day he learned he wasn't going to make it could have destroyed him, but instead of dwelling on his misfortune he decided to pursue another career. He confided in me, asked for guidance and listened hard, just as he had done as a keeper, and I helped him find the contacts necessary to further his ambition.

When Gary qualified as a physio I was thrilled. When he returned to Arsenal to undertake that role with the first team I was ecstatic. George Graham chose well because the importance of a top-class physiotherapist in the dressing room can never be overstated. On 6 June 1987 I stood beside Gary as his best man when he married Maggie. It sealed our friendship, one that had begun under a crossbar on the coaching field.

The role of coach is not just about winning. Of course it has been extraordinary to watch David Seaman collect three championship winning medals, four FA Cup winner's medals, a European Cup Winner's Cup and a League Cup winner's medal at Arsenal. In forty years at Highbury, I have been lucky enough to witness first hand, and play a part in, Arsenal winning fourteen major competitions and being runner-up in a further fifteen. Just as rewarding is the legacy that the coaching of goalkeepers has provided. When in 1976 I became the first person to specialise in the training of keepers, I never dreamt that by the new millennium every Premiership club in England and many other Football League clubs would employ full-time goalkeeping coaches, who could advance the understanding and practice of the most difficult playing position in a football team.

13
Adverts and audiences

*'Accept that someday you're the pigeon
and someday you're the statue.'*

Roger C. Anderson

'Bob for ITV Job' was the front-page headline that marked my transfer from BBC to ITV. I knew of the challenge and expectations awaiting me in my new role. ITV depends on successful prime-time programmes watched by big audiences. Without viewers, they simply cannot attract the huge advertising revenue that keeps them in business.

The initial task asked of me by Trevor East was to try to restore some credibility to ITV Sport following the criticism they received during and after their coverage of the 1994 World Cup finals in America. ITV based themselves in Dallas, Texas, and the production had been deemed less than successful.

I worked for ITV for eight years and in the first five of those, between August 1994 and August 1999, I reaped some reward following my twenty-year 'apprenticeship' at the BBC. For the first time in my TV career, I was the main presenter of football in one of the country's two main television organisations. I was extremely lucky to be in the right place at the right time. ITV's portfolio of football included the World Cup finals, European Championship, FA Cup and the relatively new and guaranteed audience puller, the Champions League.

In my private life, I was to be tested to new limits. Our

daughter Anna was fighting for her life. At no time previously had the easy smile, which I inherited from my mum, been more difficult to raise. As a family, we were in turmoil. As a television presenter, I was expected to exude a degree of tranquillity.

The rollercoaster ride I underwent was never better illustrated than in my first work for ITV. It was August. I was to interview the Arsenal manager George Graham prior to the new season. The cameras and interview position were set up in one of the executive boxes at Highbury's clock end. George was ready. As a close friend of the family, he knew all about the deep concerns we held, following the discovery of Anna's cancer six months earlier. She had undergone one life-saving operation, followed up by radiotherapy treatment. Just prior to the interview, George was asking me how my daughter's treatment was progressing. I was telling him that we remained optimistic and positive in our thinking, when the inner door to the executive box burst open and Anna appeared, followed by her husband Mitchell and Megs.

I knew they had been to Mount Vernon hospital that morning but I was unaware of the results of the scans that had been taken a week or so earlier. Anna was famous for her teasing, but on this occasion she came straight to the point. 'Dad, they're clear!' was all I heard. Amid shouts of delight and floods of tears, the four of us hugged each other in a mixture of joy and relief. George Graham went to find a bottle of champagne. The cameraman and my producer friend David Moss retired to allow us time to share the momentous news. Minutes later, a red-eyed interviewer began to put his questions to the Arsenal manager. It was difficult to take in George's answers as my mind was elsewhere. For the moment, my daughter's life was no longer in danger. The rollercoaster had reached a high point. If only it could have stopped there.

Several of my BBC pals, while wishing me well when I left, had told me to doublecheck certain areas at ITV. They intimated that standards were not always as high as those of the corporation. I never found that to be so. Both BBC and ITV employed many people of great talent in all areas of the demanding industry that is television programming.

With Anna's future looking so much brighter, I was able to give my full attention to the early stages of life at ITV. I felt at home instantly, aided by the fact that my efforts were concentrated solely on my own sport, football. After the emotionally charged interview with George Graham, my first live game was a Champions League match at Old Trafford. It was the first of many visits to the theatre of dreams where we enjoyed pre-match briefings from Sir Alex Ferguson. The United manager was remarkably forthcoming every time Brian Moore, our commentator, Jeff Farmer, Head of Football, Gary Newbon and I met with him over a cup of tea. He took us into his confidence, trusted us, and four hours before every game, Alex would tell us his team, subs and injury worries. At the end of our briefings, he never failed to take me on one side and ask for the latest news of Anna's health.

Many viewers believe ITV Sport is obsessed with Manchester United. The reality is that when United are being broadcast, they will attract a minimum of one million more viewers than any other club, Arsenal and Liverpool included. The fanatical following that Manchester United attracts has helped make them the richest club in world football. Their Champions League qualifying games in the seasons when I was ITV's main football presenter, generally produced audiences in excess of ten million viewers. The later stages were watched by additional millions. I benefited from these early days of Champions League coverage. In recent years, as interest has waned in the product, the early group games have struggled to produce half as big an audience. Huge audiences increase advertising revenue, but the downside for any TV presenter is the number of commercial breaks during a programme.

The discipline required is considerable. At the BBC, there were no restraints from the moment the opening title music had ended until the moment of handing over to the commentary team, in between which were several minutes of uninterrupted chat and analysis to promote a game. At ITV, the opening titles would end, the match would be set up and the guests introduced. There would be time to say 'Good evening', ask the two experts one question each and move to the first commercial break. At the outside, two and a half minutes would have elapsed from coming on air to the first advertisement.

Given the choice of watching the BBC or ITV on a head-to-head basis, the average viewer would prefer uninterrupted coverage, regardless of who the presenter or guests might be. Having the Champions League contract as an exclusive, however, showed how viewers are happy to tolerate adverts if there is no alternative. It was a fascinating new discipline for me to learn after my twenty years at the Beeb. On one programme, soon after my arrival, I was being counted to the close of the show, overran by a second or two and clipped the incoming commercial. Immediately after the programme, Jeff Farmer told me that the advertising company concerned might well object to losing the second or two of air time and claim thousands of pounds in compensation or a free advert. I understood the implications and never made the same mistake again.

The change in my status after becoming ITV's number-one presenter was immense. Jeff Farmer or Trevor East, would be in touch on a daily basis. They placed great store in the overnight ratings; for ITV, they were critical. Requests to chair sessions with advertisers, take part in photo shoots, appear at events on behalf of ITV Sport and many other commitments began to fill my diary. Invitations to Downing Street, film premieres and star-studded shows were part of the job.

My greatest ally at senior level was ITV's senior editor Rick Waumsley. We shared a fan's enthusiasm for the games we were showing and a desire to make ITV football the best available product for the viewers. Rick had a terrific way with words and quickly I decided that my early resolve to write my own scripts should be tempered by his brilliant input. There were times when he shared my frustrations at the senior executives' insistence that we didn't show the goals from other games at half-time or full time, for fear of affecting the late-night highlights programme. Rick, Brian Moore and I would argue the point that the prime-time live show must surely be the very best you could make it. There was nothing to stop us showing any other Champions League action. It's a source of amusement to me now that current Champions League programmes on ITV show as much action from other games as possible.

Brian Moore was acknowledged as a truly great commentator well before I arrived and I was to learn so much more about this special man. Quiet, unassuming, modest and humble, he was a person of high morals. His loyalty to the ITV cause was unswerving. So too were his deeply held religious and political views. He had his priorities absolutely right. His wife Betty and sons Chris and Simon were always foremost in Brian's thoughts. Simon worked alongside me at ITV and, like his dad, preferred a diligent quiet way of doing things rather than the dynamic. In the entire history of ITV Sport, I don't suppose any one person did more to raise its profile with the public than Brian Moore. His companionship and help from the moment I arrived was remarkable. We would travel the British Isles and Europe together and spend hours talking about every conceivable issue within work or outside. Only with Brian did I feel I could let my guard drop completely when we came to discuss the ordeal Anna was facing when her cancer returned. He would let me talk and often waited patiently as I struggled to control my emotions.

On our trips into Europe it was customary for the ITV team to eat out the night before a game, but Brian preferred to stay in the hotel and have a 'nice piece of fish'. He always asked if I would

na and Mitchell – just prior to the diagnosis of her cancer.

na in remission, 1994.

Arrival as ITV's main football presenter, 1994. Arsenal manager George Graham and Manchester United's Alex Ferguson do the honours.

A visit to 10 Downing Street during Jo Major's time as Prime Minister.

ITV's main men, still supporting their home teams – Brian Moore (Gillingham), Jim Rosenthal (Oxford United) and me (Chesterfield FC).

's 1998 World Cup team. Left to right, back row: Clive Tyldesley, Gary Newbon, Brian
ore, Ruud Gullit, me, Jim Rosenthal, Gabriel Clarke, Peter Drury. *Front row*: Barry
ison, Alex Ferguson, Bobby Robson, Terry Venables, Kevin Keegan, John Barnes.

e Bob Wilson Goalkeeping school enjoys a visit from the England goalkeeper David
man.

A family get-together with (*from left*) Hugh, Jean and Don.

The mentor, Bert Trautmann. He was kind enough to appear as a guest when I was the subject of 'This is Your Life'.

Anna – a favourite photograph, taken by Robert.

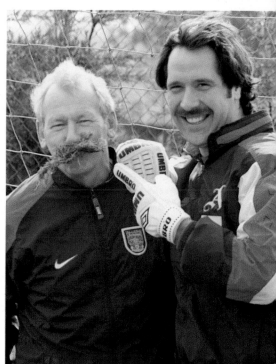

Serious times – Arsene Wenger and me on the pre-season tour to Austria, 2002.

I can't simulate the pony tail.

Another piece of history. Arsenal win the double for the third time in 2002 and for the first time three goalkeepers earn a championship medal. It all makes me very happy! *Left to right*: Richard Wright, me, David Seaman and Stuart Taylor.

Training with David Seaman is a strenuous business.

family. *Back row:* Robert and John.
nt row: Sarah, Max and Louis.

Hugh and I, on a visit to the RAF, take a
closer look at a Lancaster rear-turret.

ee of our Willow Foundation patrons. *Left to righ*t: Natasha Kaplinsky, Mary Nightingale
Linda Lusardi.

The Princess and the Woodcutter.

stay and eat with him. It's good that life does not confine the creation of wonderful friendships to days of youth. Brian Moore became a special friend when he and I were heading towards our retirement years. The tragedy was that his sudden death came so early in those days of tranquillity and satisfaction, which he had richly deserved.

He retired on the last day of the 1998 World Cup finals, and every week after that I would receive a call. 'Hello, remember me? I used to be a football commentator,' he'd say. We would laugh, exchange gossip and talk family. I was privileged to have known Brian Moore. He was a great human being.

Very quickly, ITV Champions League output became the envy of television sport. The acquisition of the FA Cup rights in partnership with Sky, and obtaining the highlights of England internationals, left BBC Sport in dismay for a time. Trevor East and ITV's parent companies deserve the praise for pulling off several coups from under the BBC's nose. The events that would always haul the corporation back into the big picture were the European Championship and the World Cup.

Euro '96, which was held in England, brought ITV and BBC together with the sharing of equipment at grounds, but pushed them apart in the pursuit of viewers. For two or three games, we were head to head. As on every previous occasion, the two broadcasters just hoped that their exclusive games would produce something special. The BBC revelled in England's defeat of Scotland, which included Paul Gascoigne's wonder goal and David Seaman's penalty save; ITV made the most of England's best display for years as Terry Venables' men thrashed Holland at Wembley.

The tournament gave me enormous satisfaction. I simply loved being part of such an occasion, in such an exalted position. I spearheaded ITV's presentation; Des Lynam fronted the BBC's. The Beeb enjoyed their three to one viewing superiority over ITV for the semi-final and final. Both channels were dismayed when England lost on penalties to Germany, one step away from a chance of glory.

Terry Venables was a regular guest on our ITV programmes alongside Glenn Hoddle and a wide variety of former players including Bryan Robson and Alan Shearer. I am often asked about the guests I have had to interview in the course of BBC or ITV programmes, and I can honestly say there were none with whom I didn't get on. They were all footballing men. All had great knowledge of the game, some held stronger opinions than others and their personalities varied enormously. Those who projected their views forcibly or dramatically were not always the best qualified. They had every right to proffer a view, of course, as could any fan, but only those who had experienced all areas of the game could fully comprehend certain situations. Jimmy Hill was the sole individual who understood chairmen of clubs, boards of directors, managers, coaches, players and fans. He had filled all those roles at one time or another. Others who could best interpret managerial decisions, coaching and playing peculiarities included Terry Venables, Glenn Hoddle, Ron Atkinson, Alex Ferguson, Kenny Dalglish and those similarly qualified. Players with no coaching or managerial experience should always be wary of the extent of their opinions.

My favourite interviewee was Bobby Robson. He gave insights into the game in such a passionate and enthusiastic way and was matched only by Brian Clough and Jimmy Hill. There was one problem for me. If Bobby was in full flow, he could easily lose track of who or what he was talking about. I would sense he'd forgotten where he was going with his views and always had to be on guard to prompt him back to the point he was making. The respect shown to Bobby by everyone was total and he produced many laughs as well. During one major tournament, he strode into the main production office, animated and cursing that he'd lost his new mobile phone. We asked if he knew the number and suggested he call it. We would alert everyone in the other offices to see if it rang in one of them. 'OK,' said Bobby, 'can I use this phone to ring the number?' Picking up a mobile off the desk in front of him, he dialled and waited. Within a second of dialling, he turned to us all and said, 'You're not going to believe this but it's engaged!' Imagine the laughter when it was discovered that it was his own phone he was using.

If Bobby's enthusiasm was infectious, Terry Venables' and Glenn Hoddle's tactical awareness was revealing. They were the analysts in September 1996 for Manchester United's Champions League tie against Juventus in Turin. The game took place on the day my eldest surviving brother underwent a major operation to remove his spleen. Don had a form of leukaemia and had to have regular blood transfusions to help the condition. This operation was more serious. He was always interested in my work and regularly expressed his delight and admiration at my successful move to ITV. 'You're in the chair now!' was a favourite saying of Don's when we talked. He was a great character and was one of the world's most dedicated amateur golfers. While I was waiting for kick-off in the Stadio delle Alpi in Turin, I received news that Don's operation had been a success, so I was relieved and relaxed as I took the programme on air.

There was always so much to do during the two and a half hours of top-class football, and time just flew by. Immediately I had finished taking the show off air, Terry, Glenn and I were joined by Brian Moore. Things had gone well and we were on a high. I told them I needed a couple of minutes to phone Megs and to get the latest news on my brother. Megs answered my call and, as ever, immediately talked about the programme.

'How's Don?' I asked. She hesitated momentarily with her reply.

'OK,' she said. I wasn't convinced.

'Megs, what's wrong? Something's gone wrong.'

There was a delay in her response. Then quietly she told me Don had died an hour earlier. Brian Moore was close to me when I let out a cry, and in the minutes that followed he helped me compose myself and encouraged me to tell him about the brother I had just lost.

I had been with ITV Sport for just over two years and we were all delighted that audiences and advertising revenue had continued to please those at the top. On the personal front, Anna's fight with her cancer had deteriorated. My concern for her future was far more important than trying to juggle my coaching commitments at Arsenal with my ITV work. Whenever circumstances permitted, Megs and I would drive down to Christchurch in Dorset where, for many years, we had a second home overlooking the Rivers Stour and Avon. On one such sortie we were in the car listening to the radio when the news revealed a surprise move by BBC's Head of Sport Brian Barwick to a similar position at the rival ITV channel following the departure of Trevor East. Megs and I both reacted in identical fashion: 'Oh shit!' As my agent, she knew the implications of the news. We were aware that Brian was a huge admirer and personal friend of Des Lynam. We both thought there would be a likelihood that he would, in time, try to persuade the great anchorman to leave the BBC. Initially, the news worried us, but when one of your children has a life-threatening illness, such concerns are of minor significance.

Brian and I were back working together as we had done during our 'Football Focus' days, except now he was Head of Sport and I was the main presenter of football. Our careers had taken us upward and we had both reached the top of the ladder. I carried on, safe in the knowledge that the contract Megs had secured took me beyond the 1998 World Cup finals to be held in France in two years' time.

ITV's domestic coverage in 1998 ended at Wembley as

Arsenal won the double for the second time in their history. It was always difficult trying to remain unbiased when the club at which I coached was playing in a game that I was presenting. Even when the World Cup got under way, I had to let my guests give their views on David Seaman's goalkeeping when my own would probably have been more objective. It was a highly unusual occurrence in television for a presenter to be quite so directly involved with the participants in the programmes. The bosses constantly reminded me to underplay my inside knowledge, and yet they were always quick to ask me to set up interviews they knew would have been declined if others asked.

The difference between the ITV and BBC coverage of World Cup '98 was considerable. ITV chose to send me to every venue in France. Our presenting positions were mostly in the open, and only occasionally in an enclosed studio. The atmosphere throughout was fantastic and, despite the difficulties of battling crowd noise, I was in my element. My schedule was testing and when Air France went on strike early in the tournament, ITV had to hire a private jet to move our six-man presentation team around the vast country.

During the first twenty-one days of the thirty-three-day tournament, I linked our live World Cup games from Montpellier twice, Bordeaux three times, Marseille three times, Paris five times, Lens twice, Lyon twice, Toulouse twice and Nantes twice, never stopping in one place for two consecutive games. In all we visited twenty-one venues. For the later stages of the tournament, we flew between Marseille, Nantes and Paris. Our tightly knit presentation team never flagged in energy levels and we never had a bad word to say to each other.

Personally, I preferred being at the event rather than in a soulless studio hundreds of miles from the action. Des Lynam presented the BBC coverage from a stylish studio in Paris, close to the Champs Elysées, a matter of yards away from the hotel where the BBC were based. It was a matter of personal preference for viewers, but for once, ITV received praise from the press for their considerable efforts to be close to the action.

Heavy discussions between the two television companies were again required to decide who covered which game. Events on the field would determine who came off better with regard to audience figures. ITV had England's quarter-final against Argentina exclusively, but the BBC would have had the advantage if Glenn Hoddle's team had reached the semi-final.

Alongside me for the Argentina game were two previous England managers. Terry Venables had been Glenn's predecessor and Bobby Robson had taken England to a semi-final shoot-out in Italia '90. For this game, we were in a studio while our reporter, Jim Rosenthal, was in the stadium in St Etienne with John Barnes and Ian Wright. It had been decided that the noise in the open gantry would make it too difficult for us to present from the stadium. Brian Moore had Kevin Keegan with him in the commentary box.

The game was dramatic from start to finish. Meetings between England and Argentina always contain plenty of grudge. David Seaman conceded a dubious penalty and Argentina took the lead; Michael Owen equalised with a wonder goal; David Beckham was sent off; Sol Campbell had a goal disallowed. It finished 2–2 after extra time. David Batty missed in the shoot-out and England lost 4–3 on penalties.

The audience figures reflected the importance of the event – 26.5 million viewers was the peak figure, the highest ever number of people tuning in to a television programme on any single channel. The average audience throughout the entire show was 23.7 million, the highest ever for an ITV programme since the channel went on air in 1955. The audience share was 80 per cent.

Rick Waumsley, Brian Moore and I were later given a

memento of the historic broadcast – a rather basic certificate stating the facts and figures. A week after we received them, Brian asked if Megs and I had found a nice spot for our memento because he was a little undecided where to place his own. 'I've put it where it deserves to go,' I told Brian, 'the downstairs loo.' He laughed and ended up replicating my suggestion in his own home. My record audience certificate and gold disc of 'Good Old Arsenal' sit nicely together to this day.

Presenting the 1998 World Cup finals was probably the greatest moment in the twenty-eight years I was lucky enough to survive in the television industry. Make no mistake, it is a game of survival and, in my view, far more demanding than anything I experienced in the football world. It was following France '98 that I was nominated as Sports Presenter of the Year by the Royal Television Society, but I didn't win. Des Lynam collected the award.

With record audiences and very satisfying advertising revenues, I never contemplated being vulnerable in my position as main presenter. The senior executives seemed to be happy with my work and they were wonderfully compassionate when Anna finally succumbed to her cancer in December 1998, four months after the World Cup finals.

During the whole of the last year of her life, it became increasingly difficult to juggle work with the essential time spent with the family, helping Anna in her struggle. The senior sports men at ITV, Brian Barwick and Jeff Farmer, never put pressure on me. They left it to me to advise them on the current situation.

In mid November 98, the ITV team were in Barcelona. I was walking away from the magnificent Nou Camp stadium after overseeing Manchester United's latest European tie. Phoning home after the final whistle had always been a priority and Anna's condition simply hastened the call. Megs latest report was frightening. During the thirty-six hours I had been away from home, Anna's breathing difficulties had necessitated another hospital visit and further emergency treatment. Megs' voice transmitted her concern. I was walking as I was talking but even before I ended the call, I knew the time had come to spend all my time at home. Our hotel, the Princess Sophia, was only half a mile from the stadium and I decided to delay telling ITV of the problems until the morning. It was a sleepless night but by 8.30 a.m. we were in the airport at Barcelona awaiting the early flight to London. In the privacy of the executive lounge, I told Rick Waumsley and Jeff Farmer that I needed time off. They knew of the problems and without hesitation told me to take as long as I needed. Sadly, events moved rapidly. Within ten days, Anna died. My friends at ITV were wonderful, full of love and support. When I returned in early February 1999, they picked me up, dusted me down and made my work so easy. Anna's courage and the memory of her drove me forward as well.

The exploits of Manchester United in Europe played a part in my regaining my appetite for work. I wasn't exactly happy that they had knocked Arsenal out of the FA Cup so dramatically, a late Dennis Bergkamp penalty miss and a Ryan Giggs wonder goal proving decisive; beating Arsenal to the championship was another blow. But to secure the treble, they had to beat Bayern Munich in the Champions League final in Barcelona in May, an event covered exclusively by ITV.

Memories of my last visit to the Nou Camp, when Anna was still alive, had to be pushed aside. I was a professional and lucky enough to be a major participant in the coverage of a piece of footballing history. Football matches rarely produce as much drama as United's final with Bayern. The German club had most of the chances. They hit the woodwork twice and were one up with only minutes to go to full time. Before the programme, I had prepared a twenty-second closing link, but it reflected a United win and compared Alex Ferguson's team with the one managed by Sir Matt Busby in 1968, United's only previous success in the European Cup. In urgent conversation with Rick Waumsley – a huge United fan – I was discussing how to adapt it when, as we spoke, United equalised through Teddy Sheringham. Rick was ecstatic. Commentator Clive Tyldesley reflected the excitement brilliantly. We started to think about extra time, but it wasn't needed. Ole Gunnar Solskjaer found the Bayern net; United were champions of Europe. As bedlam broke out all around, we needed cool heads to make the most of the moment.

It's at such times that a closely knit team of television pros call on their experience and expertise. I always acknowledged that I couldn't be seen to do the job properly without a terrific back-up team. At home, you only see the presenter's face and hear his voice. Behind it, the following all play key roles: commentators, reporters, editors, producers, production assistants, vision mixers, sound assistants, technical back-up, floor managers, cameramen, auto prompters, make-up artists, riggers, runners and many more hard-working individuals.

Only one thing prevented our coverage of the 1999 Champions League final being an unqualified success and that was commercial breaks. The advertisers buy specific time and pay huge sums for it. We had already overrun our commercial break following the final whistle, but were desperate to cover the presentation of the trophy to Peter Schmeichel. No sooner had the United captain lifted the piece of silverware into the night air when ITV cut away to adverts. We could all imagine the collective groan of the watching audience back home. The overnight viewing figures revealed that almost twenty million people tuned in.

One last minor drama occurred that night. We were keen to hear for a second time from Alex Ferguson but had only just over two minutes between coming back on air and saying goodnight. In my earpiece I could hear Rick Waumsley instructing our reporter Gary Newbon to conduct a maximum forty-second interview with the United manager so that I would get my twenty seconds to wrap up United's achievement in the most telling way. Immediately the commercial break finished, I welcomed viewers back, reiterated the 2–1 scoreline and, after a brief reaction from Terry Venables, led to Gary Newbon.

There was one minute and twenty seconds left of the programme. Mary Hutchinson was already counting me down to 'stopping talking' prior to the end titles. Even if Gary overran by a few seconds, I would still have the time needed to close the show. Gary Newbon is well known throughout the television sports industry as a forthright character with humour and a rare ego. Hearing instructions and keeping to them has never been his greatest strength. Mary continued her countdown. Gary carried on his interview with Alex and by the time a desperate floor manager successfully stopped our reporter, I was left with twelve seconds to wrap up events. I was furious but obviously couldn't show it. A bollicking for Gary could come later. Twelve seconds was too short a time to embrace United's achievement and the manner of it, but that's when presenters earn their keep and learn to think fast on their feet. The prepared lines were abandoned and I bade a hasty and inadequate goodnight.

The 1998–99 season was probably the most successful ever for ITV Sport with regard to audiences. Of the twenty television sports programmes with the highest audiences during that time, sixteen were on ITV screens. For fifteen of those shows, I was the lucky man in the chair. It was a special end to the saddest twelve months of my life.

As soon as the football season ended, allowing me a break from ITV and my coaching role at Arsenal, I was booked into the Royal Orthopaedic Hospital at Stanmore for the first of my two hip replacements. Problems with my hips had been apparent for several years, but the pain had increased and my mobility was decreasing. Kicking footballs was aided by a daily dose of anti-inflammatory tablets, and they also helped me to negotiate twelve holes of golf with difficulty. My surgeon, Tim Briggs, agreed that wear and tear from the years as a physical education teacher, footballer and goalkeeping coach had caught up with me.

Megs and I spent the summer at home in Hertfordshire and on the Dorset coast. Extra recovery time was required for the 'non cement' hip replacement in order for my own bone to knit with the prosthetic stem and ball. The pain relief afforded by a hip replacement changes the quality of your life, and the days I spent in Stanmore and recuperating at home gave me plenty of time to re-assess what was important in life and what wasn't. Anna's death affected the whole family in different ways and each of us coped as best we could.

A week or two before the start of the new football season, I received a phone call from Jeff Farmer. He told me that ITV needed to see me to talk about the forthcoming coverage of programmes. I had already received a printed schedule so found the request mildly surprising. I asked Jeff whether there was any ulterior motive for the meeting. He insisted there wasn't. ITV headquarters is situated in Grays Inn Road, just down from King's Cross Station, but when Jeff informed me that the meeting would be held at the Independent Sports Network offices on the South Bank, I should have smelt a rat. A car collected me on the Monday morning because I was still on crutches. Familiar faces greeted me when I hobbled in to the nineteenth floor offices high above the Thames. I was among good friends. I had beaten Jeff Farmer to the meeting so John Watts, ITV's top match director who, like me, had once worked at the BBC, helped me lay out my papers relating to the season's football on the office table.

Jeff Farmer appeared, shook my hand, asked how the family were coping and told John he needed the office for a few minutes in private. More or less at the same time, Brian Barwick arrived. He shook my hand but looked uneasy. Sitting down opposite me with all my papers laid out in front of him he said, 'Willow, there's no easy way to tell you this. Half an hour ago we signed up Des Lynam.'

It was a hammer blow of great proportion. The implication was obvious. Des would become ITV's number one football presenter. My fate was in the hands of the two men I faced and those in senior control of ITV above them. The premonition that Megs and I shared when Brian became Head of Sport had become a reality. My first reaction was defensive and emotive. 'You've got to be joking. He's tired, lazy and past it!' were the words that came pouring out of my mouth. I followed up this unfair abuse of the great presenter by stating the record figures that ITV had attracted during the past twelve months.

Brian quickly sought to regain control of the meeting, which was getting out of hand. He said that ITV still wanted me on board and, to prove their commitment, he produced an envelope containing a letter with an increased offer on my contract, which had only recently been renegotiated on my behalf by Dennis Roach.

I threw the envelope back at him without opening it. By now the realisation of what was occurring was sinking in and I was close to tears. I was stupidly beginning to feel sorry for myself but it was no time for that. Brian insisted that I read the new offer and delivered it for a second time in my direction. I took out the letter, glanced at the increased figure and promptly ripped it in two. The Head of Sport continued to talk, while the Head of Football said nothing. I was told that ITV would stage a press conference at Grays Inn Road at two o'clock that afternoon and that there was a press embargo until then, which would allow me time to inform my family and friends of what was happening. Briefly, the press conference that signalled my own defection from BBC to ITV five years earlier flashed across my mind. Champagne, footballs suitably inscribed with the ITV logo, a major trophy and special guests had all been a part of the act.

I was, by now, feeling sick in my stomach and humiliated but just as I was preparing to offer my resignation, my brain clicked into gear and reminded me of a phrase in my existing contact. It was the one that Megs had insisted upon which stated that I was 'ITV's principal presenter of football'. The contract had initially been for four years, but had been renewed for a further two.

'Hang on,' I said. 'I think you've got yourself a problem with the existing contract. You'd better read it. You can't do this.'

Brian listened to me intently and shot an enquiring look at Jeff Farmer as I told him the wording of which, seemingly, he was unaware. Very rapidly, Brian Barwick and Jeff Farmer left the room, having told me that the press conference would go ahead regardless. John Watts returned and could see my distressed state. As a good friend, he expressed his amazement at the morning's events. I rang Megs from the office and told her I was on my way home. I told her to inform John and Robert, the family and friends, and our solicitor.

My driver was waiting to take me home and, as we drew away, the radio news revealed that Des Lynam was about to leave the BBC to join ITV. So much for a media embargo; so much for the chance to let my family hear the news first. The twenty-five-mile journey back to Hertfordshire, which took just over an hour, was spent on my mobile phone. The first call was to Brian Moore. Expressing his shock and concern, he had no doubt about what I should do. 'Sue them for all you can' was Brian's reaction. It was so unlike him to express such a damning view of a decision made by the ITV executive. The second friend I turned to was Jim Rosenthal. His call of welcome had been one of the first I had received when I was on the way to ITV. Jim is a remarkably talented presenter of many sports including football, and he never failed to back me in my time at the commercial channel. Jim's thoughts did not concur with those of Brian. 'Don't do anything too hasty. I'll be round to your house this afternoon at four.'

271

Des duly arrived in a blaze of publicity befitting his status, with champagne, logoed footballs, a major trophy, special guests. Coverage continued for several days afterwards. They were absorbing days for me. On the afternoon of the announcement I sat in our garden, thinking hard, taking calls and receiving visitors. Jim Rosenthal insisted that I should reconsider any decision to walk out. He knew of the legal difficulties ITV faced in removing me from the main presenter role, so suggested I use that as a basis to renegotiate an improved contract and a satisfactory role within the organisation. Brian Moore began to see the sense of Jim's suggestion as well.

The biggest problem was me. I had always been a proud person. Loyalty was high on my list of essential attributes. ITV had shown me no loyalty, but I realised that many other individuals would have done what Brian Barwick did, given the opportunity to sign Des Lynam. I was almost fifty-eight years old, a year older than Des, and had surpassed, by three years, the time when I had imagined my presenting career shelf life would be over. I had achieved everything I had dreamt of in my television career.

The next few weeks were taken up with protracted talks between ITV, Megs and Dennis Roach. ITV didn't want the bad publicity that a court case would create and they did their utmost to convince me I still had a major part to play in covering great sporting occasions. The healthiest contract of my entire working life was drawn up and signed. It was for a period of three years. The words 'principal presenter of football' were not included. At the conclusion of the talks, I rang Des and wished him well.

My final three years as a television presenter were carried out in as friendly a manner as the preceding twenty-five. There was no reason for me to be anything but professional. I liked the people I worked with enormously, just as I had at the BBC. Admittedly, it was not the same after reverting to a number two role, after sampling the top job and everything that went with it. The daily phone calls from the heads of department dried up completely but the invitations to a variety of events didn't.

My new role meant that I very rarely covered 'live' games, which I so enjoyed. Now I was presenting two successive nights of Champions League highlights. The one that was transmitted live at ten was a great success; the other, which went out to the public at 11.15 or 11.30, was broadcast far too late for the majority of people. It was strange to be hosting the main highlights programme during the European Championship in Holland in the year 2000, but nothing could ever suppress my love of football and involvement with such big events.

The arrival of Des Lynam at ITV changed my profile and his. As the number one at BBC Sport, he fronted all the major sporting events including the Olympics, the World Cup, Wimbledon, 'Match of the Day', the Grand National, the boat race and 'Sports Review of the Year'. Even when the BBC's football contracts were reduced, no other sports presenter fronted such a glittering array of national events as Des Lynam.

It was a remarkable gamble by ITV to lure him to host football alone on the basis of increasing audiences and advertising revenue. Both areas had already peaked with regard to the coverage of weekly football, as the decline in viewing figures and attracting advertisers has subsequently shown. Viewers have quickly tired of the nightly games available on one channel or another, and football coverage is at saturation point; even the highest quality matches attract smaller and smaller audiences. The watching public simply cannot afford the spiralling prices demanded at the turnstiles or by satellite television.

When ITV won the rights to show all the highlights of the Premiership games, the BBC's 'Match of the Day' programme, something of a national institution, lost its main output. With much hype, it was replaced by 'The Premiership' on ITV. On Saturday, 18 August 2001, the new football show went out to the public at 7.00 p.m. in a brave but misguided attempt to prove that the popularity of our national game could outperform Cilla Black's 'Blind Date' or Matthew Kelly's 'Stars in their Eyes'.

Des opened up with typical Lynam whimsy – 'Better for you. Better for all of us. Good evening. New Season, new show, new time. You'd obviously heard.'

The general public had heard of the change of time for the football highlights programme, but they didn't like the earlier billing. Viewing figures were so ordinary that by Christmas, David Liddiment, ITV's Controller of Programmes, had re-scheduled 'The Premiership' to 10.30, the same time as the dethroned 'Match of the Day'.

Audiences and adverts remain the key to success for ITV but with the growth of satellite television, the fight for sponsorship money and commercial revenue becomes increasingly problematic. The demise of On Digital towards the end of the 2001–02 season was catastrophic for the two parent companies, Granada and Carlton. Such high hopes for On Digital crashed when the public failed to see it as a superior alternative to Sky TV, already well established.

I was surprised during the last year of my contract with ITV that Brian Barwick offered me a further one-year extension to take me up to September 2003. He asked me to look upon the proposal as ITV's 'gift' for the work I had done for them during the previous eight years, and for restoring their credibility. Heading, as I was, into retirement, I was appreciative of the gesture, which would help guarantee the future for Megs and me.

Still, I found it very difficult to enjoy the role given to me during the 2002 World Cup finals in Japan and South Korea. The live games I presented on the main ITV channel were interspersed with other matches that I fronted on ITV's digital channel, ITV2. The latter production was undermanned in every respect. It tested the patience and professionalism of all those involved. For the one and only time during twenty-eight years of presenting, I would go home and tell Megs that I wasn't enjoying the job. An exclusive interview with David Seaman following England's exit at the hands of Brazil, helped lift my spirits towards the end of the tournament. All of the media were trying to get him to comment on the Ronaldinho goal and on the circumstances at the end of the game when David was in tears. Rick Waumsley tentatively enquired if I would approach David with a view to being interviewed. I told him it was unlikely he would agree, but I would ask.

There was hardly any hesitation from my great friend. He laughed his rumbling laugh and said, 'Don't be stupid. I'll do it for you – but for you only.' Sitting in the garden of his home, I enquired whether he wished to be pre-warned on the line my questioning would take. He didn't want to know anything and preferred to react instinctively. It even came as a surprise to me when David revealed in our chat that he was seriously thinking of retiring from international duty.

By most standards the exclusive interview was really good television – a special scoop – but ITV neither trailed it adequately nor gave it the priority it merited. Had the BBC or Sky got their hands on the interview, it would have received much greater air time. I was dispirited. For three years I had called upon every bit of professionalism that had been so carefully crafted during my two decades at the BBC. I had been pleased that I could live as comfortably as I did with the disappointment I felt after Des's arrival at ITV. My credibility within football and the television business was still high. All that I had set out to achieve had been surpassed. Only the attitude of ITV Sport's senior personnel left something to be desired.

Instinctively, I knew it was the moment to go. I had just enjoyed an emotional farewell at Highbury as goalkeeping coach, on the day Arsenal lifted the third double in the club's

275

history. I had completed my ninth World Cup on television by securing the most sought-after interview of the 2002 tournament. The timing was perfect. My life on the box was over.

14
Anna's story

'In the midst of winter I finally learned that there was
within me an invincible summer.'

Albert Camus

I think we are lucky if, at sometime in our lives, we are taught
what is really important and what isn't. My special lesson didn't
begin in earnest until February 1994. That was the month and
year that my daughter Anna was told she had cancer. She taught
me until 1 December 1998, which is the date she died.

During the five years that her cancer visited her, Anna
recognised what should be enjoyed in life and the futility of
chasing the irrelevant. Her illness allowed me to spend more
time with her than would have been normal in a father–daughter
relationship. She inspired me, regularly put me in my place,
made me laugh and helped me to cry. Most dads think their
little girls are special. Anna was special. I adored her and I
miss her.

Without her wisdom I would not have been able to turn my
back on ITV so easily. I had always been driven by principle
and ambition. So many times during her illness, when I had
been challenged by apparent injustice, she would say, 'Dad, it's
not important.' I wasn't the only one in the family to benefit.
In the five years of her dying, she taught us all how to live.

Anna was born at 2.00 a.m. on 7 December 1966. England
were world champions. Unlike our eldest child John's birth

sixteen months earlier, I was present to assist the midwife as Megs brought our only daughter into the world. The umbilical cord was wrapped tightly round the baby's neck but, quickly and expertly, the midwife released the pressure, looped the cord over the tiny head and allowed life to enter our child's body. She was 6lbs 12oz and we named her Anna Louise. She was two and a half years old by the time her second brother, Robert, was born and by then had a mass of tight curly blonde hair and a cherubic face. She was always a fun-loving girl. She loved the Beatles' music, Marilyn Monroe and her two brothers.

The relationship between our three children was always a close one. Holidays, school work, friends, Arsenal FC, whatever it was, there were few secrets that weren't shared between John, Anna and Robert, and great pride in each other's achievements followed. John became the arts correspondent/presenter of the Radio 4 programme 'Front Row'. Anna qualified as a community nursing sister while Robert's skills took him into the heady echelons of commercial photography. As they all became established with respective partners, they would enjoy time together, influencing each other's taste in music and life.

Megs had created a base and home that was always there for them in times of joy, trouble or need. 'A mother's love is unconditional' is how she described her role. Most worries were the usual ones and of little consequence. Guiding children from adolescence to adulthood is never likely to be straightforward and we were not much different from any other family.

Anna had several boyfriends but none made as big an impact upon us as Mitchell Carey. The first sighting Megs and I had of Mitchell was at Anna's eighteenth birthday in 1984. A party, held at the local cricket club, was gatecrashed by two youths dressed as American baseball players. They took over the dance floor and were noisy. Later, while Megs was expressing pleasure at what terrific friends Anna had, I chirped in with, 'Just as long as she doesn't end up marrying one of those zany lads.'

Well, she did marry Mitchell Carey and for that we will be forever grateful. No one could have made her laugh as much or loved her more. Twelve months into their relationship he sent her a note. It still remains in her childhood room, a sheet of paper torn out of a diary. The date is 17 December 1985. In Mitchell's handwriting the words 'one year' are written followed by:

> I'll do anything for you
> I'd stand out in the rain
> Anything you want me to
> Just don't let it slip away.

A small red heart seals the page. It meant so much to Anna.

She and Mitchell married on 26 September 1992 in the tiny church in Knebworth Park, home of the Lytton Cobbolds. It was the happiest day of Anna's life and the proudest for me, her dad. *En route* to Knebworth in the wedding car, I started to tell her how much I loved her, but she stopped me because she knew we were both likely to start crying and unlikely to stop. She was always 'my little girl' no matter how tall she grew or how mature she became. Before we reached the church we had recalled many things, including my dancing lessons when I used to teach her to rock and roll and jive. To understand the steps required in ballroom dances I would lift Anna onto my stockinged feet and waltz or quickstep her round like a rag doll, Anna's stride joined with my socks.

The emotion attached to the father of the bride speech was neatly sidestepped by the distraction of a white hankie. Because I have been over-emotional all my life, I asked all guests and especially the youngsters to wave their napkins if they sensed a quiver in my voice and a tear in my eye. It worked like magic and created great amusement and audience participation. It became a family joke.

Anna had been married for twelve months when the earliest signs of a health problem materialised. She developed a cough that wouldn't go away. By November it had become very troublesome and was often worse after she'd been climbing stairs or lifting her patients. Swallowing became a problem and she would drink water constantly in order to help relieve the restriction in her throat.

The weekend after New Year, 1994, Anna and Mitchell joined Megs and me in Christchurch. During a walk at a local beauty spot called Hengistbury Head, Anna struggled to keep up with us. Her breathing was laboured and she joked about her lack of fitness. Mitchell made her promise to go to see the doctor, the result of which was an appointment at the Lister Hospital, Stevenage, for a CT scan. It revealed a large round shadow across the right central part of Anna's chest. The diagnosis was that she had a cyst emanating from somewhere near the trachea region and that it had grown to the size of an orange. Anna's immediate fears were quickly appeased since it was felt to be 99.9 per cent certain that, because of the spherical shape, it was benign and full of fluid. An operation to remove the media sternum cyst would be required and arrangements were made for that to take place at the renowned heart and lung hospital at Harefield. The surgeon was Mr Alun Rees.

Anna was twenty-seven when she faced this operation. It was expected to take some time, but she was back on the ward much quicker than anticipated. 'They've not taken it out,' Anna told us. We thought the anaesthetic had not worn off and that she was rambling, but when Mr Rees himself came in, he explained that more tests were needed. He wouldn't enlarge on the diagnosis until a biopsy had been performed. He was troubled by the fact that the 'cyst' had a vice like grip on her oesophagus. This indicated to him that the cyst was in fact a tumour. He hoped it was benign.

For two weeks we waited for results that didn't come, answers that didn't arrive. We refused to contemplate cancer. Our family routine tried to keep Anna's spirits high. I would finish my final 'Breakfast News' sports spot at 8.30 and be with Anna by nine. We would chat or do jigsaws, but never bothered worrying about medical possibilities. Megs would take over from me at eleven and I would return to be with the two of them in the mid-afternoon. Mitchell would get over from work as soon as he could.

The strain on the newlyweds began to show as the days went by with no further news. More biopsies were sent to Mount Vernon and the Royal Marsden for analysis but neither hospital was forthcoming with a diagnosis. Anna's breathing was worse, her trachea reduced to a quarter of its size, and she was in danger of choking.

Mitchell's humour usually saved a bad day. His individuality and talent as a graphic designer paved the way to promotion and responsibility. At his best, he would entertain a room full of people, provoking uncontrollable laughter. At his most vulnerable, his insecurities closed him down. Individually and together, Mitchell and Anna were about to embark on a five-year game of snakes and ladders.

During the second week of Anna's stay at Harefield, I was due for an overnight visit to hospital as well. My arthritic hips were to be injected under anaesthetic at the King Edward VII hospital in the centre of London in an attempt to ease the continuous pain that I was in. There was a heavy snowfall as Megs stayed with Anna while she had more tests and more disappointment at the still unanswered questions. The days seemed long and the frustration of not knowing was making everyone very tetchy. My return to Harefield next day coincided with Valentine's Day, but there was little joy in the ward as I found Anna and Megs trying to occupy their waiting time. Mitchell had disappeared and it was feared he had gone walkabout to cool off his agitation.

Suddenly, two nurses rushed through the ward shouting, 'Anna, come quick, come here!' They took our daughter to the main window of the ward, two floors up from the ground. Outside, where once had been a large grassy area, the snow lay thick and pristine. It had been broken by huge letters, ten feet tall. The 'I' and the 'U' sat either side of a massive heart in the middle of which lay Mitchell looking up at Anna's window. The desired effect was achieved and frowns became smiles once more.

Two days later, we had the news that was unwelcome. The biopsy results from the laboratories revealed that the cells were poorly differentiated and still unrecognisable, but certainly malignant. Treatment would have to be considered, but it looked as though surgery was not an option. We were unable to comprehend the enormity of it, so Anna made us all get together, hold each other tightly and cry as one. Our daughter's eyes were red from her tears. She looked beautiful but vulnerable and did most of the talking.

'Mum, Dad, I'll be OK. Of all the family, I'm the one who can cope with cancer best. You're not going to let this thing destroy you, whatever lays ahead.'

It was surreal, like being in a film or a dream. Anna talked as though she'd been released from some imprisonment, thoughts that must have been trapped inside her head during the long days at Harefield. 'And if I do die, I want to be in my wedding dress with anenomes in my hair.' Her immediate acceptance of what might happen shocked and somehow comforted us.

The nursing staff, sensitive to the situation, made up a bed for Mitchell to stay overnight. It was no time for them to be apart. I drove home, subdued, defeated, exhausted. Megs drove separately around the M25 and screamed in desperation throughout the journey. We arrived together. It was the first of many nights I would listen to my wife sobbing and crying uncontrollably, the first of many nights when sleep became impossible.

And what would be going through Anna's mind? Only five years later did we learn the truth of Anna's struggle within herself. She'd started a diary on 18 February 1994. The first entry read:

Today I was told I had cancer – how weird. We've cried, laughed, cried and cried. I thought I already knew, but kept a little dream alive that they'd got it wrong. I was wrong. I'm not scared, it's just unreal. I can't believe it's happening to me. I wonder how people will react to me now?

The days that followed brought tension, anger and irritation. Anna would vent her frustration on her nearest and dearest, Megs ending up on the receiving end of her daughter's bewildered state. I knew she wouldn't have a go at me, not 'Daddy, my Daddy!' Those were the words she had always mocked me with after we'd watched the film 'The Railway Children' together and cried as Jenny Agutter saw her dad through the smoke of a train after his release from prison.

In the midst of our confusion, Mr Alun Rees became our first hero. He burst into our family evening to tell Anna, 'I want to do something about it tomorrow. I want to operate.' He had cancelled his skiing holiday and would operate the following day. With that he waved goodbye, but I pursued him.

'Is the operation that urgent?' I asked. Mr Rees looked me straight in the eye.

'If I don't do it tomorrow, I fear that she won't be with us when I return.'

The following morning, Megs and I accompanied Anna to the doors of the operating theatre. 'Make sure you buy me a big present,' were her words. Ill she may have been; full of mischief she remained.

The courage of Alun Rees's decision to operate at first seemed to have been justified. Four hours after she went to theatre,

Anna was wheeled into recovery. Mr Rees came to see Megs and me. He was fatigued but encouraged.

'I've got it out. It's in a bucket. It's white and I don't know what it is. I've never seen anything like it before in twenty years of thoracic surgery. We'll send half of it to the Royal Marsden and half to Mount Vernon. Her trachea is free and she can breathe normally.'

Megs and I were overjoyed, overwhelmed. We shook Alun Rees by the hand, thanked him and asked if he was going back to theatre.

'Oh no,' he replied. 'I'm going to have a very stiff drink.'

Mr Rees's registrar was left to tell us more about the operation and his admiration for his boss. It had taken Alun Rees fifty minutes to prise and probe the tumour away from one part of Anna's chest, another hour to lift it gently from her trachea. The tumour had also been wrapped around the aorta and the aortic arch, but they had not found from where the tumour was emanating.

Our time at Harefield is etched indelibly in our memories. As a family, we closed ranks brilliantly but for all of us it was an experience for which we were totally unprepared. Anna, at just twenty-seven years of age, managed to face her own mortality head on. Mitchell had confronted the distinct possibility of becoming a widower one year and five months after marrying. John and Robert battled with the reality that the life of their only sister and soul mate had come close to being ended. Megs and I put on a public face full of optimism and hope, but privately we harboured differing thoughts about what lay ahead. Megs refused to believe that Anna wouldn't beat the cancer that had invaded her daughter's body. I never adopted a negative stance, but once Anna's form of cancer had been identified, I felt that one of us had to be a touch realistic.

'Malignant schwannoma. Soft tissue sarcoma. A malignant growth of the nerve sheath.' The histology reports from Mount

Vernon and the Marsden concurred. As a lay person, you try to comprehend as much medical jargon as you can. In talking privately with Mr Rees's registrar, I asked for more information about this very rare form of cancer.

'I've only heard of a similar cancer twice before,' he said.

'How've they got on?' I asked.

'Oh, they died,' came the response.

It triggered doubt and concern in my mind and, although I clung on to a belief that Anna had been lucky, the registrar's words soon came racing back into my thoughts when events began to take a change for the worse over the next months and years.

Anna underwent a six-week course of radiotherapy sessions aimed at destroying any stray tissue left after surgery and, during the summer months of my transfer to ITV, she began to appear confident of her recovery, even though her diaries later revealed to us her deep innermost fears:

> During radiotherapy I chant in my head 'kill it, kill it, kill it' constantly. Probably as scared as I've ever been right now. Thought totally on 'will I die? How long have I got?' I just know I don't want to die yet. Is it really happening to me? Sometimes I think it's not fair.

But outwardly she convinced us that she was coping and, of us all, she was the one that set the rules and led by example, insisting on laughter, fun and mischief every day. Whenever Anna felt good, she lived life to the full and when she was given the news that she was in remission, she came straight over to Highbury to share the news.

> Apparently it's gone. WOW! Went to Highbury and found Dad then got wrecked for rest of day. I'll write when I'm sober but I feel good.

She returned to her community nursing and immersed herself in the job that she loved. However, just nine months later she was in trouble again as scans revealed more areas of concern. She gave up writing in her diary as she could no longer bear to pen the reflection of her life. Her journey still had three years and five months to go. In that precious period of time we all enjoyed marvellous moments together, memories that will sustain us always. The fact that there were more bad days than good was an irrelevance simply because we still had Anna with us. For the next forty-one months, the disruption and worries were to increase steadily.

Her oncology treatment took place at the Middlesex Hospital and her surgery at the Royal Brompton, where numerous specialist doctors and nurses helped Anna through her journey of hope. We got to know many of them well and they in turn became very familiar with our daughter's zestful, madcap personality. Professor Bob Souhami was her oncologist and one of the few who was familiar with Anna's rare form of cancer. He sustained her spirit and was determined to find an answer to Anna's problems. Her cancer had returned in her ribs, back and neck area and the only alternative he could offer was surgery, since treatment by chemotherapy was not thought to be an option. He directed us towards the only thoracic surgeon who was prepared to consider her case, Peter Goldstraw of the Royal Brompton Hospital. He was exactly the sort of person Anna needed, up front and always going straight to the point.

At our initial consultation, he reiterated that Anna had received a maximum amount of radiation possible and that there was no known chemotherapy available to treat her condition.

'So I'm going to operate,' he went on. 'We have to operate. I don't know how yet, but we have to do it. If you were older, Anna, we might not consider it, but you're young and fit, so there's no reason why you shouldn't come through it.'

Anna couldn't have had two better Christmas presents. Adventurous surgery and Peter Goldstraw heightened her love of the festive season. We all faced 1996 with fresh hope.

On 25 January, Anna was admitted to the Brompton. She appreciated the single room she was given. The privacy meant a lot to her, particularly as she had a recognisable dad. We rented a flat for Mitchell close to the Kings Road so he could be at hand during what we hoped would be another life-saving operation.

Anna underwent her second thoracotomy. Peter Goldstraw had told us he knew of four areas of major concern but that these cancers were 'devious little chaps' and there might be more. The incision would follow much the same line as the first from beneath her right breast to high on the left side of her back. He would have to remove ribs at the front and at the back which would be replaced by plastic, and then try to get the tumour from her neck. We kissed her at 2.25 p.m. and as she waved a cheery goodbye, Mitchell, Megs and I hugged each other to help our anxiety.

Six and a half hours later at 9.50 p.m., Peter Goldstraw had completed his work.

'The four tumours turned out to be twelve or thirteen. It just shows that with all the sophistication of modern scans, we still couldn't detect them. The neck area had a lot of lumpy tumour and I had to cut right down to the nerve and take part of it away. I also had to take part of the tip of her lung and as much of the pleura as I could. We have flushed everything through with tap water to kill off any stray cells. All the tumours that I could see with my naked eye, I removed.'

The surgeon's report sounded so matter of fact and encouraging. Mitchell was lost in admiration and wonder but I don't think he heard Mr Goldstraw's last line – 'I cannot give any guarantees. Recurrence is very possible.' With that, and still wearing his theatre 'blues', he waved aside our gratitude and left the room, our second hero. In intensive care, Anna briefly opened her eyes and saw Mitchell's upturned thumb. She tried to respond in the same way and was thankfully asleep again before she had a chance to identify our tear-stained faces.

Over the next few days she went from intensive care to high dependency and finally back to her single room. She was watched over by caring nurses, her doting husband and remarkable mother. When Mr Goldstraw eventually told her she could go home, she thanked her mum for being 'the best nurse in the world'.

Cancer is not just a battle to be won by the patient. It tries to destroy all those who surround the person it invades. Mitchell and Anna's marriage had already been challenged and survived. Megs and I faced a similar test. Normal married life together became difficult from the day of her initial diagnosis. Megs' priority was understandably to care for her sick daughter. It was a full-time occupation and infinitely more demanding and tiring than the work in which I was involved at Arsenal and ITV.

Spring turned into summer and Euro '96 gave joy to Anna and her dad. On air, I would give her secret signals that I was thinking about her. The viewers were, I hope, blissfully unaware that a scratched ear or nose, or pen held up between both hands, were messages to Anna saying, 'Hi Anna, how ya doing? See you soon.'

Anna's life, though by no means a return to normal, was improved. She enjoyed caring for her home in Knebworth and the time that she was able to spend with Mitchell, her brothers and their friends. But by the next summer, scans revealed the reason for a cough and the growing difficulties in breathing that she had been experiencing. The tumour in her neck had returned, but it was not going to be easy to remove, due to the scar tissue surrounding that area.

Peter Goldstraw, typically, didn't delay. He operated on Anna again but this time he found that the tumour had perforated the trachea and had been growing across the breathing tube. The larger it grew, the less room there was for air to pass to and from the lungs. He removed the offending tissue but warned that there was nothing he could do to stop the same thing happening again.

Between August '96 and November '98 Anna was to return to the Brompton every few weeks as the tumour kept up its relentless determination to block her trachea and each time the surgeon used his skill in retaliation. He finally had to insert a stent, a solid tube that would help to hold open the passage of the trachea.

However, he couldn't stop the cancer advancing in its unyielding charge to all parts of her body. There were secondaries throughout her bones, particularly in her spine and her hips, making everyday tasks difficult and walking an impossibility. As the meandering menace made its way through her body, Anna's thoughts were realistic but always of others and especially for Mitchell. She said to her mum, 'I'm so worried about him. You've got Dad, but he's got to face it alone. Promise me you'll look after him.'

The pattern of Anna's life was one ever-decreasing spiral into emergency procedures, ambulance dashes and desperate sickness. The harder the cancer tried to destroy her, the more she took it head on with inspirational fervour. 'This thing will only take me kicking and screaming,' she had said during one particularly hard day. Whenever she could, she would party. Whenever she could, she would laugh. Whenever she could, she would climb into her bright red MGB sportscar with tonneau cover down, spin the back wheels in defiance and, with CD blaring loud, accelerate away from the home in which she had grown up with her two brothers. She even took a small trip on Concorde with Mitchell, a surprise gift from our friends Dennis and Jan Roach.

Even though malignant schwannoma was ostensibly a non

chemo sensitive cancer, it was decided to see if chemotherapy could stunt the growths and assist the work of the surgery. Three days after her thirty-first birthday came a moment that Anna had dreaded. The beautiful blonde curly hair that framed her face and singled her out in a crowded room, began falling out in chunks so she rang her mum and asked her to go over with her scissors.

Megs complied with Anna's request reluctantly, cutting off the bulk of her daughter's hair in one swift movement. Anna handed over a razor and demanded a shave close to her scalp. Her eyes and her high cheekbones were now the dominant features of her face, for the first time since she was a baby. She had lost her hair but her beauty remained intact. As Megs collected Anna's curls, Mitchell sat down and asked his mother-in-law to repeat the task on him. He rebutted Anna's protests and insisted he had deliberately grown it long so that they could be shorn together. Once more Megs obeyed instructions and shaved Mitchell's hair to match. Husband and wife stood in front of the mirror looking like two boiled eggs. Both laughed. Megs tried to do the same.

As her vomiting and increasing infirmity took greater hold, Anna discouraged words of sympathy but encouraged and accepted the companionship of her own and Mitchell's family. Mitchell, despite holding a senior position with a graphic design company, decided it was time to give up work and spend all his days on call for Anna's needs. The chemotherapy treatment was a last resort and, with hindsight, did little to delay the cancer's advance. Her blood count was irregular and eventually she would need transfusions to boost her failing body. The incessant attack of the tumour on her trachea needed to be relieved by surgery every month or so and the pain in her hips necessitated the use of a wheelchair, which she accepted with far more grace than we had imagined.

Television played an increasing part in Anna's days. Daytime programmes, soap operas and, of course, Arsenal games and her dad's presentations, all helped to pass the time. In May '98, David Seaman dedicated the second double in Arsenal's history to Anna while being interviewed on 'Match of the Day' and a month later she was looking forward to watching the World Cup finals in France. She insisted I go ahead with ITV's plans for me to present their coverage, which would mean my being away from home for almost six weeks. At the end of an emotional family dinner party on the eve of my departure to Paris, I told Anna it wasn't too late for me to tell ITV I couldn't present the tournament. She told me not to be stupid and impishly added, 'I promise I won't be too ill, Dad.' We held each other close for a long time and let more tears fall. As she left with Mitchell, Anna gave me a good-luck card with the message, 'Dad, you're the best!'

Within four days, and without my knowledge, the level of Anna's platelets had dropped to 18, the component that is vital in the clotting of blood, and she needed another operation on her trachea. In recovery, she suddenly found her breathing difficult and was unable to move any part of her body to alert the nurse that she was in trouble. The drug used in operations to paralyse muscles had not been reversed and she was in a panic situation that she was about to die. She began desperately to move her head, which attracted the attention of a nurse who fetched the anaesthetist to rectify the problem. The experience lasted forty seconds but in that time, Anna later laughingly told us, all she could think about was who would take over her dad's place in the presenter's chair if she died and he had to return for the funeral!

I did make two flying visits home to see Anna but my delight at getting back from the World Cup was partly tempered when Anna and Mitchell were unable to come with us to David and Debbie Seaman's wedding celebrations at Castle Ashby. The Goalie had asked me to be his best man, despite an age difference of twenty-one years, and Anna helped me prepare my speech, which centred on the age gap, our hair styles and changes in football between my era and his. When I learned from David's mum and dad that he had been blond as a little boy, Anna persuaded me to take her wig and place it in on David's head so that everyone could see how he would have looked. Anna couldn't be there in person but she played a little part in what was an unforgettable wedding.

No sooner had Megs and I returned from Castle Ashby than we were on our way back to the Brompton. Anna had a bad infection of the lung and her trachea was almost blocked yet again. With Mr Goldstraw away, the operation had to be performed by his senior registrar. The procedure proved incredibly difficult. Anna haemorrhaged badly and was immediately put on a ventilator. It was clear that she had experienced another close call, but once she was released from intensive care and back on the ward, her reaction was to joke and try to relieve the family concerns. 'You know, it's far harder for you, when I'm having an operation, than it is for me. I'm asleep and know nothing, while you are all on tenterhooks.'

Late August and early September brought a period of calm and Anna was able to have quality time in the warmth of an English late summer sun, enjoying the house and garden that brought her so much pleasure. Her hair was starting to grow back strongly and she sported a healthy looking tan. However, coughing up blood became a daily occurrence, and her struggle for breath, her struggle to move and her struggle to eat had all become a way of life.

It was in mid October that Anna called her mum and told her she needed to get to the Brompton. If Anna volunteered to go to the hospital, we knew it had to be serious. Tests undertaken revealed that she was very poorly with a bad infection, a low platelet count and a very high temperature. However, she had to wait until her platelet count could be increased by transfusion, but in the meantime she was becoming much worse. Mr Goldstraw was called to her room where he found her in a very bad state.

'Speak to me, Anna,' he said.

She whispered, 'I just want to be able to breathe.'

'Anna, we're between the devil and the deep blue sea, but you give me no alternative. I'm going to operate. I want you in theatre now.'

Our fears heightened rapidly and as Mitchell, Megs and I walked alongside her to the theatre doors we wondered if this was the last time we would talk to her. 'Take care, darling, God bless, I love you, see you soon.' It was all so inadequate. She was in pain, unable to breathe, as near to death as she had ever been. The chances of her pulling through seemed slim.

We waited back in her room as an electric storm with huge flashes of lightning lit up the Chelsea skyline. We joked that Anna was putting up one hell of a fight. An hour and three quarters after leaving us, Mr Goldstraw's junior doctor came to tell us that the operation had been terribly difficult. A blood clot had been sitting in the centre of her trachea, the tumour had grown round the top and bottom of the stent, blocking her airway, and there was huge bleeding.

'We thought we'd lost her twice,' he said. 'Mr Goldstraw managed to insert a new stent but there could be damage to the lungs. She's on a ventilator.'

Mitchell started to ask if he could see her and whether he'd be able to take her home. The doctor attempted to ease a negative reply by saying, 'We hope so Mitchell.' It wasn't the time for anything but the truth so I asked just how serious it was. This time the doctor told it straight.

'I'm afraid there's little chance of her surviving the night. I'm sorry I need to ask you this question. In the event of a cardiac arrest, how vigorously do you want us to resuscitate?'

It was so unreal, even though we thought we were prepared.

We agreed there should be no resuscitation and were told we could see Anna in intensive care very soon. We immediately phoned John, Robert and his partner Sarah telling them to get to the hospital as soon as they could. Mitchell phoned his mum, dad and brothers. All had arrived by the time Mitchell, Megs and I were allowed to see Anna. She looked calm on the ventilator, there was no struggle for breath. Anna the invincible was now hanging on to life by the finest of threads.

Back with the rest of the family, we tried to console ourselves with the fact that Anna no longer had pain. We waited through the night and tried to rest, taking it in turns to visit intensive care where the staff were keeping Anna comfortable. At breakfast, just after I'd rung the closest of family and friends to warn them that Anna was expected to die, her physiotherapist ran towards us and said, 'You're not going to believe this but Anna's just opened her eyes. She's waving to everyone and wants to know where you are!'

She had defied all odds one more time but was soon aware of the drama that had occurred. Concerned for us that we should all have been through agonies, she asked, 'But did you have a laugh?' It was important for her to know that we hadn't given up on our sense of humour. We assured her that our time through the night had produced some amusing moments through the obvious hours of anxiety. While I left to fetch Mitchell and the boys, Anna continued to assure her mum that she would be OK and added, 'By the way, we are still going ahead with "This Is Your Life" aren't we?'

Behind my back, Anna, Megs and the boys had spent the last month working with the BBC team to piece together my story and find a convenient time in Anna's treatment to get Michael Aspel to present the famous red book. It was 2 November when Megs bade me farewell from home with the words, 'Have a nice day.' I found her choice of expression strange, but dismissed it, just happy that she could smile again since Anna's return home.

David Seaman told me, prior to training, that a BBC film crew were making a documentary about him. I was used to such minor distractions where he was concerned. During our warm-up session, the first-team squad ran as a tightly packed group towards the goal where I was coaching, which was unusual. When they stopped abruptly, I turned to see Jill Dando emerge from the middle of the pack.

'What on earth are you doing here?' I asked of my lovely friend.

Before she answered, I was astonished to see Michael Aspel appear behind her, clutching the big red book and saying the famous words at me. My mind was in turmoil. 'This Is Your Life' at a time when Anna's life seemed to be fading fast. After smiling politely, I asked for the cameras to stop recording.

'I don't want to do this,' I said. 'Anna is too ill.'

But the reason Jill was part of the catch was precisely because Megs and Anna had anticipated my reaction.

'It's Anna who's planned it, Bob,' said Jill.

Moments later my mobile phone rang to confirm her words. The face of the phone showed 'Megs Mob' was calling me. It wasn't my wife on the other end but Anna, my mischievous, madcap, amazing Anna, saying, 'Dad, I'm ready to party.'

And party we did. As I stood behind the big screens with Michael, the title music playing, I took out my white hankie in readiness to wave should I lose control. I was confronted by a collection of family and friends led by John, Anna, Mitchell and Robert. As I hugged John, he fiercely whispered in my ear, 'Dad, don't cry.' It wasn't easy to obey. As I moved back from an embrace with Anna, her smile dissolved and her look of love and pride for 'Daddy, my Daddy' gave way to emotion. Robert and Mitchell were as concerned as John at how we would all hold up to the occasion.

It was fantastic, simply fantastic. For the next forty minutes and at the big party that followed, we experienced shared joy that we couldn't have thought possible. During the programme, I was greeted, surprised, moved by tributes delivered by those who had played a part in my life – family, team-mates, college friends, TV colleagues and sporting heroes. It was an event at which Anna could be normal, join in the gossip, catch up with cousins and hold hands with her Grandpa Miles, Megs' dad. She was wheeled from group to group, laughing and smiling. I'm certain she knew that it would be the last time she would see most of her family.

Here she was, three weeks after being on death's doorstep, the life and soul of the party. To all observers, she appeared to have no pain, no worries. Her adrenaline rush and excitement lasted ten full days. On every one of them, Megs and I arrived at her home anticipating a deterioration in her condition, but she appeared better than she had been for weeks. All she wanted to do was talk about our magical day, gossip about friends and family and share experiences of the day, an activity that seemed to work better than all the medication that lined her cupboards. When her symptoms and pain returned to take up residence, she spent precious time talking to all of us, often individually. She told me that she couldn't 'do this thing any more' but that she needed time to talk with Mitchell, John and Robert in order to be sure that they understood how she felt. She seemed to know now that it would be soon. We discussed letters that would help her husband and brothers, should that time arrive.

During the last week in November, Anna found herself back in the Brompton as the tumour in her trachea made its presence felt once more. She began, for perhaps the only time during her five-year battle, to open up the barriers that she had kept shut for so long, and admit that she had really had enough. Through the trauma of the last five years, she had been strong for all of the family, concerned only for our welfare. At the hospital, as the signs and symptoms looked bleak, she and her mum spent time talking through their despair and, for the first time, Megs and Anna cried together.

We were all reacting differently to the growing concerns. As I went to Barcelona for a Champions League programme, my body was covered in a strange rash. By the time I returned home, I was on my temporary leave of absence from ITV and Megs and I were now both at Anna and Mitchell's beck and call.

Anna was sent home, having been plied with large doses of steroids, which enabled her to spend a much more comfortable weekend with Mitchell, appreciating his attention and inimitable humour. On the Monday, Megs was shocked when she received a call from Anna asking if she could take her to the local shopping centre. It was the last day of November and Megs and Anna had a lovely time at Habitat as Anna managed, via her wheelchair, to fill a trolley full of goodies with Christmas presents for everyone on her list.

The next day, 1 December, we took her to the Middlesex Hospital for radiotherapy treatment, aimed at stopping the tumour from bleeding quite so much. We had a long wait before Anna was seen and we didn't get back to Knebworth until three in the afternoon. She was a very different Anna from the day before, exhausted and very unwell. Megs and I left to go home at four but soon got a call from Anna telling us her breathing was changing and that we might need to get to the Brompton.

Back at Knebworth, we found her sitting on the bottom step of the stairs, looking frail. Anna had decided we should not try to go straight to the Brompton but seek advice on her condition in casualty at the local hospital, the Lister, where she had trained. She knew just how serious the situation was.

Two paramedics helped us take her inside and were already administering oxygen as we were led to the resuscitation room. It was 6.30 but neither Megs' instructions through Anna's carefully prepared emergency page in her filofax, nor a direct line to the Brompton, could prevent the moment we had feared and dreaded for such a long time. I try to convince myself now that Anna's distress at this moment was minimal, that her struggle to breathe was no worse than on many other occasions. I pray she knew very little of what was occurring. The memory will haunt me forever. As numerous doctors and nurses busied themselves around the bed, Mitchell stood holding her left hand, I stroked her forehead and hair, Megs continued to pass on instructions from the Brompton phone line. Anna's discomfort was obvious, but as her right arm made to thump her chest, as she so often did to relieve a clot that had stuck there, a high-pitched tone replaced the sound of her pulse from the monitor. It was sensitively switched off and silenced.

I had already made my way to Mitchell's side while Megs held Anna's other hand. Mitchell's grief was physical and agonised as he cried, 'Has she gone, Bob, has she gone?' As gently as I could, I told my son-in-law 'Yes, Mitchell, she's gone.' We had travelled such a long road since she entered the Lister hospital as a trainee nurse, full of enthusiasm for her chosen career. This was also where she had first encountered the face of her foe and where that evil enemy finally seized her life.

For an hour we stood in a side room and looked down on her beauty. I asked a male nurse to help me wash her mouth while Mitchell removed her wedding ring and handed it to Megs. It was the same ring that Megs' father had placed on her own mother's hand in 1936 to seal another loving marriage. It was so difficult to walk away from Anna. Numb, we made our way back to Knebworth and waited for John, Robert and Sarah and Mitchell's parents to arrive. Mitchell produced four letters, one marked to himself, another two to 'John' and 'Robert', the last one addressed to 'Mum and Dad'.

Anna would have been proud at how her husband and two brothers coped with her death. John and Robert were consoled knowing that the three of us were holding her when she slipped away. All five of us acknowledged that the experience of Anna's fight and the manner in which she conducted it had enriched our lives and would never destroy us.

Mitchell's family joined us and we spoke together of the joy of the gift of Anna. Her life had been relatively brief. In six days' time she would have celebrated her thirty-second birthday, but in the last five years she had been able to tell us all how to get the best out of life.

There was one last poignant moment for Megs and me on this saddest of days. We opened her letter:

Mum and Dad,

I'm sorry I've not been able to say things to you face to face and that it now has to be via a letter – it just always seems too hard, too emotional – and you know what I'm like about 'not letting my barriers down'.

I love you both so very, very much – you have both been amazing – not only through this illness but through my whole life – I am so very proud of what you've both achieved, of who you are – you really have given us all everything you could – thank you.

I'm sorry you've been the ones taking a lot of my anger/black moods etc – nothing was meant personally towards you – I should have been loving/hugging you both – you deserve better.

Obviously if you're reading this, then the inevitable has happened. I'm really not frightened about it – we've all got to go sometime – and one day we will be together again – it's just I'll probably be younger and better looking than the rest of you! Please don't let your lives stop or be ruined by this – you must carry on together – talk together – don't ever push each other away – please be happy – and don't forget I'll be there watching, just to make sure!

I love you more than you'll ever know.

See you later
Anna X

15
Under orders

'A day without a smile is a day wasted.'

Charlie Chaplin

The first day of December had always begun the most exciting month in Anna's year – the first day of Advent, six days before her birthday, twenty-four days before Christmas and thirty days before New Year. It was the month she and Mitchell first went out together and the month in which they had become engaged. The fact that it was the date of her death gave added poignancy to our sadness. Not that we were allowed to dwell on grief for long because we were all under Anna's orders. Her letters to her husband and brothers reflected the same sentiments as the one Megs and I treasure.

We also had to react to other instructions left meticulously by Anna in her filofax. She had planned her funeral in minute detail. Her wish was to be cremated at a private family service, dressed in her wedding gown, her feet bare and with her head covered by a circle of anenomes. She had even written, 'No flowers. Donations? Cancer I guess.' Her mischief lived on.

Robert read a favourite poem of my mum's:

And I said to the man who stood at the gate of the year
Give me a light that I may tread safely into the unknown and
  he replied

*Go out into the darkness and put your hand into the hand of
God
That shall be to you better than light and safer than a known
way.*

As her younger brother spoke, a shaft of sunlight pierced
the window and seemed to indicate Anna's presence among
us.

An hour after the cremation, the family joined a packed
throng at the tiny church in Knebworth Park, where a lone piper
reflected Anna's Scottish ancestry and her love of bagpipes. She
wanted her service of thanksgiving to replicate as much as
possible her wedding day, at the same church just six years
previously. Megs was ordered to wear the same pink suit she'd
worn on what Anna described as the 'happiest day of my life'.
To all in attendance she had asked that the message be read
out, 'PLEASE BE HAPPY'.

We achieved her wish. Barely three weeks earlier, Anna and
I had talked about the main address at her funeral. She asked
me if I could cope with the emotion of it and asked if I would
mention certain special people including her mum and Mitchell.
Finding suitable words for Megs was easy for me. Delivering
them, more demanding.

*First the mum, whose love for her daughter knows no bounds,
no barriers. Pre-illness days, it was Megs who nurtured and
shaped the femininity of Anna, the common sense of Anna,
the sensitivity that is Anna and the fun that is Anna.*

*Post-diagnosis days it is Megs who has dedicated every minute
of her life and every ounce of energy to sustaining Anna in her
determination to fight on; fight on until the love of having
her with us is challenged and tempered by compassion and
realisation that it is better to let her slip away. How does any
mother accept that? Let alone a mother as special as Megs.
How Anna loves you and thanks you, through me, for always*

being there from day one to the one day you, her mum, never deserved to face.

I was driven by the memory of Anna telling me that there must be no white handkerchief waving on this occasion, but it was hard when it came to expressing gratitude to Mitchell.

Anna's greatest worry was not in dying. That's never been her fear. Her worry was and is, how Mitchell will cope. Well my darling daughter, have no fear. Of course, it will be with difficulty, but Mitchell will cope. All who love him will make sure he'll cope. Mitchell, we marvel and thank you for completing and truly fulfilling Anna's life and happiness. Six years as man and wife is not enough, but eternity would not have been enough for you two.

And so little Willow, continue to show us all the way. Smile as you've always smiled and fill our lives daily, until we meet again.

We were amazed to see how many people had come to celebrate Anna's life. The little church was filled to overflowing and many more stood outside in the sunny but cold air as the service was relayed to them. Afterwards, we all moved into Knebworth Park's medieval barns with specific orders, straight out of the filofax. 'Party!' was what Anna had written and we did so as her favourite music rang out.

Nurses in uniform from the Lister, staff from the Brompton, top personnel from ITV Sport, half the Arsenal team plus the manager and coaching staff, former Arsenal players, close friends, distant friends, patients and many others whose life Anna had touched in some way – all mixed with Anna's family, laughed and remembered a special girl.

The days leading up to Anna's farewell were filled with great love, personal visitors, phone calls and more than a thousand letters. At any time that we could find time together during the day, I would sit and read aloud to Megs every letter and card of condolence. They came from every corner of the British Isles and beyond. They included a personally written letter from the Prime Minister and a touching note written on an order form from the local milkman.

In the weeks and months that followed, it was difficult to fill the void that had opened up in our lives. We missed her, and still do. At the start of a day and whenever we are at home, we light a candle alongside Anna's photo. It's symbolic but keeps us in touch. The one thing Megs would always love to know is whether Anna is OK. Occasionally, we like to believe she's tried to let us know that she's absolutely fine. When she was ill, she was once touched by a story on television about white feathers supposedly being left by angels. At that moment, Mitchell had walked into the room and found her in tears and asked her why. When she explained what she'd been watching, he opened his palm and asked, 'What, you mean like this?' There was a feather he'd just picked up from the bedroom. 'It's the pillows, Anna, they're leaking,' he said, trying to bring some lightness to Anna's emotional state.

Three weeks after Anna's funeral, I returned to ITV and my coaching role at Arsenal. One day I was about to be interviewed for a football programme, standing by a goal out on the training ground. Miked up and ready to go, I suddenly spotted something falling towards me. The camera stopped rolling as I put out my hand to let a white feather fall gently into it. There have been many such occasions and it would be easy to read too much into such moments, but when they occur, they offer comfort and draw a smile. We are happy to accept any sign that Anna is around, is still watching us.

The most intriguing event followed a phone call with Kevin Keegan's wife Jean. She told me she'd been contacted by Betty Shine, a well-known medium, and that I should talk to her. I was sceptical but decided to phone, listen and just take notes on what Betty had to say. She told me she had been visited by a lovely girl with curly blonde hair, that her name was Anna and her dad was Bob Wilson. Various other details were given which could have been read in any of the many articles that had been written about Anna since her death. She told me that Anna would be likely to reveal her presence to us through water or electricity and unexplainable things could happen. Betty's words shocked me because twenty-four hours earlier, Megs' new computer had suddenly failed and all attempts to restore life to it through back-up support were fruitless. I didn't let Betty know about the computer, but was fascinated by her words. The next day, we went down to our place in Christchurch and when we arrived we discovered our home to be without electricity. We laughed but at the same time wondered why our house should be the only one on the marina to be affected. For three hours, the local electricity board called upon all their expertise but were unable to restore power. It took several days and a new main cable to remedy the problem.

Some people had an extraordinary gift when it came to giving us support. One was Sir Alex Ferguson. Even before a letter was delivered, he called us personally. He was concerned enough for me but doubly concerned about Megs. Sir Alex helped her at a time when the enormity of her loss was at its height.

Jill Dando was a former work colleague whose friendship and regular phone calls I particularly cherished, especially after Anna's death. We were so thrilled that Jill had met someone so special that she was starting to make wedding plans. Jill and her fiancé Alan Farthing were absolutely perfect together and an evening spent with them at Hampstead was full of fun and laughter. Within a matter of weeks, Megs and I had just got home when our neighbour phoned to tell us a news bulletin had just reported that Jill had been attacked and shot. We were transfixed as we watched the subsequent report of her death. It was shocking, appalling, a frightening extinguishing of the life of someone who had been blessed with beauty, talent, sensitivity and humility.

A private service attended by Jill's family and close friends was held in Weston-Super-Mare the day before the 1999 FA Cup final between Manchester United and Newcastle United. ITV rehearsals were delayed so that Megs and I could pay our last respects to our lovely friend. Getting there by helicopter was the only way we could attend the early afternoon service and still be back at Wembley Stadium by six for the rehearsal. I was honoured to be asked by the family and by Alan to pay a small tribute to Jill at a thanksgiving service held in All Souls Church, Langham Place, a few weeks later.

Jill's death provided another example of the fragility of life. She had helped Anna and Megs spring the 'This Is Your Life' surprise on me and, during the actual programme, sat alongside another work friend, Helen Rollason. Helen, the first woman to present 'Grandstand', was fighting her own battle with cancer and had often phoned Megs and me to compare her experience with Anna's. Helen died in the summer of 1999. Between December and August, three young women, each in the prime of her life, had been lost to us, one in a senseless moment of madness, two from sheer bad luck.

Throughout this time, in coming to terms with the loss of one of our children and two other close friends, Megs kept remembering Anna's words about not giving up on life. 'Don't let this thing destroy you. If anything, go out and make use of what you've learned.'

Terry Mitchinson, the editor of the local newspaper, the *Welwyn and Hatfield Times*, had been very moved by Anna's story and got in touch. He wondered if we had thought of doing something in her memory. We too had toyed with the idea but it was only six months after Anna's death and we were still struggling to cope with everyday life. Megs felt that any memorial should be something that was needed and worthwhile but that was not readily available, so suggested a meeting with the chief executives of the local hospitals and hospices.

She asked them if there was anything that the NHS could not provide and yet would be invaluable. The reply came back that hospitals could provide diagnosis and treatment but could not give quality of life. Wouldn't it be wonderful if there was a service that could send a seriously ill patient out for a massage, a hair-do, a meal with friends, to the theatre, or for a day out at a sporting occasion?

The idea began to excite us as it reflected Anna's own philosophy of having quality time with those closest to her. It had been proved time and again that when Anna had a special day, either at a concert, a football match or even at her dad's special tribute programme, an adrenaline rush of excitement would give her the means to cope with all that an evening or day out entailed. If Anna smiled, all those around her smiled. If she was enjoying herself, it would reflect on everyone else and make life that much more bearable. Megs suggested that if it worked for Anna, why shouldn't it work for others. Through our experience, we knew there was an age group that was not well supported when illness struck, those between sixteen and forty. There were many wonderful charities that helped sick children up to the age of sixteen, but over that age, the support was very limited.

So we decided to set up a charity that would fund and provide special days for seriously ill people between the ages of sixteen and forty. It was also important to us that serious illness did not just mean cancer, but all life-threatening conditions. The charity needed a name and for that we turned to Mitchell who suggested we called it 'Willow Foundation'. He was in the habit of calling Anna 'Wills' and 'Willow' as a reflection of her maiden name, but was unaware that it was also my nickname as a player at Arsenal.

Terry Mitchinson had promised his paper's full support and was persuaded by Megs, once the charity had been launched, to print a new story about it every week for the first year. We in turn promised to go to every fundraising event put on by the people in the area, no matter how big or how small. We decided the charity should start its life in north and east Hertfordshire, the area in which Anna lived and practised her community nursing.

On 25 August 1999, the Willow Foundation was launched at Brocket Hall in Hertfordshire with the help of golfer Laura Davies, there to play in her own golf tournament. It was an emotional moment as we saw the birth of an idea created in Anna's memory and conceived out of her needs during illness.

Megs and I owe a huge debt of thanks to the people in the Welwyn and Hatfield area who made sure that the Willow Foundation got off to a great start by their imaginative fundraising efforts. In the first year of the charity's life we met groups in pubs, clubs, schools and workplaces, to receive monies raised in so many different ways. There were raffles, head shaves, parachute jumps and motor-cycle rallies, coffee mornings, marathons, football matches and quiz evenings. All who supported us did so because the vision of the charity had touched an area of their own lives. Most people knew someone who had a serious illness, and could appreciate that a little quality time puts smiles on the faces of those most affected.

It was heart-warming to receive such overwhelming support for the idea of Willow and, although my having a recognisable face helped the charity's growth, it was other people's compassion and understanding that allowed it to expand so rapidly. After only four months of fundraising, we were able to give our first special day. It was for a young lady whose one wish was to go to the theatre with her husband. Megs organised for a taxi to pick them up and take them to London where they were to be met at the theatre by the manager, who would show them to their seats. They were doing something normal at a time when normality had become a cycle of illness and treatment. They were so delighted with their evening out, and the fact that everything had been organised for them, that they sent the charity £30 as their donation to our work. Two months later the young lady died, but her husband was left with a very special memory.

The Willow Foundation is now four years old and in that time has grown beyond our wildest dreams. What was once a small local charity provides a service to the whole of the south east of England. It has funded and provided over 400 special days, all unique and of the recipients' own choice. They range from weekends in London taking in the special sights, visits to sporting events, thrills and spills at motor-racing tracks, birthday parties, relaxation at country retreats and pampering at health spas; every one is organised to meet the individual's needs.

It has helped that our celebrity friends have rallied to the cause, eager to help when required and willing to give time to others not as fortunate as themselves. Sometimes the special days have to be taken at home if the recipient is too ill to go out. The father of one young gentleman applied to the charity for his son to meet David Beckham. When we got in touch with the England captain's agent we were told that David would be willing to meet the young man at the England training session that week. It was explained to him that the young man was not well enough to leave his bed so it was asked if a phone call would be acceptable. The father was delighted and at an arranged time the phone call came through. The young man was able to talk to his hero for ten minutes, thought to be an almost impossible task for him since he was on a respirator. David asked him how he spent his time and when he learned it was often playing his Play Station, the footballer offered to send the latest game to him. It duly arrived and so too did a signed shirt. The effect of the 'special day' on the young man was dramatic and his fight with his illness received a massive boost.

The letters we receive from those who have benefited tell us how much the special days meant to them and their families at a time when quality time was not easily available. The Willow Foundation reflects all that Megs and I learned during the five years we were privileged to witness our daughter's strength of character during her illness. I feel strongly that the experience, however sad, has helped enrich our lives and, in my case particularly, made me appreciate what is of importance in life and what isn't.

Sometimes as a footballer at the highest level of the game, you are not always the most pleasant person. The television world is even more cut-throat. So many people have this image of Bob Wilson as a nice sort of guy with a ready smile, but I always had an underlying competitiveness. It could overlap into real life and it took Anna to knock it out of me. The way she faced up to everything made me realise what is important in my relationships.

I can't say that it has been all plain sailing since Anna died. It hasn't. In the early weeks and months I owed a huge debt to the Arsenal players and staff. I would arrive for my coaching sessions, try to smile and enjoy the banter, change into my training kit and go to make sure the footballs had the correct pressure in them. Out on the field beside the goalposts I would sit on the ball, wait for the keepers and weep. The sadness was better out of me than kept inside. My goalies would arrive and we'd laugh and work in equal measure. They helped me live again in the way that Anna would have wanted.

John and Robert took the loss of their sister badly. Only four years separated the three of them and the boys were extremely close to their sister. John's little boy, Louis, is doted on by Megs and me and he was always spoilt by his Auntie Anna and Uncle Mitchell who loved him dearly. Louis's mum Jane was worried how he would react to her death. She had thought carefully about how she should tell him the news that Anna had died. At breakfast the day after her death, Jane broached the subject.

'Louis, you know Anna has been poorly?'

'Yes Mummy,' Louis said with nonchalance.

'You know she's been very poorly?'

'Yeah, yeah!' he said, impatient at her repetition.

'Well Anna was so poorly that she died.'

'You mean Anna's dead?'

'Yes and she's now in a really lovely place called Heaven.'

Louis jumped down and went over to his toys and began playing. After ten minutes he said, 'So Anna's dead, Mummy?'

'Yes, darling.'

He continued to play for another few minutes.

'So is Anna an angel?'

With much relief that Louis seemed to be getting the right idea, Jane confirmed the fact. It was fifteen minutes before Louis said, 'Has Anna got wings?'

'Yes she has.'

'And is she still in her wheelchair?'

The picture he painted was perfect. Louis remembers his Auntie Anna and always will.

Our other grandson, Max, will have to be told about her one day. Max is the son of Robert and his wife Sarah. They were as close to Anna and Mitchell as anyone, sharing weekends, holidays and lots of memories during her five-year struggle. One of Anna's last wishes was to live long enough to see their wedding day, but it wasn't to be. When the big day did eventually arrive, the ceremony was conducted on the farm in Lincolnshire belonging to my nephew – exactly where Anna would have approved. Robert and Sarah, with Anna and Mitchell, had stayed at the shooting lodge by a lake and that's where they chose to become man and wife. The service took place at the water's edge beside a willow tree; at its base was a lit lantern, given as a present to Rob and Sarah by Anna and Mitchell. They now have a son, Max.

Anna would be proud of how her humorous but vulnerable husband has followed her orders. She gave him strict instructions to move on with his life and not wallow in the material aspects that represented their time together. She was afraid of how he would react and she had given us special instructions to watch over him. There is no doubt that it has been a difficult journey for Mitchell but, with the amazing support of his own family and friends he has achieved more than could have been imagined. He now has two sons of his own with Debbie, one of Anna's good friends, who understands the trauma of his past life and the need to create a future. They will always be a very special part of our family.

The loss of Anna hit Megs and Mitchell hardest. It had to. Everyone has admired Megs' strength of character in creating something so worthwhile out of the experience of losing a daughter, but life will never be quite the same for her. Megs is still learning to live without her daughter. She has always been an extrovert, inheriting the fun that was her father's trademark, but I'm often told by those who know her well that since 1 December 1998 'she smiles without smiling' and that something is missing. Well there is and she admits it. Her life has changed irrevocably but in one respect only. Sons, grandchildren, families and friends remain and are all there to be enjoyed.

As for a boy named Primrose, as a child he was strictly forbidden ever to hold on to a miserable face for too long by a mum who simply refused to give up on life because it had briefly betrayed her trust in it. He has cried plenty but still knows the true worth of a smile. That smile always becomes especially warm in answer to any question about how many children Megs and I have. 'Oh we're so lucky,' I reply. 'We have three children.'

Index

313